W9-BDF-827

The Story of Lynx

CLAUDE LEVI-STRAUSS

The Story of Lynx

TRANSLATED BY CATHERINE TIHANYI

THE UNIVERSITY OF CHICAGO PRESS
Chicago & London

Claude Lévi-Strauss is professor emeritus at the Collège de France. His previous books published in translation by the University of Chicago Press include the four-volume *Mythologiques* and *The Jealous Potter*. Catherine Tihanyi is assistant professor of anthropology at Simon Fraser University.

The University of Chicago Press, Chicago 60637
The University of Chicago Press, Ltd., London

© 1995 by The University of Chicago
All rights reserved. Published 1995
Printed in the United States of America

04 03 02 01 00 99 98 97 96 95   5 4 3 2 1

ISBN (cloth): 0-226-47471-2

Originally published as *Histoire de Lynx,* © Plon, 1991.

Library of Congress Cataloging-in-Publication Data

Lévi-Strauss, Claude.
    [Histoire de Lynx. English]
    The story of Lynx / Claude Lévi-Strauss ; translated by Catherine
Tihanyi.
      p.   cm.
    Includes bibliographical references and index.
    ISBN 0-226-47471-2 (alk. paper)
    1. Indians of North America—Folklore. 2. Folklore—Structural
analysis. 3. Lynx—Folklore. 4. Indians of South America—
Folklore. 5. Tales—Québec (Province) 6. Tales—Northwest,
Pacific. I. Title.
E98.F6L57718   1995
398'.08997—dc20   94-34811
                                                 CIP

♾The paper used in this publication meets the minimum requirements of the American National Standard for Information Sciences—Permanence of Paper for Printed Library Materials, ANSI Z39.48-1984.

Sed prius haec fuere: nunc recondita
senet quiete, seque dedicat tibi,
gemelle Castor, et gemelle Castoris.
Catullus, IV: *Dedicatio Phaseli*, 25 – 27.

Contents

Translator's Acknowledgments

I would like to express my heartfelt gratitude to Claude Lévi-Strauss for his thorough final review of the English text, from which this work has greatly benefited. It must also be noted that there are a few small differences between the English text and the French one as the author has taken this opportunity to correct some minor errors that had cropped up in the original French edition. Many thanks also to Claudia Rex, production editor, and to Mary Laur, copyeditor, for their outstanding work and, last but not least, to T. David Brent, senior editor at the University of Chicago Press, for his insightful comments and kind encouragements.

Preface

This book begins with the image of the chessboard, an image offered both as clarification and apology. The apology is for the possibly arduous reading of the opening chapters. Before the argument could begin, it was necessary to devote certain pages to that which is known in chess as the opening and which, in the course of ten or fifteen moves, sometimes repeats beginnings of games already played and known. Likewise, the reader somewhat familiar with my other books on Amerindian mythology might feel that the first chapters of this one are standing still. This is because I too must deploy my pieces, the elements of the myths to be used in the start of a new game.

Against whom is this game played? This point requires clarification, as the nature of the game itself is puzzling. Is it like chess, or should we rather compare it to solitaire, a game in which one submits to certain constraints and follows certain rules so as to order a finite number of elements—the cards—whose original distribution was accidental? But the card game is passive, and the chance distribution of the beginning stems from the initiative of the card-shuffling player.

A very different situation confronts the analyst of myths. He is not the author of the disorder he has the task of reducing. Not only does this disorder owe nothing to the analyst's intervention, and precede it, but even that which appears to him as disorder is not really so. Rather, it is a different order, one obeying constraints and rules distinct from those the analyst is going to use. To him, myths are adversaries and the question is which of two strategies—theirs or his—is going to prevail.

We play against myths, and we should not think that myths, coming to us from very far away in time or in space, can only offer us already-played-out games. Myths do not consist in games finished once and for all. They are untiring; they begin a new game each time they are retold or read. But, as in chess, the at-first-inscrutable strategy of one of the adversaries is unveiled as the game progresses. Toward the end, when this adversary's only remaining choices are a limited number of moves, the player nearing victory can even anticipate this now-transparent strategy and force it to model itself on his own.

What is the use, some would ask, of breaking down, of analyzing, of outmaneuvering a strategy that myths have repeated without renewal for dozens or perhaps even hundreds of millennia at a time when rational thought, when scientific method and techniques, have definitively supplanted them in explaining the world? Did myths not already lose the game a long time ago? This is not certain or, at least, it is not certain anymore, as it has become doubtful that an unbridgeable distance separates the forms of mythic thought from the well-known paradoxes that the masters of contemporary science, faced with the impossibility of making themselves understood in any other way, put to ignorants like us: Schrödinger's "cat," Wigner's "friend," or again the allegories invented to put within our grasp the paradox EPR (and now GHZ).

I mean no irony in speaking this way about scientific thought, in which, to my eyes, lies the greatness of the West. It only seems to me that in societies without writing, positive knowledge fell well short of the power of the imagination, and it was the task of myths to fill this gap. Our own society finds itself in the inverse situation—one leading to the same results though for opposite reasons. With us, positive knowledge so greatly overflows our imaginative powers that our imagination, unable to apprehend the world that is revealed to it, has no other alternative than to turn to myth again. In other words, between the scientist who through calculations gains access to a reality that is unimaginable and the public eager to know something of this reality, which is evidenced mathematically but entirely against the grain of sensible intuitive perception, mythical thought again becomes a mediator, the only means for physicists to communicate with nonphysicists.

We are told that an electron pulsates seven million times per second, can be at once wave and corpuscle, and exists simultaneously here and elsewhere; that chemical reactions occur in a measurable time, but one in which a second corresponds to a second only in relation to thirty-two million years; that at the other end of the cosmic ladder, our universe has a known diameter of ten billion light-years and our galaxy and its neighbors move in it at the speed of six hundred kilometers per second, pulled by bodies or by sets of bodies that have been given fabulous names such as Great Attractor or Great Wall, and assumed to be massive enough to produce this effect (but whose order of magnitude would contradict all our previously existing ideas about the way the universe was formed). These propositions make sense to the scientist who doesn't feel the need to translate his formulas into ordinary language, but any layperson even only slightly prone to intellectual honesty must confess that these are for him empty words, corresponding to nothing concrete or nothing from which he could as much as formulate an idea.

Consequently, scientists imagine events to help us bridge the chasm that has formed between macroscopic experience and truths inaccessible to ordinary language. Big Bang, expanding universe, and so on all partake of a mythical character to the point at which, as I have shown for myths, thought engaged in one of these constructions immediately generates its opposite. Thus, we have notions of a universe that, according to some calculations, is doomed to expand endlessly or, according to others, to contract to the point of annihilation.

For several centuries, science was dominated by the idea of a reversible time, of an immutable universe in which the past and the future were identical by right. Only history was left as refuge to mythical thought. But now we are learning—first through the theory of evolution and then through the new cosmology—that the universe and life itself are also in history, that they had a beginning and are subject to becoming. And yet this raises such enormous problems that this uncontestable knowledge leads us to doubt that we will ever understand what came before, what will come after, or how things really happened. That billions of events, each one highly improbable, have in the course of seven million years ensured the passage from a world in which all life was absent to first a world of RNA and then a world of DNA seems so difficult to admit that even some well-known scientists are reduced to making up myths. The first seeds of life, they claim, would have arrived on Earth 3.8 billion years ago (to which should be added the number of light-years required to make the journey) on board a spaceship originating from a distant planet and piloted by beings already very superior to us in science and technology . . . Similarly, ordinary words used to try to explain phenomena occurring on the quantum scale shock common sense much more than the most extravagant mythological inventions. As a contemporary physicist writes, the world of quantum mechanics differs not only quantitatively from everyday life but qualitatively as well:

> Common language has no words for it. . . . The quantum world [is] no less real than the classical world. And it teaches us that the reality of the common experience in the classical world is only a small part of what there is.[1]

A supernatural world thus exists again for humans. Though physicists' calculations and experiments demonstrate its reality, these experiments take on meaning only when transcribed in mathematical language. In a layperson's eyes (that is, to almost the whole of humankind), this supernatural world offers the same properties as that of myths: everything in it happens differently than it would in the ordinary world, and more often upside down. For the man in the street, for all of us, this world remains out of reach, except through the means of ancient modes of thinking that the scientist consents to restore for our use (and sometimes, regrettably, for his own). In the least expected manner, the dialogue with science makes mythological thinking actual again.

꙰

Several readers who seemed to have taken an interest in books such as *The Way of the Masks* and *The Jealous Potter* have complained to me that they are difficult. I could have understood this for *Mythologiques,** but I was surprised that this reproach was addressed to these two other books (and the present one is in the same vein) because I have been thinking of them as halfway between the fairy tale and the mystery novel, genres that are not thought to be particularly difficult.

After reflecting on this, I came to wonder if the difficulty did not stem mostly from the names of tribes found throughout these texts and that, since they do not represent anything to these readers, gave them the same impression they would have if they were bumping into Hebrew or Chinese words in the middle of a French text. But I have no choice but to use these names, as those of my colleagues who are involved in the same studies need them. Non-Americanist readers simply need not pay them as much attention. It will be enough for these readers to note that we pass from one people to another and from one linguistic family to its neighbor. The names, taken by themselves, seldom present an intrinsic interest. More often than not they are the result of historical chance or convention.

No doubt these names are sometimes those the people gave themselves, such as Sanpoil (in spite of its French consonance), Kalispel, Lilloet, and so on. Some, very difficult to pronounce, have defeated even specialists who, rather than repeat page after page of names such as Ntlakyapamux or Utamqtamux, preferred to call the peoples who use these names Thompson River Indians (from the name of a famous fur dealer from the beginning of the nineteenth century) or, in short, Thompson Indians, specifying, if need be, "Upriver" or "Downriver." A suffix meaning "people" (anglicized into *-ish, -mish*) is found as well in names whose mean-

---

*TN: This French title for the four-volume series *Introduction to a Science of Mythology* is commonly used even in English texts.

ings remain unknown to us, such as Salish, the name that the Flathead gave themselves and that is used as a generic term to refer to all the peoples of the same linguistic family, or again Skitswish, the real name of the Coeur d'Alene. We recognize the same suffix in the names that the peoples of the Puget Sound bore or were given by their neighbors. Thus Skokomish (a subgroup of the Twana), "people of the river"; Skyomish, "people from upriver." Other names, either French or English, are either nicknames or their translations: Tête Plate or Flathead (not because their anatomy was abnormal but because they would not deform their skull into the shape of a sugar loaf* as did several of their neighbors); Blackfoot (because of the color of their moccasins); Pend d'Oreille; Nez Percé; and so on. Indians who were also referred to by English speakers by the French name Coeur d'Alene were said to believe they had a small and pointed heart as a sign of toughness; it was possibly a mark of courage claimed by the Indians themselves, or an accusation that they are said to have thrown at the White traders with whom they conducted business. This last example well shows the often-anecdotal nature of the names of tribes. There is nothing in this that should confuse the reader's mind.

꽃

This book, which is not a big one, has a rather long history. It stems from two questions that I had asked myself across a gap of several years without noticing their connection. In 1944 I wondered about the nature of dual organizations in South America (see pp. 235–38 below). At the time I was writing *The Elementary Structures of Kinship,* and the comparative data I was using (chap. 6) suggested that dual organization in other areas of the world raises similar problems. Articles published in 1956 and 1960 [2] and my lectures of the years 1957–59 at the Ecole des Hautes Etudes [3] mark the stages of this reflection.

Later, as I was working on *The Naked Man,* I encountered a

*TN: In other words, an oblong shape.

problem that I first thought to be specific to the mythology of the Salish-speaking peoples in the Northwest of North America. This problem appeared so special that I first resigned myself to set it aside. I have, however, alluded to it in various places (see the index of *The Naked Man* under the entries for "Wind" and "Fog"), all the while promising myself to come back to it someday. In 1968–69 I interrupted my teaching program so as to draft the main lines of this problem in the form of an *intermede** (I called it an interlude) in one of my courses at the College de France.[4] On this occasion, I became aware that the two problems—that of South American dualism and that raised by the mythology of the wind and the fog in a specific area of North America—were really only one and that the second formed a test illustrating and confirming, through a particular case, the solution that I had proposed for the first.

Still in the same vein, I believe that it is now possible to trace Amerindian dualism to its philosophical and ethical sources. It draws its inspiration, it seems to me, from an opening to the Other, an opening that manifested itself in a demonstrative manner during the first contacts with the Whites, even though these latter were driven by very opposite motives. To recognize this as we are about to commemorate an event that—rather than the discovery—I would call the invasion of the New World, the destruction of its peoples and its values, is to engage in an act of contrition and devotion.

This book is a synthesis of reflections scattered in the course of the years, and its writing was laborious. I thank particularly Eva Kempinski, who, before and during her typing of the manuscript, brought to my attention a number of mistakes and inconsistencies in the complicated palimpsest I had handed over to her, in which so many successive versions had intermingled that I was not able to reread myself anymore.

*TN: Translates into English as "interlude" or "one-act play."

PART ONE

On the Side of the Fog

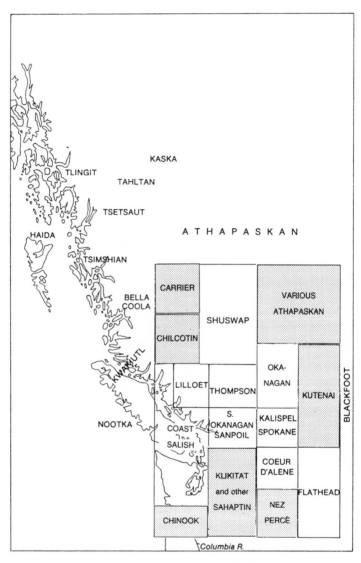

FIGURE 1. "Chessboard." The squares occupied by the people not belonging to the Salish linguistic family are colored gray.

1

An Untimely Pregnancy

O n the schematic map shaped like a chessboard on which the pieces will make their moves, we shall move the first pawn from a bottom case located very near the middle. In principle this choice is arbitrary, but it can be justified in parts. The Nez Percé Indians who occupy this case, and whose language is related to that of their Sahaptian neighbors, tell two very different versions of the myth that will be discussed throughout this book. One is a shortened version that could even be called minimal, while the other, developed to the point of self-division, turns into two stories that, even though imbedded into each other, fulfill distinct etiological functions. These two states of the myth—one contracted and one expanded—exist among the same people and enable us to perceive in a single gaze the basic common motif in all versions, the one we can describe as a constant, and they make it thus possible to assess the spread and properties of the semantic field in which the myth unfolds.

First, here is the short version.

In olden days, in a village peopled by animal creatures, lived Wild Cat (another name for Lynx). He was old and mangy, and he was constantly scratching himself with his cane. From time to time, a young girl who lived in the same cabin would grab the cane, also to scratch herself. In vain, Wild Cat kept trying to talk her out of it. One day the young lady found herself pregnant; she gave birth to a boy. Coyote, another inhabitant of the village, became indignant. He talked all of the population into going to live elsewhere and abandoning the old Wild Cat, his wife, and their child to their fate. Wild Cat covered his head and did not leave his cabin anymore; there was no food. In the end, Wild Cat felt sorry for the young woman. He told her to dig a hole nearby and fill it with water heated up with burning stones; he bathed in it, and then he immersed himself in the cold water of a stream. All the scabs covering his body fell off. He appeared as a handsome young man and went hunting. From this day forth, there was abundance in the household.

About one month later, Magpie, another villager, wanted to know what had happened to the unfortunates who had been left behind. On the old village site, he saw a child eating a piece of fat. The hungry Magpie stole it from him, the child started to cry, and his mother invited Magpie to eat. She even gave him food to take home and invited him to come back with his family, but on the condition that he keep the encounter secret. Indeed, ever since Wild Cat had uncovered his head, a thick fog had fallen on the new village. It made hunting impossible, and famine reigned. Thus Magpie's family's feast was met with surprise, and he had to tell all. On Coyote's order, the animals returned to the abandoned village. Wild Cat gracefully welcomed his former companions. He decreed that henceforth there would be no more fog, and he became head of the village.[1]

The antagonism between Lynx and Coyote, which is implicit in this version, comes to the front in another version. However, this is not the only difference between the stories. The heroine of the version I summarized above has crude manners. The heroine of the developed version is a modest and properly raised young girl; instead of living in the same cabin as a sick and repulsive old man, she lives in the cabin reserved for young ladies. One night, as she goes out to urinate, Lynx sees her and urinates in turn on the same spot. The young girl becomes pregnant without understanding why. She bears a son who cries constantly. Coyote orders all of the men of the village in turn to take the baby in their arms. He plans to pacify the child by surreptitiously putting bone marrow in the baby's mouth and thus to be acknowledged as his father, but the ploy fails. The men fail one after another. Lynx, whose conscience is uneasy, stands cautiously aside. When he is forced to try the test, the child calms down immediately.

Coyote, who hates Lynx, demands another test: a hunting competition that Coyote is to lead. He takes advantage of his responsibilities to cheat: he kills his game ahead of time and hides it in a hollow tree. But at daybreak, Lynx pulls out one of his own whiskers and sticks it into the ground. A thick fog falls, making it impossible to see anything; Coyote searches in vain for his hiding place. The weather clears up only after Lynx has made a kill and been the first to bring back his game.

It turns out that the woman was a bird, a member of the genus *Vireo*. Coyote, full of resentment, excites her family against Lynx. The birds attack Lynx and make mincemeat out of him. But he had had a premonition of this fate, and he had advised his wife to find a fragment of his body, even a minute one. Now, having become a bird again, she perches on a tree and waits for Coyote and the other inhabitants to leave the scene of their crime. She finds a tiny piece of bone, wraps it up carefully, and builds a cabin to shelter herself along with her child.

Day after day, she hears faint sounds coming from the deerskin in which she had placed the bone. Finally Lynx emerges from it, his body hurt and covered with wounds. Steam baths heal him. And then Coyote comes seeking news. He finds Lynx in the deserted village, protests his innocence, accuses Bear of being the guilty one, advises Lynx to seek revenge, and promises to help him. Lynx accepts; Coyote goes to see Bear, gives him perfidious advice, and causes his five sons to fall into an ambush. Lynx kills them with one arrow made with a hair from his mustache, an arrow that pierces all five bodies.

Understanding this his brother Coyote has betrayed him, Bear chases him and wounds him. Coyote transforms himself into a repulsive old man, infested with vermin, accompanied by a dog covered with sores—both so hideous that no one dares come near them. Bear arrives but does not recognize Coyote, who talks him into stepping on a footbridge made of twigs. It breaks. Bear drowns in the river that flows beneath it. Coyote and his fellow, Fox, bake him in an earth oven. Bear's wife, who has lost her husband and her sons, henceforth lives as a recluse.[2]

A New World genus, *Vireo* comprises, in the Northern Hemisphere, about one dozen species, some sedentary and some migratory. They are small, insect-eating birds, slow and a bit wary, of variable but always subdued colors. The magpie of the other version is on the contrary an excitable bird and, as we have seen on various occasions, singularly lacks reserve.

In both versions, Lynx appears as the master of the fog: he can bring it on and lift it at will. And it is yet another kind of fog, one that is beneficial rather than harmful, warm rather than cold—namely, steam—that heals Lynx and gives him youth and handsomeness. To these paired elements the second version adds the earth oven, dug into the ground and heated with hot stones (like the warm water bath, thus replacing the sweat lodge also mentioned in this version). Fog, sweat lodge, and earth oven thus form a triangle in which the fog, in the realm of nature, corresponds to the sweat lodge and the earth oven in the realm of culture.

The text itself shows that it is no accident that the motif of the earth oven is introduced in the second version: well before killing him, Coyote and Fox plan to cook Bear in this manner. Even better yet: Lewis and Clark, who at the very beginning of the nineteenth century were the first White visitors of the Nez Percé, tell that it was customary for these Indians to bake bear meat on a bed of hot stones. Meat and pine branches were layered on top of each other. The mound was then covered with pine branches wetted with water and topped with earth about ten centimeters deep. Cooking took about three hours and made the meat more tender than if it had been roasted or boiled, but it did have a taste of resin.[3]

A Nez Percé myth tells that Raccoon dug an earth oven to cook bear meat.[4] The same culinary technique is found among the Klikitat, who also speak a Sahaptin language, in a myth borrowed from their Cowlitz neighbors. In it, an old man named Bake-on-Hot-Rocks successively throws three female bears in the fire, saying to each one: "That is how you will be bear in the future. They will bake you on hot rocks."[5]

The required use of pine branches, which gave meat "a distinctive flavour, unpleasant to most Whites,"[6] raises a problem that I am temporarily setting aside (cf. pp. 115–18 below).

Yet other divergences between the two versions must be noted. Why do Lynx and the heroine live in the same cabin in one version, while in the other they live in cabins that custom requires to be very strictly separated? Why is one heroine modest and good and the other the opposite (since, remaining deaf to the objurgations of Lynx, she grabs his cane to scratch herself)? The storyteller of the second version indirectly provides the answer when drawing the moral of the myth: "She who is considered by others to be superior and difficult to win in marriage, she who considers herself better than other women, she will be taken in marriage by a homely and poor man."[7] Indeed, in this version, Lynx comes back to life and heals but becomes again what he was in the beginning: poor and ugly. Moreover, he disappears from the last third of the plot. Attention is then directed to his enemy Coyote, who experiences one success after another. In the end Coyote triumphs alone over Bear, even though this game is usually the object of a collective hunt; this is the reason its meat is eaten communally.[8] It is thus Coyote who plays the role of the hero, in contrast to the first version, in which the mismatched marriage with Lynx turns out to the advantage of the heroine: physically, since Lynx changes into a handsome young man; economically, since he becomes a great hunter; and socially, since he ends up the chief of his village.

The means used in this first version are located closer to the side of culture: a cane, means of impregnation, and a hat or the flap end of a piece of clothing, means of making the fog, are fabricated objects, which are opposed in the second version to urine, means of impregnation, and a whisker, means of bringing on the fog, both organically produced. And just as the second version constructs a triangular system with the fog, the sweat lodge, and the earth oven, it constructs another one with urine, the whisker planted in the ground, and the whisker shot as an arrow. This opposition between vertical and horizontal axes is reinforced by the fact that, in its second use, the whisker pierces the five bear cubs in one blow and is thus the horizontal instrument of a superlative hunt, while the whisker planted vertically brings on the fog, to which the myth gives the explicit function of rendering hunting impossible.

The relation between the hat and the fog is particularly deserving of attention. This relation appears again at the other end of the Northwest, where so many mythological motives common to the region's diverse peoples circulate (or perhaps one should say stagnate). The Tlingit of Alaska and the Tsimshian of British Columbia attribute to the demiurge a brother who brings on the fog when he takes off his hat and puts it upside down in a canoe.[9] Their Kwakiutl neighbors believe that twins are able to incorporate fog into their bodies by picking it up in their hats and pressing it against their chests.[10] Indeed, in American Indian thought and probably also elsewhere, the hat has the function of a mediator between up and down, sky and earth, the external world and the body. It plays the role of intermediary between these poles; it can either unite or separate in different instances. This is also, as I have written in the past, the role of the fog, which is alternately disjunctive or conjunctive between up and down, sky and earth: "a mediating term conjoining extremes and rendering them indistinguishable, or coming between them to prevent them growing closer."[11] This can also be expressed as "key of water," a role identical to one that other myths express in terms of "key of fire"* and assign to the domestic earth:

> By its presence, cooking fire averts total disjunction, since it *unites* the sun and the earth and saves man from the *world of rottenness* in which he would find himself if the sun really disappeared; but its presence is also *interposed,* that is to say, it obviates the risk of a total conjunction which would result in a *burned world.*[12]

In the region of North America that is of particular interest to us here, the concept of a four-storied world predominates. The fog occupies the layer immediately above our own.[13] Still, accord-

*TN: *Key* is used in the musical sense.

ing to the Thompson Indians, the terrestrial world was originally hot and windy; it was very dry.[14] According to the Tsetsaut, it was flat and hot, without water, rain, snow, wind, or fog. Hunger reigned. This situation lasted until the animals tore up the celestial roof and freed rain and snow.[15] In mythical times, tell the Coeur d'Alene, the climate was not the same as today: windy, hot, and dry, there was neither rain nor snow.[16] No snow, either, according to the Kutenai.[17]

Even though they disagree on the existence of the wind, these narratives evoke a time when fog was unknown—fog that other myths personify under the name of Fog Man, the great hunter.[18] All of these beliefs appear to give the fog a positive connotation. In this framework, one can bring up numerous myths in which fog, erasing the boundaries between sky and earth, enables a given protagonist to escape from his pursuers (indexed in *The Naked Man* as M_{557a}, M_{598a-g}, M_{644a-b}, M_{667a}, M_{668b}, M_{667}, M_{349}, and so on). Celtic legends attribute this same ambiguity to the fog: at times opening and at times forbidding access to the other world.[19]

ॐ

The two versions of the story of Lynx that have occupied us up to now come from the Nez Percé, inhabitants of the eastern side of the Sahaptin linguistic area. What happens on the other side? The Klikitat are the Cowlitz's neighbors. The Cowlitz are representatives of the great Salish linguistic family lying northward as far as the coast and the interior of British Columbia. Both peoples tell the story of Lynx in almost the same terms and diverge from the versions of the Nez Percé on two main points. First, Lynx (called Wild Cat here), infested with vermin and scabs, impregnates the chief's daughter by spitting from on high into her mouth while she begins to chant a ritual song. However—most significantly—while, as in other variants, he uses a steam bath to heal himself and even to acquire youth and handsomeness, nothing indicates here that he is the master of the fog; the famine present in the village of his persecutors remains unmotivated.[20]

The Coeur d'Alene, northern neighbors of the Nez Percé and

Salish speakers like the Cowlitz, tell that Lynx impregnated the chief's daughter through his thoughts, or (in another version) that he took her for his wife without her father's consent. The means for corporal impregnation (scabs, urine, saliva) thus disappears. The sweat lodge disappears as well: in the Coeur d'Alene versions, Lynx, trampled and reduced to only his skin, buried by hostile villagers, instead massages and beautifies himself. A new motif appears at this point in the narrative, one to which, as shall be seen, the other Salish versions give a large place: the wife clumsily interrupts the treatment that Lynx is administering to himself, and his face remains wrinkled and retains a residual ugliness.

The motif of the fog is missing as well; the myth does not explain the famine that reigns in the village. However—and this through an effect often noted when crossing a linguistic boundary—the motif doesn't simply disappear; it becomes inverted. The chief's daughter agrees to welcome and to feed her remorseful father, but in one version she demands that he give her in exchange "Bluebird's blue coat" and in another version this same bird's "pretty and blue necklace."[21] This bird, called a bluebird in Canada, is a Turdidae of the genus *Sialia* that, according to the Coast Salish, sings when it rains.[22] This song perhaps announces the return of fair weather, as the bird's coat or necklace, pretty and blue like a cloudless sky, is not far removed from the coat mentioned in certain Coast Salish myths (a coat that makes "the noonday sun glorious and resplendent").[23] Should this link be valid, it would follow that the blue coat of the Coeur d'Alene myth and the fog in the Nez Percé myths are in a relation of symmetry and that, through the complementary means of the cleared fog and the resulting clear sky, the myth ends everywhere on the return of fair weather (see pp. 163–66 below).

The difference in the two conceptualizations concords well with Teit's account. He claims to have found among the Coeur d'Alene no trace of beliefs regarding the origin of light and darkness, nor that of clouds and fog.[24] The same author, however, thinks that according to these Indians the world was in the past plunged in darkness and men moved by groping their way around.

And as he then goes on to write about the origin of the sun and the moon, one could conclude that native thought correlates darkness (nocturnal) and fog (diurnal) on the one hand and the moon and the sun on the other—a hypothesis that the following mythological transformation confirms.

The sweat lodge—but not the fog—reappears northwest of the Coeur d'Alene, among the Sanpoil. They tell that Lynx, ugly and covered with oozing sores, lived alone. One day he surprised the chief's daughter—who was refusing all suitors—lying down and asleep in a small underground cabin. He spat in her mouth, with the predictable result. Beaten, hurt by the inhabitants of the village, Lynx locked himself up in a sweat lodge, but his wife entered it too soon: "His body had become soft, delicate, and pretty. The wounds had disappeared. But his face remained drawn up around his eyes."

Lynx captured all of the animals, and there was a great famine among the guilty in the village. One of them, Raven, came to reconnoiter at Lynx's camp. Lynx's child was playing with a piece of fat. Raven tried to take it away. He was knocked out by the mother, and the shock caused him to lose part of his large intestine. The woman grabbed hold of it, filled it with fat, and fried it. Raven regained consciousness and the woman offered him this sausage; he almost died when, upon returning to his village, his children started to eat it.[25]

East of the Coeur d'Alene, the Flathead, who are also Salish speakers, ignore the motif of the fog, while that of the sweat lodge appears there only in the very weakened form of the blankets in which the wife envelops the remains of her husband "to keep him warm." According to the same version, Lynx accidentally impregnates the heroine by letting some of his saliva dribble on her.[26]

The presence or absence of the motif of the sweat lodge calls for some remarks. Several neighboring tribes in the middle of the Salish area believed in the divinity of the sweat lodge. Kwilsten, which means "sweat lodge," was the name of the demiurge of the Sanpoil and the Okanagan. Upon departing, he had told these Indians' ancestors:

I shall have no body, no head; nor will I be able to see. Whoever desires to construct me will have the right to do so. The one who builds me may pray to me for good looks. . . . I am Sweat Lodge, for the help of human beings.[27]

The Thompson prayed to Sweat Lodge, who for them was also the Wind, one of their tribal gods.[28] The Shuswap called the spirit of the sweat lodge Swalus, a word perhaps meaning "open face" or "face not hidden."[28] For the Lilloet, Quailus, the spirit of the mountains, was also the god of the sweat lodge.[30]

In contrast, it does not appear that the steam bath held an important place with the Salish-speaking peoples settled in the coast and in the Puget Sound area.[31] The Twana did not give it much import; it was in their eyes "a secular or lay, not shamanistic, therapy."[32] The Puyallup–Nisqually did not see the steam bath as an obligation, nor even a social convention, but as a simple matter of individual taste.[33] Farther north, the Lilloet did not make use of steam baths as often as their neighbors in the interior, the Thompson and the Shuswap.[34] It might have even been unknown to the Nootka, a people speaking a Wakashan language and settled on the western coast of Vancouver Island.[35] When going over the Salish language area from east to west, we thus see the use of the sweat lodge weakening until, perhaps, disappearing beyond it.

However, in the center of the Coast Salish area, the Snohomish have a version of the myth that is idealized in several respects. This version smoothes out the myth's angles. While Lynx (here named Wild Cat), a hideous old man covered with sores, has impregnated the chief's daughter with his saliva, he has done it involuntarily, by accident. Moreover, in the course of the test to identify the father, he takes care to request a feather blanket so as not to contaminate the child when he takes it in his arms. When the villagers abandon the couple, Raven hides an ember so that they can relight the fire. Old Lynx wants to free the woman from his presence and leaves. Filled with pity, she goes out to look for him (even though he had ordered her not to) and after several days finds him in a sweat lodge, where he has become young and handsome. But because she arrived too soon, Lynx keeps a sore on his forehead.

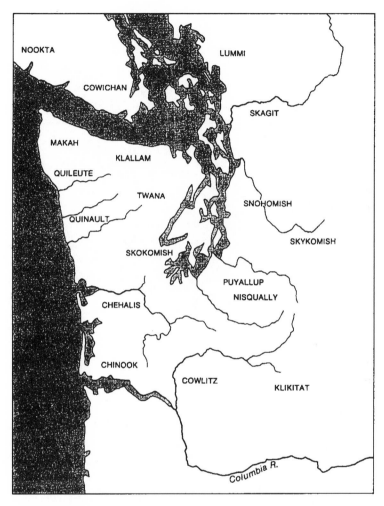

FIGURE 2. Peoples of the Puget Sound and the southern British Columbia area

FIGURE 3. Canadian lynx (*Lynx canadensis*)

Instead of causing famine in the village of his persecutors (as he did with the fog in the Nez Percé version and by imprisoning the animals in the Sanpoil version), Lynx becomes a creator: he transforms garbage in the old village into human beings of all ages and all social conditions, and they build cabins, carve canoes, plait baskets, and weave blankets. This is the origin of the arts of civilization. Following this, the persecutors' village disintegrates and the villagers are forced to return to the old one.

Finally, the Snohomish version presents itself as the myth of the origin of the sweat lodge:

> Wild Cat decided that the sweat bath should be of the greatest use to the people. Everybody could see what it had done for him. It had cured all his sores and made him young. It should do this in

the future. The sweat bath shall make people clean and shall let them regain their strength.

In conclusion: one must respect the elders.[36]

Considered as a whole, the mythical field thus seems to be the locus of a double pendulum swing. One oscillation pertains to the sweat lodge—at times a supernatural mediator with a place in the pantheon, at others a hygienic practice whose legendary origin is narrated in one version. The other oscillation pertains to Lynx's character, which has varying connotations ranging from the negative mode (when he causes famine through fog, making it impossible to hunt, or when he imprisons all the animals, which amounts to the same thing) to the positive mode (as creator of a new humankind and the arts of civilization). In this later stage, his character corresponds almost to that of Moon, whom the Coast Salish regard as the civilizing hero *par excellence.* The interest of this link will become apparent later on (see pp. 140–42 below). Moreover, in almost all of the other versions, Lynx's nature is ambiguous: old, ugly, and sick at the beginning, young and handsome at the end.* Yet his face remains afflicted with a residual ugliness corresponding, it seems, to the Indians' aesthetic views of

---

* "Ulcers, or open sores, are cured by a plaster or salve made from the ashes of the hairs of a wild-cat mixed with grease. I am not aware what particular virtue there is in wild-cat hair over any other; but they have a belief to that effect, and consider a wild-cat or a lynx skin to possess remarkable medicinal properties" (Swan, *The Northwest Coast,* p. 178). Is this belief at the origin of the myth—or at least the origin of the name given to the main protagonist—or is it the result of the myth? This cannot be ascertained. Pliny (*L'Histoire du monde,* pt. 28, p. viii) attributes sedative properties to the ash of Lynx nails.

Regarding Swan's equivocal expression "a wild-cat or a Lynx skin" [TN: in English in the French text], it must be noted that two kinds of the genus Lynx exist in North America: *Lynx canadensis* (in English, rather lynx or wildcat) and *Lynx rufus* (in English, rather bobcat; "rather" because informants appear to use these vernacular terms in a fairly vague manner). Given the more southern habitat of *Lynx rufus* (from the extreme south of Canada to Mexico), it is probable that, generally, *Lynx canadensis* is the hero of our myths.

the animal itself (the Kutenai call the lynx "Short Face").[37] Another aspect of the same ambiguity: although accounts from southern California all the way to the northern Athapaskan oppose lynx meat, which is generally looked down upon, his fur is held to be the most precious of all.[38]

2

Coyote, Father and Son

We have seen that a myth centered around the character of Lynx can grow to make room for another character, Coyote, and tell of their squabbles. The duality of the protagonists comes out even more clearly with the Thompson, so much so that these Indians sometimes divide the myth into two stories, one dealing with Lynx and the other with Coyote's son. Let us begin by looking at the entire myth, whose episodes I will number so as to make it easier to assign them to one of the two stories, which are here consolidated into a single narrative.

1. In a village, a young and beautiful maiden rejects all her suitors. Tired of enduring their courtship, she leaves one day with her younger sister to take refuge with their grandmother, Mountain Sheep (*Ovis canadensis*).

2. After several days of walking, they pass near Coyote's cabin. He causes the temperature to become very cold so as to induce the sisters to warm up in his house. For dinner, he serves them something that he claims is fat but is in fact his own dried sperm. The older girl is suspicious, and she throws this substance into the fire and notices that it sizzles instead of burning; she refuses to eat it. Her younger sister lets herself be tempted and becomes pregnant. The sisters then resume their journey. Coyote runs ahead of them and four times has recourse to the same trick. Finally, the younger sister is on the verge of giving birth. Coyote states that he will kill the baby if it's a girl but raise it if it's a boy. The older girl leaves her sister, who has become Coyote's wife, and continues her journey alone.

3. The grandmother, having through her magical powers become aware that the young girl is near, sends Hare to meet her with some provisions. Hare hides behind a tree fallen in the middle of the path, over which the traveler trips. Hare, ambushed underneath her, can see her red vulva and mocks her. She hits him and pierces his nose with her stick, giving the animal's nose the shape it has kept since that time.

4. As soon as the young woman appears, the grandmother organizes a race among the various animals (including Lynx) who live in the village; the winner will have the granddaughter for a wife. Hummingbird is about to win when the grandmother outdistances him; she drags her granddaughter to her cabin and locks her up in it.

5. Lynx, who is young and handsome here (in contrast to the previously summarized versions), makes a hole in the roof over the bed of the young girl. He impregnates her by spitting on her navel. She gives birth to a handsome son, and no one knows who the father is. It is decided that all of the males of the village are to present their bow and arrows to the baby. The child is not even interested in the splendid weapons that Coyote has made for the occasion. Lynx keeps to himself at a distance. He is pushed forward, and, even though his weapons are plain, the child accepts them and thus recognizes him as his father.

6. Furious at their failure, Coyote and the other villagers throw themselves on Lynx and disfigure and trample him. He is abandoned with the mother and child. The mother takes care of Lynx and heals his wounds except for his face, which remains ugly and contracted.*

Before leaving the village, some inhabitants who feel sorry for him leave behind a bit of dried-up fish. Later, Lynx's son, who becomes a great hunter like his father, thanks them by supplying them with fat.

---

*"Closed up like a fist," says Jules Renard of the cat's head. Jean Dutourd gave me this quote one day while we were discussing cats.

7. As for the younger sister, Coyote's wife, she gives birth to four sons named collectively the Tsamu'xei (meaning unknown).* Only the youngest, who inherits magical powers from his father, bears a name of his own, whose meaning can be rendered as "mighty foot." By hitting tree stumps with his foot, he can make fire spring forth in various places so that his companions can warm themselves.

8. One day, the oldest of the four brothers wants to marry the daughter of a fearsome sorcerer named Cannibal. Under the pretext of helping him cross the river, Cannibal, who lives on the other shore, invites the young man to jump into his canoe. It tips over and he drowns. Two other brothers meet with the same fate. In turn, the youngest, this time helped by his father, decides to attempt the adventure. Both succeed in jumping into the middle of the canoe without causing it to overturn.

9. They manage to protect themselves from the fire Cannibal has lit to kill them by surrounding themselves with blocks of ice. Cannibal then consents to the marriage; but, along with his friend and assistant Kwalum, he plots against his son-in-law.

10. Thanks to the advice of Short-Tailed Mouse, the young man first avoids a fire lit by Kwalum by standing in the middle of a path. He next escapes a tree whose sides were closing up on him while he was working to split it, and then he escapes from a half-human, half-fish aquatic monster. (A fourth test is missing here, forgotten by the narrator.)

11. The next day, Cannibal and Coyote challenge each other. They both resist fire, water, and wind. Coyote finally triumphs by causing a drastic drop in temperature, which freezes Cannibal, his daughter, Kwalum, and all the members of their village. Avenged, Coyote and his son return home.[1]

---

*In another group of myths in which Coyote is opposed to Antelope (see pp. 157–58), Coyote's children each have an individual name while Antelope's do not; cf. on this point *The Naked Man*, p. 399.

⅔

Even though the plots merge on two occasions—the two sisters are both prey to the schemes of Coyote, who is as well the leader of Lynx's enemies in Mountain Sheep's village—it is clear that the sequences numbered 2 and 7 to 11, and those numbered 3 to 6, form separate stories for which sequence 1 provides a common introduction. Of these two stories, the one devoted to Coyote's adventures is the more developed. Difference in narrative styles further accentuates this disequilibrium. Lynx's story *per se* unfolds freely; it is free of formal constraints and has the allure of a small novel. I have elsewhere mentioned the affinity of Lynx's story with the style of the novel and showed how, by collating several versions, one could see the myth transforming itself into legend, into a pseudohistorical narrative, and finally into a novel.[2]

FIGURE 4. Coyote (*Canis latrans*)

In contrast, Coyote's story makes use of narrative devices characteristic of mythical narratives and more generally of oral literature. It offers what musicologists would call a *carrure:* a bar made perceptible to the listener by the consciousness of a periodicity. This periodicity manifests itself through the means of stereotypical formulas. Thus the foursomes succeed one another: four identical tricks by Coyote to bewitch the heroines; four sons; their four attempts to marry Cannibal's daughter; four means used by Cannibal to kill his son-in-law; four tests in which the adversaries confront each other and from which Coyote comes out a winner along with his son . . . A fragment version of the same myth tells that, suspecting her sister's pregnancy, the older girl makes her leap four times into the air; she gives birth on the fourth leap.[3]

In most of the versions, as well, Coyote utters a stereotypical phrase—"If it's a girl, I'll kill her; if it's a boy, I'll keep him"—but we will see later that sometimes he inverts it. This phrase raises complex problems, not only from the standpoint of its geographical distribution but as well from that of its signification in the myths of both North and South America. We will come back to this later (see chap. 5 below).

Even in comparison to the other versions of Lynx's story, versions that I have characterized as minimal, the one that I have just summarized appears to be an abbreviated one. Several episodes disappear, notably those pertaining to the sweat bath and to the fog. Those events that occur, so to speak, on Lynx's side and that are lacking here are put back in the much more extensive versions of the myth whose study will be broached in the next chapter. If the present version highlights Coyote (and his son), it is because it aims to bring out not Lynx's meteorological connotations but rather those of Coyote, who is presented here as the master of cold: he surrounds himself with ice blocks to survive the fire lit by Cannibal; he triumphs over this same Cannibal with the intense cold that he alone can stand. Coyote's son shares this same talent since, by kicking tree stumps, he causes fire to burst out, not for culinary ends but, as the myth specifies, to warm up his companions.[4] Thus this has to do not so much with the origin of fire as with the production of a comforting heat, which is opposed to the deadly fires set by Cannibal. Both terrestrial, these two fires are in a relation of symmetry with two modes of celestial fire because, according to other myths of the area, the Sun, which in the past was excessive and destructive (through either excess or lack), let itself be convinced to emit henceforth a moderate heat that would warm up humans without killing them.[5]

Two versions show this link directly. The Shuswap are the Thompson's northern neighbors, and they limit themselves to the story of Lynx *stricto sensu:* Coyote does not intervene in the plot. The heroine is a female Elk (*Cervus canadensis*). It is either her parents who reject all of her suitors or she herself who rebels against marriage (in different versions). She goes to her grandmother, who pretends to organize a race for marriage and spirits her granddaughter away thanks to the fog or to the night, which she makes fall at high noon. According to one version, it is believed that the Sun has kidnapped the young lady.[6] This detail can be found in another shortened Thompson version of the story of Lynx, in which the heroine also belongs to the Elk family.[7] This version comes from the Upriver Thompson, who are nearest to the Shuswap; it is probably the same version but transcribed by different researchers (on the substitution of the Elk for the Mountain Sheep, cf. p. 71 below).

As we shall see later in this book (see chap. 13 below), it is often in exchange for a human spouse that the sun accepts to emit henceforth a beneficent warmth. This motif is already sketched out in the very midst of the story of Lynx.

❦

The readers of *The Naked Man* might remember that the Thompson versions of the myth called "The Bird-Nester," whose richness I noted,[3] also have Coyote and his son as protagonists. But in that myth they are pitted against each other, while here they are in solidarity: far from wanting to appropriate his son's wives, Coyote helps him obtain a spouse.

In this area of America, and particularly with the Thompson, the myth of the bird-nester ends with a long and complex episode. It explains why the people settled downriver from the falls and cascades have salmon as the basis of their diet, in contrast to the people settled upriver, who are deprived of salmon and have to eat mountain sheep. To avenge himself of his father, Coyote's son causes Coyote to fall into the river. Coyote, dragged away by the current, discovers and frees the salmon imprisoned in the estuary. Ever since then, these fish travel up the rivers. Coyote, who guides their first journey, spies young maidens at their baths. He calls to them and offers them salmon backs. He copulates with those who accept this food from across the river, thanks to his long penis. However, when other young women farther away from the estuary state that they prefer mountain-sheep meat, Coyote creates breaks in the river with falls that the fish are unable to cross and causes mountain sheep to multiply.[9]

The myth thus establishes a relationship between the circulation of salmon and that of women: only those people who accept exogamous unions are to have salmon. The symmetrical myth on Coyote and his son's adventures inverts this proposition, though in an implicit manner. In this latter myth, a young girl rebellious against marriage (who continues to show this disposition by refusing to eat Coyote's dried sperm, which in the register of aridity corresponds to the long, luxuriant penis) takes refuge with her grandmother. This latter is a Mountain Sheep who, under pretext of marrying off her granddaughter, uses a trick—a race between various species of animals—to avoid such an exogamous marriage for her granddaughter. She pretends not to participate in the race, but she is sure to win "because Mountain Sheep can beat any animal in running in a broken country"[10]—that is, on the very type of ground that includes falls on the rivers, preventing salmon from traveling beyond them.

To back this interpretation, one can cite a myth that is found in the whole of the area, an area encompassing in its northerly orientation the low valley of the Columbia River up to the high valley of the Fraser River and, from a west-to-east orientation, the Pacific coastline up to the foothills of the Rocky Mountains. I have discussed elsewhere this myth, referred to as "The Story of Salmon," and showed that it partakes of a vast ensemble of myths that could be labeled "ecological" and that deal with the unequal distribution of animal species in various parts of this territory. However, these myths unfold in a manner that inverts the preceding ones. Instead of explaining why salmon and mountain sheep are not found in the same places, the story of Salmon imagines new conditions under which, during certain times of the year, salmon and wolves (mountain animals like mountain sheep) can be found together. Keeping this difference in mind, we can still observe a remarkable parallelism between the story of Salmon and that of Lynx. Openly in one case, surreptitiously in the other, the hero competes with other animals to obtain his spouse. In both cases the frustrated rival avenges himself by attacking the winner. This latter either heals from his wounds or dies from them, but not without having produced a son (who in the story of Salmon frees his mother, who had been taken away by the wolves).[12]

Other aspects will come to the fore when we discuss the more complex versions. For the time being, I will limit myself to mentioning the existence, in the narratives we have looked at so far, of a set apparently pertaining to details only but providing a good illustration of the modus operandi of mythical thought.

On the way to her grandmother's village, the heroine trips over a tree fallen in the middle of the path. A fragment variant already mentioned (see p. 18 above) substitutes another incident for this one. Having reached the village, the heroine sits down unnoticed at one end of the log her grandmother is in the process of splitting; the granddaughter causes it to tip under her weight, and thus her presence becomes known. Later in this narrative, Coyote's sons want to jump into a canoe. They land in one end of the boat (and not in the middle as they should have), causing it to overturn, and they drown. Finally, the last son protects himself from a forest fire by standing in a cleared path in front of which the fire stops for lack of combustible material. (Or, according to Kutenai versions, the fire crosses the path without stopping.)[12]

Beginning with the end, we start with a major opposition between the absence of trees (the unburnable path) and their presence (in the other cases). When present, the tree is either hollow (the canoe that turns over)* or convex. When convex, the tree materializes in two forms, between which there is a relation of correlation and of opposition: the tree log on whose end the young girl sits and that she causes to overturn, and the tree fallen in the middle of the path that she steps over clumsily and that causes her to trip (in which case she is herself overturned).

We would yet come closer to closing the system if we could demonstrate the following (but these are only hypotheses): (1) An unburnable path is the opposite of an earth oven because the earth oven is dirt that burns while the path is dirt that does not burn; and (2) a tree fallen across a path is the opposite of a treacherous canoe, just as a convex trunk presenting an obstacle to the path of the traveler is to a concave one that turns over under her feet. Absent or present, convex or concave, placed lengthwise or across, all of these aspects of the tree participate in a set that the myths systematically exploit.

---

*There is a boundary between the area in which canoes are built with single, hollowed tree trunks and that in which bark canoes are used. This boundary diagonally divides the region whence our myths generate. The Thompson Indians knew and used both types of canoes. At any rate, a canoe, even if made out of bark, evokes the image of a hollow tree, though it is then a reconstituted tree.

I. Shells of the genus Dentalium. *(These have the same overall shape but are of a different species from the one fished by the Indians of the Pacific coast.)*

II. Mannequin with the clothes and dentalia necklace of a Thompson chief, collected in 1903. Royal British Columbia Museum, *Victoria, Catalogue nb. 1267 (necklace). Reprinted with the kind permission of the museum.*

III. Nisqually woman (Puget Sound area) wearing rich dentalia adornments, photographed in 1868 next to a White child entrusted to her care. Thomas Burke Museum, Seattle, Catalogue nb. L4233. Reprinted with the kind permission of the museum.

IV. Haida sleeveless shirt made of commercial cloth and embroidered mainly with dentalia shells representing a bear, acquired in 1979. Royal British Columbia Museum, Victoria, Catalogue nb. 16537. Reprinted with the kind permission of the museum.

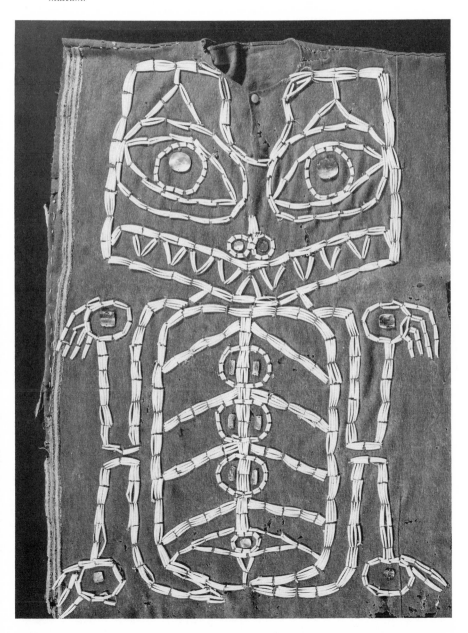

3

The Dentalia Thieves

We have seen how the story of Lynx, reduced to its essential outlines, can be imbedded in a more complex narrative in which Coyote, Lynx's adversary, is the main character. We will now broach a third state, which diverges from the preceding ones in two ways. First, it reestablishes equilibrium between the protagonists by reintegrating everything that, "on the side of Lynx," was lacking in the plot of the second state. Then, and more important, while the first state fits into the second, this second in turn fits into the third state, which is enriched with new episodes. The image of Russian wooden dolls containing one another illustrates this relationship well.

For the sake of convenience, let us label this new group with a code name: "The Dentalia Thieves." * This time, again, it is with the Thompson Indians that we find the most typical forms.

In these mountains in olden days, away from any human dwellings and without any family, there lived a man and his two sisters. He was a great hunter; he brought back an abundance of fatty meat and hides. Every day he bathed in a neighboring stream and rubbed his body with pine boughs. The needles that fell changed into shells of the genus *Dentalium*, which he brought back to his sisters. But he forbade them to visit the place where he bathed. Curious, the younger one talked the elder into going there, and they picked up handfuls of the shells lying at the bottom of the water. Their brother was angered and decided to leave them. He lifted the slab of stone on the hearth; this stone hid an opening through which he descended into the lower world. (Another ver-

*TN: In the French feminine form; that is, the thieves are female.

sion locates the scene in a higher world, and it is into our own world that the hero descends.) Intrigued by the behavior of their hunting dog, the women leaned over the opening, from which a mighty wind was blowing. They discovered their brother playing ball with the people from below. The older of the sisters reproached the younger one; they both cried abundantly, and their tears, fallen into the hole, wet their brother. This surprised him because, in these mythical times, rain did not yet exist (see p. 9 above). He went back up to console the young women; they asked to follow him. He agreed, but three times in a row they were unable to keep their eyes shut during the descent, which caused them to go back up. Discouraged, the brother advised them to go instead to Elk, their aunt. And he advised them not to stop along the way.

From this point on and except for details, we are rejoining the Thompson myth, the principal subject matter of the preceding chapter: four successive stops at Coyote's; the younger sister becoming pregnant ("If she has a female child I will rear it; but if a male I will hang it up in the branch of a tree"); the episode with Hare; the arrival at the aunt's home; the race for the marriage in which participate all of the quadrupeds and birds, except for Coyote, Lynx, Hare, and Deer (*Odocoileus;* the species is not specified). The Elk aunt passes them, drags her niece away, and locks her up in a basket suspended above her bed.

The rest of the story is identical to the others, except that Lynx, nursed and healed by his wife, does hunt for his family but imprisons all the game on a hill: "Puma, Wolf, all the best hunters . . . could find no game, and a famine began to reign." A final sequence, already encountered with the Sanpoil (see p. 11 above) and used in this version, tells of Raven's visit and the return of the remorseful villagers, whom Lynx supplies with large quantities of game: "He gave most meat and fat to those people who had formerly treated him kindly; but to Raven, Coyote, and others he gave very little."[1]

The Thompson also have several variants of this story, of which we will mention only the most notable. In one story, the hero encourages his sisters to come join him in the lower world, "a fine country [where] there is neither rain nor snow; nor heat nor cold." But the women are afraid to go down, and the hero, feeling sorry for them, goes back to them.[2]

A very different version (but cf. p. 198 below) tells that a hero named Tcîskíkik (probably a tit; species *parus*) had a sister who kept following him while he was hunting and, in spite of his interdiction, would throw herself on the barely killed game to eat it. Angered by this behavior, he wounded the young girl, who took flight and changed herself into a *kaqwa* bird (possibly a golden plover, genus *Pluvialis*). The brother bemoaned his loss, and since then the song of the bird *tcîskíkik* seems to say: "Oh! My younger sister!"[3]

More different yet, a third version has two brothers. One disappears one day into the happy chthonic world of the Ants, where ball games are played all day long. The other brother succeeds in joining him through the hole of the hearth. They live there, united and happy, in the world of the Ants.[4]

❧

The Okanagan, eastern neighbors of the Thompson, begin the narrative in the same manner as their neighbors but continue it differently.

After the two sisters have spied on the hero and stolen his shells (in this version, so as to adorn their dolls), the latter is indignant, and he persuades his parents to abandon the guilty ones (this version includes a complete family). Only the dog remains, and he digs in the earth next to a rock. The young girls lift this rock and see their parents in the lower world. They cry and beg; the mother feels sorry for them and asks her son to go get them. He tries to descend with one girl under each arm, but they cannot keep their eyes shut as they should and he fails three times in a row. He suggests they go live with their grandmother and advises them not to accept any rancid food that might be offered them along the way. The sisters set off, arrive at a river, and call out to a ferryman. He pretends that his canoe is broken and points them toward a ford downstream.* They arrive at his camp, where he serves them a dish of fat that only the younger sister tastes. "If it's a boy, let us spare him; but if it's a girl, let us drown her!" the man exclaims immediately. Upon hearing these words, the elder girl realizes that her sister is pregnant. She leaps up four or five times and orders her sister to imitate her and to make sure to come down exactly into her footsteps. The younger sister misses and gives birth to a boy; she remains with her seducer along with the child.

The older sister continues her journey. She spends the night in a hut and finds in it some fat left there by Hare, whom Lynx had sent to meet her; but she eats only her own provisions. Hare, hidden under a fallen tree, sees the woman's sex as she crosses over it; he makes fun of her vulva, which is white (and not red as on p. 18 above). The woman hits his nose with a digging stick.

She arrives at the home of her grandmother, who is splitting wood, and sits down unnoticed on the log. The old woman discovers her presence because her ax blows sound different from before. She hides her granddaughter, but the secret is soon known; all of the young men of the village want to marry her. One day when the grandmother is absent, Lynx, the shrewd one, climbs on top of the roof and urinates on the planks. One drop falls into the mouth of the sleeping woman. She soon gives birth to a boy. This version shows a more open approach than the other ones as the villagers assemble to celebrate the event. The baby passes from hand to hand. Owl steals it, carries it away, and raises it without anyone objecting because Owl is a powerful character feared by everyone.

The child grows and becomes a good hunter. Finally someone succeeds in talking to him and convinces him to return to his family. Owl goes out to look for him, but the fugitives, who had crossed a river on a tree trunk fallen across it, beg Wood Worm to gnaw on it. The trunk breaks, Owl falls into the water, and Crabs

---

*His name means "gull." The trait might be more suitable to the water ouzel (who holds the same role in the Kutenai and Coeur d'Alene versions), as this bird is capable of walking underwater.

throw themselves on him and keep him from moving. He drowns. The happy fugitives arrive near a lake; the weather is very hot. The young man—who, we must not forget, is Lynx's son, whose story as told here matches that of Coyote's son—wants to bathe and goes away from the shore in spite of the warnings of his mother. He is called back, but he pretends not to hear and dives under the water, to reappear transformed into a Loon (genus *Gavia*).[5]

East of the Okanagan, the Kutenai, who form a separate linguistic group,* have versions that are quite different. I summarize these next.

Deer orders his sisters Doe and Fawn to throw into the water the cartilage from the game he was bringing back; these parts transform themselves into dentalia. One day, the young women steal them. Angered, their brother and the other inhabitants of the village decide to emigrate to the lower world without allowing the culprits to follow them. The sisters themselves then leave, cross a river by using stilts, and accept the hospitality of Water Ouzel. The bird makes the younger sister, Fawn, pregnant by giving her cooked blood to eat. Ordered by her sister to walk in her footsteps, Fawn inadvertently takes a misstep and gives birth to a son. Doe sends her back to Water Ouzel, whose head Fawn holds underwater to avenge herself.

Doe continues the journey alone. She meets Hare, who refuses to take her to her grandmother, Frog, unless she agrees to call him her spouse. Frog hides her granddaughter, whom Lynx surreptitiously impregnates. (Another version narrates how: Lynx sticks four of his hairs into the ground where the young woman goes to urinate.) Doe gives birth to a boy. The three of them are abandoned. Lynx brings back plenty of game, while in their new village

---

*Due to an unexplainable error in the publication process, in the Skira edition of *La Voie des masques,* the part of the map of the tribes (pt. 1, p. 79) marked with crisscrossed lines bears the label "Sahaptin" instead of "Kutenai." Gone unnoticed, the mistake has been repeated in later editions (Plon, 1979, p. 44, and Presses Pocket, 1988, p. 38), the map having been reproduced without change.

the inhabitants are suffering from famine; they thus come back. The child is passed from hand to hand, and then Frog and Owl take it away. Doe pursues them, takes back her son, hides with him in a tree, and pits her dog (which is a Grizzly Bear) against his kidnappers. Later, Doe and Lynx have another son (one version attributes twins to them). The two sons become the Sun and the Moon, which, according to one version, Crow and Coyote attempt to embody. They do not succeed because they are either too cold or too hot, too slow or too fast.[6]

With the Coeur d'Alene, southern neighbors of the Kutenai, we reenter the Salish linguistic area, which we had left temporarily. These Indians turn the story of Lynx and that of the dentalia thieves into two separate ones. I will not repeat their version of the first myth, summarized previously (see pp. 9–10 above), except to remind the reader of the motif in which the fog and the resulting famine lead to the origin or the return of fair weather. As for the Coeur d'Alene version of the dentalia thieves, it is made up of parts from the Kutenai version (the means of production of the shells) and of parts from the Okanagan version (the transformation of the hero into a bird). Here it is.

The head of the village of the Eagles demands that all the families give him the bones from the game they have eaten. He orders his two daughters (Eagles like himself) to make a hole in the ice covering the river and to throw in the bones without looking. Intrigued by a "mu, mu, mu" noise, one of them disobeys and sees at the bottom of the water the bones transformed into dentalia. She tells her sister about this. Together they secretly build a cabin in the forest, where they pile up the shells. Day after day, they thread them on strings made up of vegetable fiber. One of the sisters, pretending to act on behalf of her father, the chief, has enormous quantities of this fiber given to her by each household. Becoming suspicious, the father spies on them. When he discovers their scheme, he summons the whole of the population: "Not for my own, but for your sake, I asked you to bring me the bones. Now my own children have stolen them." He orders that the culprits be abandoned. When they return in the evening from their cabin, they find no one: all of the dwellings have been destroyed, the village abandoned. The sisters then set forth and come upon the bank of a river that forks into two streams. They call to a ferryman (probably a Water Ouzel, as in the Kutenai version); he pretends not to have a canoe and directs them to a ford.

At the ferryman's house the two sisters are offered some soup made of cooked blood. The older pretends to eat some of it but gets rid of it through a dentalium shell that she has attached to her chin and that works like a small funnel. The younger sister is less careful and, after the meal, has trouble following her sister. They argue and backtrack. A ferryman invites them to climb into his canoe, but he does not come to the shore. The older refuses to get wet and shoves the ferryman. He falls into the water and drowns. She then leaves her sister and carries away all the shells they have taken along.

She meets Mudhen and offers her a dentalium shell (whence the shape of this bird's beak). Mudhen alerts the group with which she travels that a stranger is not far off. The chief promises the girl in marriage to whoever wants her. Mudhen schemes so that her grandson, Red-Headed Woodpecker, becomes the groom in spite of his shyness. The woman gives birth to a boy whom everyone spoils. The Four Man-eating Sisters take advantage of the situation to kidnap him.

The young mother, carrying dentalia as a provision, sets off in search of her son. Meadowlark gives her information and receives as a reward Bluebird's necklace. The child has become an adult and a great hunter. The mother surprises him as he is taking a steam bath, introduces herself, and persuades him to leave his captors. The Man-eating Sisters are in the habit of encircling their quarry and making themselves invisible by surrounding themselves with smoke. The hero fools them by leaving a mannequin in his stead, and he runs away with his mother.

Together they cross a river on the woman's untied belt. Invited to do the same, the cannibals drown when the hero's mother suddenly pulls out this footbridge. The four sisters are transformed into Terns: "You'll no longer be cannibals," states the woman.

"You'll be animals that live along the river. When people come, you will not fly up." As she is thirsty, the woman sends her son to get her some water; he is slow to return and plays while bathing. His mother becomes impatient and decides to leave without him:

You will be Hell-diver;* I will be Robin (*Turdus migratorius*). You like the water too well to live with me. When the wind blows, you will fly. You will make the sound "yaxa yaxa."† As for me, I will be a ghost. I will sit on a tree near the houses of the people and make my sound there when people have a death. Since you like the water, you will live in water. As for me, I will live in the brush."[7]

We have so far offered in bulk a large package of myths, the telling of which might have seemed fastidious. But how else could this be done? They form the substance of this book. The reader might think, not without reason, that it is high time to take an overall view and to justify the attention that has been given to them.

These narratives have enabled us to see how the story of Lynx, in its reduced form, gradually takes its place in a larger plot whose two initial protagonists are two sisters, of whom one will become Coyote's wife and the other Lynx's wife. The story either stops at this point or continues with the narrative of either Coyote's or Lynx's son (sometimes doubled into twins), or again of both of them.

However, this set appears homogeneous only if one takes a bird's-eye view of it. When it is looked at closely and in detail, one can make out a first fault line. In one group of myths, the two sisters (or, more precisely, the older followed by the younger) are

---

*"Hell-diver" is a common name for all grebes, particularly the horned grebe (*Podiceps auritus*) and the pied-billed grebe (*Podilymbus podiceps*). This latter is less widespread in the interior of British Columbia; thus we are probably dealing with the first one. These two species spend the summer by lakes and marshes and the winter by the seashore.

†The cry of the grebe is a sign of wind.

FIGURE 5. Horned grebe (*Podiceps auritus*)

difficult girls, rebellious against marriage. In another group of myths, the two sisters (or, more precisely, the younger followed by the older) are indiscreet: they spy on their brother while he, away from all gazes—particularly those of women—makes himself undergo initiation tests, at the end of which he is to acquire his guardian spirit or spirits. This is how the ethnography of people of Salish language and culture leads us to understand the episode of the bath followed by the rubdown with pine boughs. In this sense, one could say that the behavior of the two sisters comes close to incest.* The loss of the dentalia shells is the result. Let us

---

*This would be even clearer if we could generalize on the basis of the observations coming from the areas surrounding the Salish one. Among the Carrier to the north and the Hupa to the south, both members of the Athapaskan family,

remember that the Inland Salish did not know the real origin of these univalve shells, whose length is about three to six centimeters and which resemble miniature elephant tusks. They were getting the shells from the Chilcotin, who themselves received them from the people of the coast.[8] Dentalia were found only in the Puget Sound and north of it. But there was much demand for them to the south, all the way down to California, where they were part of the same set of beliefs but with one essential difference: the Inland Salish saw dentalia as precious jewels, while the Californian tribes sought them mostly as money, which was hoarded and which played a major role in the competition for prestige and in economic and social exchanges.* However, one could not imagine a better gloss on the Thompson myths than the following account pertaining to the Yurok of California, located about one thousand kilometers to the south:

> When he [a Yurok Indian] goes down to the river, he stares into it, and at last may discern a shell as large as a salmon, with gills working like those of a fish. Young men were recommended to undergo these practices for ten days at a time, meanwhile fasting and exerting themselves with the utmost vigor, and not allowing their minds to be diverted by communication with other people, particularly women. They would become rich in old age. . . . The Yurok hold a strong conviction that dentalium money and the congress of the sexes stand in a relation of inherent antithesis.[9]

---

dentalium was worn by men while women wore mother-of-pearl from abalone. This same opposition has been reported among the Salish, but only for earrings (the opposition is inverted with nose plugs). In all cases, consequently, the sexual polarity of shells used for adornment appears strongly marked (cf. Morice, pp. 725–26; Goddard, pp. 19–20; Hill-Tout *The Natives of British North America,* pp. 86–87).

*This passion for dentalia was not limited to this area of the New World. Treasures of 1,400, 2,200, 2,100, and 4,500 dentalia respectively have been discovered on the shore of the Black Sea in Bulgaria, in the necropolis of Varna, which dates to around 4000–5000 B.C. (Catalogue from the exhibit *Le Premier Or de l'Humnité en Bulgarie, 5e millénaire.* Paris, Réunion des Musées nationaux, 1989, numbers 218, 230, 279, 300)

It is also indeed by bringing the sexes closer (even if it is at a distance, but made worse by the fact that this rapprochement occurs between brother and sister and in circumstances that make it highly sacrilegious) that the Thompson, Coeur d'Alene, and Kutenai versions of the myth of the dentalia thieves explain why the Indians lost the possession of these precious shells, or at least why their production stopped.

And yet, things are not quite so simple because, east of the Thompson and thus further inland, the Coeur d'Alene and the Kutenai versions substitute one interdiction for another: the families cannot throw away certain parts of the game they consume (the cartilage portion or the ribs or, more vaguely, the bones from the game), but they must turn these over to the chief. However, these myths do not turn hunting into a ritual activity, in contrast to the initiation rituals mentioned in the other versions. When these various versions are thus compared, a triple opposition seems to come to light:

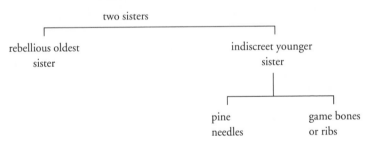

The last opposition raises a problem that I am not yet able to resolve given the available evidence. Do bones from the game invert the dentalia shells, which are "bones" that contain meat (not enough for human consumption, but there are mythical beings with minuscule mouths who feed off them; cf. *The Jealous Potter*, pp. 103–4), while game is meat that contains bones? Nothing in the myths supports this hypothesis, which would at any rate leave the cartilage unexplained. Should we rather look to history? The formula with the ribs or the bones from the game could have come from the Kutenai. This interpretation is tempting, as the Coeur d'Alene, the Kutenai's neighbors, are the only ones among Salish speakers to have adopted this variant. But this would not resolve the problem because the Kutenai themselves are an enigma. They form an isolated linguistic group, wedged in between the two large linguistic families, Salish in the west and Algonkin in the east. Perhaps the Kutenai once lived east of the Rockies next to the Blackfoot (an Algonkin people by language, Plain Indian by culture), with whom in the nineteenth century they still maintained relations, at times hostile and at times those of marriage and trade. This being the case, one might make out in the formula of the ribs or the bones of the game a sort of distant echo of beliefs reported for the Algonkin people of the Atlantic shore, according to which the shells used to make beads called *wampum* would have been carnivorous and even cannibalistic. This hypothesis is the more attractive in that the same belief, this time relating to dentalia, has been noted in northern California among the Yurok, whose language, like that of their Wiyot neighbors, seems to belong to the Algonkin family.[10] To which we can add that only in the versions with the bones of the game are the hero's captor or captors labeled as cannibalistic.

In addition to this problem, another one is raised by the aquatic birds that seem to burst in groups into several versions of the myth. A character named Gull or Water Ouzel replaces Coyote in the Okanagan, Coeur d'Alene, and Kutenai versions. In the Okanagan and the Coeur d'Alene variants, Lynx's son is metamorphosed into a Loon or a Grebe; according to the Coeur d'Alene, his captors become Terns. A group of versions "with Waterbirds" overlaps in parts with the group "with pine needles" as well as with the group "with game bones" without matching any of them:

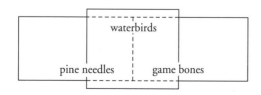

In the segment to the far left in the schema—that is, among the Thompson—the myth continues with the adventures of Coyote's son (who is a great sorcerer) and only makes an allusion to Lynx's son becoming a great hunter. In the segment to the far right—that is, among the Kutenai—Lynx's son or rather his twin sons become the Sun and the Moon. But in all cases, among the Okanagan (pine needles + Waterbirds), as well as among the Coeur d'Alene (game bones + Waterbirds), as well as among the Kutenai, the transformation of Lynx's son into a Loon or into a Grebe, or that of his sons into celestial bodies, occurs as a consequence of the kidnapping of the child by an Owl (Okanagan), a Frog and an Owl (Kutenai), or again four cannibalistic sisters (Coeur d'Alene)—from which yet another fault line cuts through the myths. I will temporarily set aside the motive of the kidnapped child and deal with it later (see chaps. 7 and 8).

4

A Myth to Go Back in Time

The family of myths that I have divided into two groups labeled "The Story of Lynx" and "The Dentalia Thieves"—the second one encompassing the first—illustrates, in northwestern North America, a set of myths found in both hemispheres. As we have known for a long time, surprisingly similar forms of these myths exist in North America, Brazil, and Peru. Some versions were collected in the sixteenth and seventeenth centuries, others in the nineteenth or even the twentieth. In spite of this time spread, the myth remains easily identifiable, and it is striking how little these distances in time and space have affected it.

To show this, I will call upon a version that is also the first myth of the Indians of Brazil that came to be known to Europeans. Thevet collected it around 1555 from the Tupinamba of the Rio de Janeiro area and published it in 1575. We owe to Alfred Métraux a new annotated edition of this myth accompanied by previously unpublished versions from a manuscript.[1] The myth is truly an American Genesis, and the motifs that have concerned us up to now form only one episode—or, more specifically, one sequence—placed in the middle of the narrative. However, it will be seen that this sequence is articulated on those that precede and follow it, so that the narrative forms a whole in spite of Thevet's admission of having kept only some incidents and omitted others he was told.

I thus do not think that Thevet has "welded into a single myth several different ones and even different versions of the same myth."[2] Every myth has a structure that attracts attention and has an impact on its hearer's memory. This is the reason myths can be transmitted through oral tradition. This not only holds for native listeners, enabling them to repeat the myth, but to a lesser extent it holds as well for listeners as poorly prepared as a sixteenth-century French Franciscan monk must have been; Thevet's choice of what he heard and remembered was not haphazard. Instead, in the myths collected in the nineteenth and twentieth centuries one can often recognize the debris of a more coherent mythology whose existence can still be witnessed here and there (such as that collected in our time by Nimuendaju from the Apapocuva and by Cadogan from the Guarani, two peoples that are close kin of the ancient Tupinamba).

And so, Thevet tells us, at the beginning of the world, the god Monan, whose name specifically means "the ancient one," was living among the human beings and bestowing his favors upon them in great number. But the humans were ungrateful, and the god made them perish through a fire of celestial origin. He also molded the land in relief, because in those days the earth was smooth and flat; neither the sea nor the rain existed. Only one man was saved, whom Monan transported to heaven. Giving in to the entreaties of the survivor, the god drowned the fire with a deluge, from which the sea and the other water bodies originated. Monan created a woman for the man so that the couple could reproduce. Thus was born a second race and, most important, the demiurge Maire-Monan ("ancient transformer"), master of all arts, of whom the Whites, superior to the Indians because of their culture, are the "true children." It was Maire-Monan who granted to all living things their present aspect and their distinctive character.*

*Thevet's not-very-explicit text implies that in mythical times human beings and animals were part of one single family; the role of Transformer consisted of introducing generic differences into this confused mass. I have shown elsewhere that his South American geste of the Transformer (all the beings he meets in his travel wish for his death because they refuse to be changed into a Deer, or a Monkey, or a Tapir, or one kind of plant or another) is found in all its details in the Northwest of North America, notably among the Chinook and the Salish. Cf. "De la Fidélité au texte," p. 130.

Rebelling against their transformation, Maire-Monan's contemporaries killed him by burning him on a pyre. He went up to heaven and became Thunder, leaving some of his descendants on earth. One of them, Sommay (= Sumé), had two sons named Tamendonaré and Aricouté. One of the sons was of a peaceful nature, while the other had an aggressive temperament. A conflict between the two brothers resulted in a flood of terrestrial origin. The two brothers and their spouses took refuge on top of a mountain; all of the other human beings and animals perished. From one brother and his wife descended the Tupinamba; from the other couple, their hereditary enemies. Each brother was able to relight his hearth thanks to the fire Monan had taken care to place between the shoulders of the Sloth (*Bradypus tridactylus,* called "scapular sloth" in Brazil on account of the yellow spot between its shoulders).[3]

All this might, at first sight, appear unconnected to the North American myths discussed in the preceding chapters. The link will shortly become clear: the following leads us back to the North American myths.

In the village there lived one Maire-Pochy. He was "an intimate of the great Monan" in spite of his condition as servant or even slave. He was ugly and disfigured but possessed magical powers. One day, as he was bringing back some fish, his master's daughter decided to have a taste of it; she became pregnant and soon gave birth to a beautiful baby boy. All of the men of the village assembled to find out from whom the child would accept a bow and arrows, thereby identifying his father; it was Maire-Pochy. "There were grumblings against him," and he was abandoned with his wife and child. But "the place where this Maire lived was plentiful in all things, while the place where the others lived was sterile and lacked all fruits, so much so that the unfortunate people died from hunger."

Feeling sorry for them, Maire had his wife take them food, and he invited them to come for a visit. The fertile gardens of the host made them so envious that they looted them; Maire transformed the visitors into various animals on the spot. The incident permanently turned him against his in-laws and even against his wife: "He got rid of his disfigured and ugly body, becoming the most handsome of human beings, and went up to heaven to live in peace."

Maire-Pochy's son, also called Maire, who was a great sorcerer like his father, wanted to go with him to heaven. This son transformed himself for a while into a rock separating the sea and the land so as to prevent anyone from following him.* Later he returned to a human shape and remained among the Indians. Among other marvels, he made a diadem out of flames. A companion who was too much in a hurry ripped it from Maire's hands to try it on; the imprudent one caught on fire, threw himself into the water, and was transformed into a Rail, a small wading bird with red legs and feet. Finally, this Maire went to join his father (whom Thevet here calls Caroubsouz; compare in Lingua Geral, *coaracy;* in Guarani, *quaraçi, kuarahy,* "the sun"; in Tembé-Tenatehara, *ko'ar-apo-har,* "the Creator of the world"); he left on earth a son called Maire-Ata, who married a local woman. She liked to travel and wanted to see the country even though she was pregnant. The child in her womb conversed with her and told her the way; but because she refused to pick for him certain "small vegetables" he fancied, he became silent. The woman got lost and arrived at Opossum's dwelling. He invited her in and, taking advantage of her sleep, impregnated her with another son, "who kept company in her womb with the first one."

I abbreviate the end of the myth, which has many parallels in both hemispheres that are of less direct interest to us. The woman left Opossum and got lost among ferocious Indians, who killed her and, before eating her, threw the children extracted from her

*In the Peruvian version, also dating from the sixteenth century and collected in the province of Huarochiri, it is a woman—whose slot corresponds to that of Maire's mother in the Tupinamba version—who, disgusted with her husband (as Maire-Pochy was with his wife), transformed herself along with her daughter into a rock at the bottom of the sea (Avila, p. 25). On the role of "semiconductor" of the rock in the middle of the water, cf. *The Naked Man,* pp. 434, 444–47.

womb into the trash. A woman found them and raised them. They avenged their mother by drowning her killers, who became the wild beasts of today. After this, they set out in search of Maire-Ata, whom they both believed to be their father. In order to recognize them as his sons, Maire-Ata imposed tests on them, in the course of which Opossum's son showed himself vulnerable while Maire-Ata's son was invulnerable, capable even of resuscitating his brother each time he died.[4] The versions collected in our time in Paraguay, as well as in southern and northeastern Brazil, evidence the extraordinary stability of this myth. Tupi-speaking groups have maintained it intact for centuries, and the distances separating them have not affected the myth either.[5] It even spread to peoples of languages and cultures different from that of the Tupi. Thus the episode of the fire diadem is found unchanged among the Gê (*The Raw and the Cooked,* p. 292; on the Gê, cf. chap. 5 and pp. 235–38 below).

❧

It has often been noted that the story of Maire-Pochy prefigures very exactly the myths collected three or four centuries later in North America, thousands of kilometers away from southern Brazil. The Salish versions of the story of Lynx offer a striking example of this: everything is there. "Ugly and disfigured" (as in Thevet) at the beginning or in the course of the plot, the hero transforms himself into a handsome young man in the middle or the end of the story. The test for recognizing the father is based on the same device: each man offers the child his bow and arrows. The defeated rivals abandon the hero along with his wife and child. This works out poorly for the rivals, as they are soon prey to famine while their victims live in plenty. The hero, feeling sorry for them, welcomes and feeds them but without forgetting his grievances. He changes his persecutors (or some of them) into animals; or, according to some North American versions, he reduces Coyote and Raven to the condition of carrion-eaters.[6]

No less significant is the episode in the Tupinamba myth in which Opossum, a stinking animal (replacing the Coyote of the

North American versions), seduces a woman who has lost her way. Coyote serves her his dried-up sperm for a meal. A South American version originating in the Chaco area involves a similar trick: the trickster, who is a Bird here, deposits on the woman's path his sperm, which is so dried up that she takes it to be salt, picks it up, and licks it. This version includes as well the test for recognizing the father by presenting bows and arrows to the child.[7]

In the North American versions, Lynx's twin sons become the Sun and the Moon. When Lynx has only one son, the latter becomes a Waterbird. In the Tupinamba version, Maire-Pochy's son, the equivalent to Lynx's son, becomes the Sun, while one of his companions is transformed into a Waterbird.* All of the South American versions, moreover, establish a close relationship between twins and the two celestial bodies. The Guarayu of Bolivia[8] express this in almost the same way as the Kutenai, who live in the northern Rockies (see p. 31 above). These versions, like those of the Tupinamba, pertain less to the origin of the sun and moon than to their proper behavior—whether it be (as in the North American versions) the setting of their daily or nightly succession or (as in the Tupinamba myth) the sufficient distancing of the Sun so that it would not burn the Indians as it did the overly impatient companion of Maire-Pochy's son. Maire-Pochy still exists under his name (Mbae-Pochy) among the Mbya–Guarani of Paraguay. They assign him the job of punishing couples who have offended the gods. How? By causing them to give birth to twins . . .

There certainly are differences between the North American versions and those collected in the sixteenth century in South America. The first of these have as central characters two sisters,

---

*Today, the Mbya-Guarani of Paraguay still tell a version of the myth in which a demon, victim of the same fate as Maire's companion, is reduced to ashes— except for a piece of his intestine, which becomes the partridge *tataupa,* mistress of fire. *Crypturus tataupa,* a different bird from the Old World partridge, has a bright red beak and light red legs (Cadogan, p. 83; Ihering, entry "Inambu chintau"). Montoya's Guarani-Spanish dictionary (1640) translates *tataupa* into the Spanish *fogon*—that is, "hearth."

one who is impregnated by Coyote, the other by Lynx. Each one gives birth to a boy; the two children are thus parallel cousins. The other versions—for instance, the Tupinamba myth—have Opossum impregnate a woman already made pregnant by her husband, and her children are then born as twins:

$$\begin{bmatrix} \triangle = O = \triangle \\ | \quad | \\ \triangle \quad \triangle \end{bmatrix} \Rightarrow \begin{bmatrix} \triangle = \overline{O \quad O} = \triangle \\ | \quad \quad | \\ \triangle \quad \quad \quad \triangle \end{bmatrix}$$

And yet the children are not, properly speaking, twins, as they have been procreated by different fathers. We must note, however, that North American mythology conceptualizes the two fathers' relationship as somewhat akin to twinness. Perhaps alike originally—that is, twins from an anatomical perspective—the animals decided to become differentiated: Lynx lengthened Coyote's nose and legs, while Coyote pushed in Lynx's nose and shortened his tail.[9] One comes across this motif in many places in North America: its area of dispersion ranges at least from the Shuswap in northern British Columbia to the Pueblo of Arizona and New Mexico (see p. 229 below). It is clear that Lynx and Coyote in North America, and Maire and Opossum in South America, fill complementary but opposite functions. The first separates the positive and negative aspects of reality and puts them in separate categories. The other acts in the opposite direction: it joins the bad and the good. The demiurge has changed animate and inanimate creatures from what they were in mythical times into what they will be thenceforth. The trickster keeps imitating the creatures as they were in mythical times and as they cannot remain afterward. He acts as if privileges, exceptions, or abnormalities could become the rule, while the demiurge's job is to put an end to singularities and to establish rules that will be universally applicable to all members of each species and category. This explains the metaphysical importance myths assign to the trickster: he always keeps to his role, whether he is extracting the less good from the better or introducing the worst (cf. *The Raw and the Cooked,* p. 172 and p. 293 n. 1; *From Honey to Ashes,* pp. 83–84; *The Naked Man,* p. 385).*

Alfred Métraux has been very interested in the story of Maire-Pochy and has compiled its distribution map for South America. He believes it to be of Peruvian origin. Ehrenreich thought likewise.[10] It is true that there are very similar versions collected in the sixteenth century by Spanish missionaries in the provinces of Huamachuco and of Huarochiri.[11] (This last version, which I have already discussed, is closest to the story of Lynx.) There are also other clues from which one can surmise that Peruvian influences might have been at play all the way to the Tupi of the southern coast of Brazil and through Bolivia and the Chaco region. Yet even while accepting this distant origin, one should recognize that the Tupinamba have reserved for the story of Maire-Pochy a precise spot in their Genesis, a location where it could best be organically integrated and articulated into the rest of the myth. Though many episodes of this Genesis are lacking, there are enough left in it for us to grasp its general economy and to convince us that the whole was solidly constructed (as still is the part that we know). Thus the two deluges that Ehrenreich, and Métraux following him,[12] proposed to consolidate into a single one are really of very different natures: celestial healing water (putting an end to a destructive celestial fire) in one, terrestrial destructive water in the other (see

---

*A comparison between the faults of the trickster and the fall of Adam could be pursued. Both create the possibility for all knowledge and mark the end of original innocence. But in one case the one who falls is the last of the gods, while in the other he is the first of men. In addition, Adam falls all at once; his fall has the character of a catastrophe. On the contrary, the trickster falls in stages. He commits his errors in spurts, which are told in the cycle of "The Bungling Host"; whence the highly sacred value the Indians give to this cycle (a value that has often intrigued commentators). The trickster gradually discovers that he can no longer accomplish the same supernatural feats as other supernatural beings can. This is because of his linking his destiny to that of men, and it is this factor that could lead to broadening the comparison.

p. 44 above). And while the first destructive fire of which the myth speaks has a celestial origin, the second (the pyre on which dies the demiurge) is of terrestrial origin. We can thus write the following within the sequence of the unfolding of the narrative:

1. destructive celestial fire (putting to an end the first humankind);
2. repairing celestial water (origin of the sea and waterways);
3. destructive terrestrial fire (the pyre);
4. destructive terrestrial water (sprung from the ground);
5. relighting of the hearth (domesticated terrestrial fire);
6. the sun pushed back to a safe distance (domesticated celestial fire).

It can be seen that the myth methodically exploits a system of multidimensional oppositions—fire/water; celestial/terrestrial;

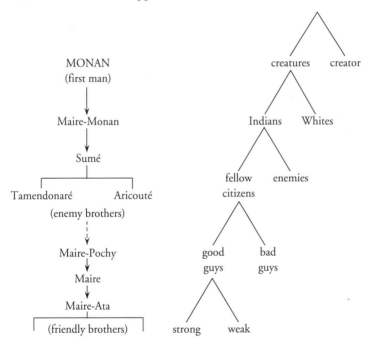

FIGURE 6. Two-way splits in the Tupinamba myth

destructive/repairing; extreme/middle—and that a satisfactory equilibrium is established between all these terms in the end. Ehrenreich, followed by Métraux,[13] considers (probably with good cause) that the divinities who succeed and replace one another in the course of the narrative are really only one; that they are, as Métraux puts it, doubles of one another, and that the two pairs of twins (issued respectively from Sumé and from Maire-Ata; see pp. 45, 46–47 above) should also be reduced to one. Though this might possibly be right, it doesn't lessen the reality of their diffraction, since each of these hypostases fills a special function. The twins of the first pair are antagonists who are always in conflict; those of the second pair are friends, associated in all of their endeavors in spite of their unequal abilities. As for the demiurges who succeed one another on the scene of the myth, they all perform a dividing action between terms whose extension and comprehension gradually diminish or whose nature changes. In creating the first human being (if this is the right term to use for a time when animals and human beings were still undifferentiated), Monan establishes a primordial division between celestial divinities and terrestrial creatures. His successor, Maire-Monan, lives among the latter, but their ingratitude causes a new split: one between the Whites and the Indians. Sumé, the son of Maire-Monan, and his children, the first twins, split the Indians into fellow citizens (the Tupinamba) and strangers (the Timimino, the sworn enemies of the Tupinamba). In charge of twinness, according to present-day Guarani (see p. 49 above), Maire-Pochy introduces a new distinction within the group of fellow citizens: on the one side, the good guys who live in abundance; on the other, the bad ones punished by famine. The fifth demiurge, Maire, ensures the mediation between heaven and earth by settling at a good distance from the earth. His son, Maire-Ata, the sixth and last demiurge, fathers the more intelligent and stronger twin in one pair, while the other twin, Opossum's son, bears the stigma of illegitimacy. Moreover, Maire-Ata had chosen a local woman as his spouse, but she had the desire to travel "in faraway lands."

Thus her own nature is equivocal and is a prefiguration of the differentiation of her children.

In this way, the principle of a dichotomy manifests itself all along the chain. This dichotomy constitutes the invariant element of the system; the myth, as we know it, continues to evidence this invariant element in spite of the mutilated form in which it has reached us.

5

The Fateful Sentence

Let us pause on one of the rungs of this dichotomous ladder, right where the demiurge's creatures are divided into Whites and Indians. In Brazil, the Indians of the linguistic family Gê are a possible stratum of the archaic population that the Tupi might have pushed back to the interior when they occupied the coast. The Gê, too, have a myth that purports to explain the origin of the separation of the two races. Several versions of it have been collected, and these have been conveniently assembled by Johannes Wilbert in his *Folk Literature of the Gê Indians.*[1]

A woman (whose social status varies from one version to the next—I'll come back to this) is pregnant with a child who, while still in her womb, talks with her or even leaves and returns to the maternal body at will. During his excursions or after his birth, according to different versions, the child named Auké shows he possesses magical powers: he transforms himself into persons of various ages or, again, into often-frightening animals. The terrified villagers—and, more prominently, the maternal grandfather or uncle of the child—make him die on a pyre. When the mother goes to collect the ashes, she discovers that her son is quite alive and has come into possession of all the treasures of the Whites. He offers to share these with the inhabitants of the village. According to different versions, they either refuse him, whence the superiority of the Whites, or they become gradually civilized in the company of Auké. Two versions identify Auké with the emperor of Brazil, Pedro II (1831–89). Twentieth-century native storytellers were thus narrating the myth in the form it had taken in the nineteenth century.

Two substantial studies have already been devoted to the myth of Auké. In one, R. Da Matta compares two versions and interprets their differences in the functioning of the social organization of the Kraho and Canela groups, whence the different versions originated. In the other study, M. Carneiro da Cunha performs a subtle analysis of the transformed and supposedly relived versions of the myth that the Canela place at the origin of the messianic movement and uprising of 1963. I refer the reader to these studies[2] while here I look at the myth from a different angle. There are perceptible similarities between the Tupi and the Gê myths. What do these consist of? The answer jumps out when we compare, episode by episode, Thevet's version, such as he transcribed it, and the version we have of the myth of Auké. The Gê tell the same story as the Tupi, but they reverse it.

Both peoples feature a woman whose pregnancy is of problematical origin: in the Tupinamba version, rape by Opossum; in one Gê (Kraho) version, revelation by the Serpent of the practice of sex to the first human couple that lived on earth; or, again, in other Gê versions, uncertain paternity because the woman is a village prostitute. All the versions, moreover, emphasize the supernatural aspect of a pregnancy during which the child talks with his mother (as, for instance, Maire-Ata in the Tupinamba version; see p. 46 above) or, better yet, leaves and returns to his mother's body at will.

Whether this happens before his birth (thanks to his ambulatory gifts) or immediately after, the child terrifies the villagers, particularly his maternal relatives, because he takes the forms of several animal species. He is burned on a pyre. Traveling backward along the plot of the Tupinamba myth, we thus rejoin the corresponding episode in which the demiurge Maire-Monan too is burned on a pyre, not because *he was transforming himself* into various animals, but because he was thus *transforming* the Indians, who here were his companions instead of his relatives. To punish them, he deprived them of all cultural goods and reserved those for the Whites. In Auké's story, Auké himself becomes a White:

the White *par excellence,* master and distributor of their wealth. Thus we have two sequences that are doubly inverted, in the order of the narrative as well as in the content of their conclusion:

TUPI	GÊ
The demiurge refuses the Whites' treasures to the Indians,	Auké offers the Whites' treasures to the Indians
because his companions have burned him on a pyre	...his relatives burn him on a pyre
because they are terrified that he is transforming them into various animals.	Because they are terrified that he is transforming himself into various animals...
His last descendent converses with his mother while still in the womb.	Auké converses with his mother while still in her womb.

Is it possible that one of these inverted versions of the same plot antedates the other? Is one primary and the other derivative? In contrast to the Tupinamba demiurge, the Gê hero creates neither the Whites nor the Indians and, as well, he is not responsible for their separation. Thanks to his magical powers, whose origin we do not know, Auké comes back to life, or, apparently unharmed from the pyre, reappears as the master of the Whites' treasures. According to some versions, he succeeds in convincing the Indians to benefit from this and thus, to put it in anthropological jargon, to become acculturated. In this sense, the myth of Auké, collected in the twentieth century in a form dating from the nineteenth, appears less radical than the myth collected in the sixteenth century from the Tupinamba. We can guess the reason for this: the Gê came into sustained contact with the Whites only in the eighteenth century, two hundred years after the Tupi of the coast, at a time when the Portuguese settlers were firmly established and could subject the Indians to a stronger and more brutal pressure than had been the case in the sixteenth century, when the Whites, still few in number, had to seek acceptance from the natives. A myth accounting for the Whites' existence and their technological superiority was already extant when the Gê found themselves in a situation in which they needed to look to it for inspiration. However, as often happens when crossing a cultural and linguistic boundary, the myth turns over: the end becomes the beginning, the beginning the end, and the content of the message is inverted. I have given many examples in *Mythologiques* and elsewhere of this phenomenon, which the comparatists have long ignored.[3]

It is thus all the more intriguing to see reappear in this final state of the transformation one sentence already encountered in several versions of the story of Lynx and of that of the dentalia thieves. Coyote, having impregnated one of the two sisters, exclaims, "If it's a boy, I'll rear him; but if it's a girl, I'll kill her"—except in one version, in which he inverts the sexes.[4] It is in this latter form that the sentence appears in one version (Canela) of the myth of Auké. At the time of delivery, the mother (who is a village prostitute; this condition did exist among the Canela) exclaims, "If you are a boy, I'll kill you; if you are a girl, I'll raise you."[5] The child is a boy, but he talks his mother into sparing him. Thus we face a double problem: Can one explain the recurrence, in areas of the New World very distant from each other, of the same motif, collected several centuries apart? And how are we to understand that the terms of this motif are inverted in only one version out of the six we have for British Columbia, and that it reappears under this inverted form in eastern Brazil?

Let us begin with this latter point.

We have two versions from the Thompson that include the sentence, one in its straight form (the boy will be kept, the girl killed) and the other in an inverted form (the girl will be kept, the boy killed). In what additional way do they differ? In both cases the sentence is spoken by Coyote, but the son comes to the fore in only one version.[6] It is possible that the narrator of the version in which the son is missing, aware that the rest of the plot will not include this male character, decided it more efficient to get rid of him at birth. Unfortunately, the other version, which leaves the sentence unmotivated, does not offer us any element backing this interpretation. Moreover, when we compare the first Thompson version, which belongs to the group of the dentalia thieves, with that of their Okanagan neighbors, we note that in this latter narrative, it is Lynx's son rather than Coyote's who occupies center stage.[7] The interpretation of the divergence between the two Thompson versions proposed above thus cannot, as the hypothesis would require, also account for the divergence between one of these versions and the Okanagan ones.

We are not any luckier with the myth of Auké. The sentence is only present in one version out of the two featuring the mother as a village prostitute (the other versions present her as a married woman, or else they do not specify her condition). Thus we cannot find any motivation in the mother's social condition, although it is the main difference between the versions.

Let us then attempt to broaden the field of the inquiry. The sentence, which I will call fateful, does not properly belong to the group of myths discussed so far. It is found in myths belonging to the same area of North America, narratives in which the motif is given a clear motivation and other uses. At times a father speaks it in fear that his wife will give birth to a boy who, later on, will have a specific reason for hating him. At other times, in matrilineal groups, it is a maternal uncle who fears that his nephew, having become his rival, will want to take his place with his wife and usurp his authority. The motif is diffused uninterruptedly in western North America, from the Eskimo to the Shoshone, including the Tlingit, the Tsimshian, the Kutenai, the Sahaptin, and the Chinook.[8] It also exists in the East, among the Iroquois and the Algonkin.

One Chinook version sends us directly back to the dentalia thieves. A chief was killing all of his male children and only spared girls. One of his wives had a boy whom she succeeded in saving by having him wear girls' clothes. She entrusted him to her mother, who went to live far away with her grandson. Every time he took a bath in the lake (as was his habit), the water would fill with dentalia shells. The grandmother kept these secret, and, in order to be able to string them, she would go from house to house begging for the sinew strings (cf. p. 31 above). This begging irritated the villagers. The young hero gathered them and distributed the precious shells to them. Thunder-Bird had given him magical powers and even a whale. He became a great chief in the place of his father.

The fact that this myth makes the hero the ancestor of an Athapaskan tribe, formerly neighbors to the Chinook, is even the more interesting in that dentalium has a northern origin and it was the Athapaskan—in this case, the Chilcotin—who provide it to the Salish of the interior (see p. 35 above). The Chinook myth could thus be an echo of the myth of the dentalia thieves, reverberated far to the south. I have noted elsewhere the syncretism of Chinook traditions. Masters of the great fairs of the lower Columbia River, they welcomed distant tribes and lived in a cosmopolitan ambiance that permeated their mythology.[9]

After all these comments, one might, for once, be tempted to breach the fundamental rule of structural analysis—that is, the requirement that any detail, no matter how insignificant, fulfills a function. Could the fateful sentence coming from the trickster's mouth be nothing but an allusion, evoking on the plane of humor myths otherwise imprinted with a tragic greatness, in which fearsome characters, such as ogres or cruel chiefs, utter or even execute it? Its attribution to Coyote would then be derisory.

Without completely excluding this hypothesis, I am inclined to believe that in our myths the sentence has a specific signification. To show this, I will start by introducing something that could well be a state of the same transformation. In spite of geographic distance, a myth from the Kutenai, inhabitants of the foothills of the Rockies, bears a striking resemblance to the South American myth of Auké.

Yaukekam, the civilizing hero of the Kutenai, is not the master of the Whites' treasures as Auké is. However, Yaukekam plays an analogous role in that he is the inventor and the distributor of elements essential to the native culture: arrow shafts, arrow feathers, flint points, sinew strings. All of these things used to be animated. Yaukekam turns them into technical objects, and he transforms the beings who used to personify them into the animals of today. Like that of Auké, Yaukekam's birth has a supernatural character that upsets close relatives (particularly a paternal uncle filled with bad intentions). In both myths, the grandmother takes in and protects the child. Having become an adult and a powerful sorcerer, Yaukekam terrifies the people around him. He is killed and his body thrown into the water (for the same reason, thus, that Auké's relatives kill him on a pyre). Like Auké, Yaukekam comes back to life, but he becomes a great chief among his own people (while Auké, also becoming a great chief, becomes one outside his group, as he becomes identified as a White).

While he is still a child, Yaukekam's mother sends him to live with his grandmother. The grandmother is asleep, but upon awakening, she becomes aware through several clues that a child has entered her dwelling, which perplexes her: "No one knows if it's my grandson or my granddaughter." To find out, she lays out two toys, a small bow and a little basket; then she gets back to sleep. From the choice the child makes when he comes back while she is asleep, she reaches the appropriate conclusion.[10]

This is a strange episode (one would have rather expected the old woman to await the child's arrival as she did in the other myths), and it would be difficult to account for it without recognizing in it a transformation of the fateful sentence, one that fits quite well in the same stream as those we have already discussed. A being not yet born, or already born but not yet seen, has only a virtual existence, which leaves its sex undetermined. This being contains a double nature; only its passage to actual existence can clear up this ambiguity. The being is, so to speak, twin to itself: it must be born or must show itself in order to acquire individuality.

A Salish myth (akin to those including the fateful sentence, but coming from the coast) tells that Blue Jay, the trickster, separated Siamese twins: "If he had not meddled," concludes the myth, "twins would still be born attached to each other." In contrast, a myth from California features an already-born child who requests to be cut vertically in two and thus is transformed into twins.[11]

The fateful sentence and the test devised by the grandmother do not separate two beings merged into one, but they ascertain the sex of a unique being who in its initial state virtually contained both.

There is a great mythological cycle found from the Atlantic to the Pacific coast to which American mythographers have given the code name "Lodge Boy and Thrown-away." This cycle has twins as heroes, and the circumstances surrounding their birth indicate that they are to have opposite temperaments. This myth is close to that of the Tupinamba: in both places, an ogre kills a pregnant woman and extracts twins from her body (see p. 46 above). In the North American cycle, he leaves one twin in the cabin and throws the other one into the stream, where he is found. They are raised together, and the two boys have many adventures, in the course of which, as with the twin sons of Maire-Ata in the Tupinamba myth, their original difference continues to manifest itself.

From the image of twins who are identical in a virtual state but who show their differences when acceding to actual existence, we pass easily to another image: that of a child in which both sexes merge until birth (or recognition) makes differentiation possible and reveals which one of two beings promised to opposite destinies he is to be. Among the Kutenai, for whom the myth of Yaukekam is inseparable from that of the dentalia thieves, the cultural hero and his friend, Coyote, attempt in the course of their adventures to take up the role of the Sun that the animals want to create. They are rejected because Yaukekam, who irradiates a red light, is not warm enough and Coyote is too hot. However, as might be remembered, in the Kutenai version of the dentalia thieves, it is the twin sons of Lynx who alone are to succeed in fulfilling to everyone's satisfaction the roles of the Sun and the Moon (see p. 31 above). Through this, we link up with Tupi mythology, in which the divine twins personify the two celestial bodies.

꙳

León Cadogan has collected in native language, translated into Spanish, and published a Genesis from the Mbya-Guarani Indians of Paraguay. In it we find some of the perfectly recognizable elements of the version collected four centuries previously from the Tupinamba by Thevet. Cadogan makes a very pertinent comment. If twins are defined literally as children sired by a single father and given birth to at about the same time, it is hard to understand the prominent place that the Tupi-Guarani and many other South American peoples give to twins in their mythology. Indeed, the Mbya and generally the Tupi held the birth of twins to be maleficent: they put them to death as soon as they were born.[12]

Without always going so far, almost all the peoples of South America—with the exception of the ancient Peruvians and a few groups within the influence of the great Andean civilizations (Aymara, Mojo)—fear the birth of twins. The Inca felt a sort of sacred horror for twins that went as far as to turn into their worship.[13] In what are commonly labeled the low cultures of the tropical forest, usually only one twin was put to death: the girl if they were of different sexes, or else the "older" or the "younger" of the two children. In this sense, we might say that the fateful sentence expresses in a diachronic mode that which the differential fate reserved to twins of opposite sexes accomplishes synchronically. We thus understand why in the Tupinamba and the Gê myths that invert each other (see pp. 55–57 above) the first resorts to the motif of unequal twins while the second makes use of the fateful sentence.

The usual reason given for the murder of one twin is that a woman can procreate only one child at a time unless another man in addition to her husband has impregnated her. As we have seen, this theory is illustrated in the myths, even though none of them advocates the killing of one of the twins, who are both called upon to play essential roles in putting the world in order.

But, as Cadogan emphasizes, these twins are not really twins. In the Mbya-Guarani Genesis, an only son, the future Sun, uses his divine power to give himself a younger brother, who will become the Moon.[14] The Tupinamba Genesis gives to different fathers the job of siring the "twins," who only appear such because of the circumstances surrounding their birth and who are even the less twins in that the Tupinamba attributed an exclusive role in conception to the father. And when finally the myths feature real twins, they quickly differentiate them by attributing to them opposite abilities and characters: one is aggressive and clever; the other stupid, clumsy, and heedless.

What, indeed, is the underlying inspiration for these myths? Our schema in figure 6 sheds light on it. These myths represent the progressive organization of the world and of society in the form of a series of dual splits but without the resulting parts at each stage ever being truly equal: in one way or another, one is always superior to the other. The proper functioning of the system depends on this dynamic disequilibrium, for without it this system would at all times be in danger of falling into a state of inertia. What these myths implicitly state is that the poles between which natural phenomena and social life are organized—such as sky and earth, fire and water, above and below, Indians and non-Indians, fellow citizens and strangers—could never be twins. The mind attempts to join them without succeeding in establishing parity between them. This is because it is these cascading distinctive features, such as mythical thought conceives them, that set in motion the machine of the universe.

This is valid even for details. A contemporary version of the Tupi Genesis, collected in 1912 in southern Brazil, tells that one of the twins, too eager to nurse, deformed one of his mother's breasts. Since then, women have asymmetrical breasts:[15] even breasts cannot be twins! In North America, the Nez Percé version of the story of Lynx (see p. 7 above) purports to explain the origin of mismatched marriages: they are those in which the respective spouses are not twins, whether physically or socially.

Among the series of dual splits the myth enumerates, that of the Indians and the Whites deserves particular attention. Indeed, it is remarkable that only half a century after the arrival of the first Whites in Brazil, native mythology had already integrated them at a very appropriate spot within a Genesis in which everything nonetheless happens through the work of the demiurge.

There is more. Métraux had good reasons to note in regard to a myth from the Toba–Pilaga Indians, inhabitants of the Chaco (whose hero, called Asin, corresponds closely to the Gê hero, Auké):

> In this myth, the Pilaga explain the difference between Indian and White cultures. A similar myth appeared in many Indian tribes after conquest, myths which are of great interest as we cannot attribute the resemblances between these numerous versions to direct borrowing.[16]

Light is shed on the problem formulated by Métraux if the myths of Amerindian origin do rest upon the framework I have attempted to extract. The myths, I have argued, order beings and things through the means of a series of dual splits; ideally twin at each stage, the parts always reveal themselves unequal. No disequilibrium could have appeared more marked to the Indians than that between the Whites and themselves. But they possessed a dichotomous model enabling them to carry over this opposition and its consequences into a system of thought in which its place was in some ways already reserved, so that, as soon as it was introduced, the opposition would start to function.

Twins occupy a prominent place in Amerindian mythology but only in appearance. Indeed, the reason for their importance and for the role the myths assign to them comes precisely from the fact that they are not really twins, or else because the incompatibility of their temperaments contradicts their supposed condition of twinness. The fateful sentence from which this discussion started comes down in the end to the implicit affirmation that all unity contains within itself a duality, and that, regardless of what we might wish or do, when this duality becomes actual, there cannot be true equality between the two halves.

6

A Visit to the Mountain Goats

The bringing together of North and South American myths
has allowed us to reopen the debate on the place of twins
in the myths of both hemispheres. It also encourages us to attempt
one of those experiments whose value is crucial for the analysis of
myths. Starting from a set of transformations whose existence in
South America I have demonstrated, could we uncover in North
America a myth indicating that there, too, one can find the same
set of transformations?

The story of the dentalia thieves contains striking analogies to
a South American myth from the Bororo. Indexed M_{20} in *The
Raw and the Cooked*, this myth, like that of the dentalia thieves,
deals with the origin of body ornaments. It features an indiscreet
woman who spies on her brothers while they invent adornments
by piercing shells with a sharp stone found in the bottom of the
water. The myth specifies that this activity is of a ritual nature and
that the brothers lead a happy life in cabins made out of feathers,
evoking a celestial sojourn. As might be remembered, the hero of
the North American myth spied upon by his sisters is also engaged
in ritual activity. He finds shells in the bottom of the water but
has no need to pierce them since dentalium comes in the form of
naturally opened tubes.

In both cases, one or several brothers separate themselves from
their families: in the Bororo myth, by throwing themselves on a
pyre where, as soon as they are consumed, they rise to the heavens
transformed into Birds; in the North American myth, by descend-
ing into a lower world where the hero leads a happy life and where
his sisters, who wet him with their tears, are not able to rejoin

him. (Here, water is the result of the separation and replaces fire as its means.)

In *The Raw and the Cooked* (pp. 83–90, a demonstration summarized again in *From Honey to Ashes,* pp. 20–27), I have established:

1. that this myth, whose armature rests on the disjunction of brothers from their sisters and these sisters' husbands, $\triangle \overset{\prime\prime}{\frown} \bigcirc = \triangle$ transforms a group of myths (indexed M_{15}, M_{16}, and M_{18}) existing among the Bororo's neighbors, myths that pertain to the origin of meat and, more particularly, that judge wild pig as the best meat and the one holding the main place in the diet;

2. that if, within an identical armature, the message is inverted when passing from M_{15} and M_{16} to M_{20} (food → body ornaments), it is because the first two myths come from patrilineal tribes while the third comes from the Bororo, whose mode of descent follows the maternal line.

Indeed, those who are kin in direct line in one case become affines in the other: in a matrilineal system, the father is affine to his son, the same way the mother is affine to her son in a patrilineal system. The analysis of the myth confirms that, in the case of an invariant message, a breach occurs in the function of the mode of descent—that is, either between kin or between affines. In contrast, in the case of an invariant armature, it is the message that becomes inverted. A myth (indexed M_{18}) coming from the Kayapo–Kubenkranken, who are matrilocal, confirmed the rule in this particular case: if the myth (M_{18}) maintains intact the message carried by M_{15} and M_{16} (origin of meat), it is at the price of an inversion of the armature (*The Raw and the Cooked,* pp. 88–89).

$$M_{16}\left[\triangle \overset{\prime\prime}{\frown} \bigcirc = \triangle\right] \quad \Rightarrow \quad M_{18}\left[\triangle \overset{\frown}{} \bigcirc \neq \triangle\right]$$

Now that all this has been brought back to mind, we are justified in proposing a hypothesis regarding only the following two conditions.

If the North American myth of the dentalia thieves and the Bororo myth M_{20}, which both pertain to the origin of body ornaments, are homologous; and if the Bororo myth is a transformation of a myth on the origin of meat from one of their neighbors; then there must exist in North America, very close to the myth of the dentalia thieves, a myth on the origin of meat that is homologous to it, with the qualification that its armature be inverted:

$$\text{origin of ornaments} \left[\triangle \overset{\prime\prime}{\frown} \bigcirc = \triangle \right] \Rightarrow \text{origin of meat} \left[\triangle \frown \bigcirc \neq \triangle \right]$$

We will see that all of the characteristics required by the hypothesis exist in a myth found among the same people who have given us the story of Lynx and that of the dentalia thieves. However, without the hypothetical and deductive procedure used above, it would have been difficult and perhaps even impossible to perceive that this myth and the others I have just cited make up the stages of the same transformation. The only clue would have been provided by the place—larger than elsewhere—that these myths reserve to the great ungulates, Elk and Mountain Sheep (see pp. 17, 22 above), to which we must now add the Mountain Goat (*Oreamnos americanus*).

Like the wild pigs in South America, these goats were much prized as food and were the object of numerous beliefs. The Kutenai described them as very shrewd, difficult to hunt but a choice food.[1] The Plateau Thompson and the Coast Salish observed the same rites for a goat hunt as they did for a bear hunt.[2] One of the Coast Salish people, the Squamish, whose myth we shall discuss, looked upon the goat hunt as dangerous and requiring special physical and supernatural abilities from both the hunters and their dogs. The much-prized goat's fur served as a matrimonial gift: a suitor would offer it to the parents of his betrothed. Capes woven out of goat hair were symbols of wealth and were worn only on special occasions.[3] All of these details match the information provided by naturalists: these goats live above the tree line in rocky areas inaccessible to any other animal of similar size.[4]

It is possible that most or some of the Shuswap Indians weren't interested in goat meat except when they didn't have anything else to eat.[5] However, their myths too poeticize this hunt, though their narratives contain, in relation to those of their neighbors, certain anomalies, to which I will come back later (see p. 72 below). These differences justify giving them a separate place in a set of versions that are, moreover, very homogeneous. It is now time to present these. Here is, for instance, a Thompson version coming from the group Utamqt, of the lower Fraser River.

🐐

In olden days, goats were of the same nature as the Indians; they took on human or animal appearance at will. The Indians knew it, and this is why they continued to observe special rites when they killed a Goat, as well as a Black Bear or a Grizzly, animals who also have this double nature.

One day, a man with two wives—one a young mother and the other pregnant—went out to hunt. He chased Goats, lost them from sight, and was very surprised to meet two young women who denied having seen the Goats (because they were the Goats themselves). They invited the man to follow them, made him able to climb along a sharp rock face (by putting saliva on the soles of his feet), and had him enter into a cave at the mountaintop. Many people lived there. He married the two young women, but they refused to have sex with him: "We have sex only during a very short time at a certain season of the year." His parents-in-law sent him out to hunt; he was supposed to kill only one Goat each time, which would feed all of the inhabitants of the cave. This lasted several months. The man began to suspect that the Goats he killed were in reality his brothers-in-law, of which only the "goat part" would die while the "human part" would come back home in the evening. To ascertain this, he cut up the nose of a dead Goat;

FIGURE 7. Mountain goat (*Oreamnos americanus*)

one of his brothers-in-law came back that evening with a bleeding nose.

Finally, the rutting season arrived. It was announced by the traveling upstream of a species of Salmon ("dog salmon"; *Onchorynchus keta*), a run lasting from mid-August to the end of November. The Goats' rutting season occurred in November,[7] but the myth is set in the mountains, where the Salmon arrived only at the end of their journey. Weighed down by the heavy fur with which he had been clothed, the hero did not succeed in participating in the rut. His wives gave him a lighter fur, and then he could copulate with all the females.

Months passed; one of the wives gave birth to a child who, when still small, asked to visit his human grandparents. The hero set out with his wife, his son, and one of his brothers-in-law, named Komús ("two-year-old goat"). He carried with him mittens filled with meat and fat.

The man had been away for almost two years, and he was thought dead. At first invisible, he then made himself known to his fellows. They all feasted on the fat and the meat, which magically kept increasing. To the Goat woman and her brother they offered their usual food: a soup of black and white moss. But the young Komús stuffed himself, swelled up, and made a fool of himself while playing ball. He was mocked, trampled on, and farted at in the face. When Komús was through digesting, he took the ball and ran away to the mountain. He was pursued, and he caused an icy wind to kill his pursuers. The Goats reprimanded Komús, who agreed to bring his victims back to life, but he farted in their faces to avenge himself. Finally he returned to the Goats with his sister. The hero and his son remained in the village.[8]

Because of its construction, this myth bears a striking resemblance to those South American ones also dealing with the origin of meat or rather, more specifically, with the origin of the hunt for the best game. In olden days, not only was this game human or humanlike, but these myths identify it as a brother-in-law, a relation of kinship stressed as well in another Thompson version. Before sending the hero back to his own people, the Goats promise him that he will become a great hunter, capable of crossing the sheerest of cliffs, on the condition that he scrupulously observe certain rules:

> When you kill goats, treat their bodies respectfully, for they are people. Do not shoot the female goats, for they are your wives and will bear your children. Do not kill kids, for they may be your offspring. Only shoot your brothers-in-law, the male goats. Do not be sorry when you kill them, for they do not die but return home. The flesh and skin (the goat part) remain in your possession; but their real selves (the human part) lives just as before, when it was covered with goat's flesh and skin.[9]

That in the two Thompson versions the armature is of the type $\triangle \ \overline{O} \neq \triangle$ comes out through the way the first version concludes: the wife and the brother return to the Goats; the hero and his son remain with the human beings. The final episode of the second version unfolds the same way, though in a slightly different form. After coming back to his own people, the hero goes out to hunt and wants to kill a female and her young, who are in reality his Goat wife and his son. She reprimands him and reminds him that he must respect the rules. He then kills a male and, upon his return to the village, pretends that the female escaped him.[10]

A third version replaces the Goats with Deer, and an Okanagan version does not distinguish clearly between these families.[11] We have already encountered myths in which a people of Elk replaces a people of Mountain Sheep (see p. 22 above). These substitutions are explained by a belief, whose existence has been evidenced among the Lilloet, that in mythical times Deer were so wild and fast that they could not be hunted; the Deer people, in addition to all the genera of this species, included the Mountain Sheep, the Mountain Goats, the Horses, the Bison, and so on.[12] It is thus not surprising that the Thompson version dealing with the Deer subjects their hunt to the same rules as those for hunting Goats. The hero has killed and then brought back to life his Deer wife and their child: "Only kill your brothers-in-law," she reminds him.[13] One of the immediate neighbors to the Thompson, the Lilloet, have a version that specifies why the hero's Goat wives cannot follow him when he wants to return to his own people with the two sons they gave him: "We will not keep you [they say]; you can take your two sons with you, but we stay behind. We cannot accompany you; we are not the same as you. The boys are of your blood, and so can go with you, but we cannot."[14] It is thus clear that in all these myths disjunction affects affines—either spouses or brothers-in-law.

Finally, a comment on the episode featuring Komús occurring at the end of the first Thompson version summarized above. This big-bellied character sends back to another one likewise afflicted with a protuberant stomach who, in a Coast Salish myth, causes a thick fog to fall.[15] As for Komús, he brings an icy and murderous wind, and he emits intestinal gases after having been the target of such gases himself. In a meteorological register, wind is opposite to fog, while in a physiological register, farts are the fog's equivalent because the fog too stinks (see p. 92 below). Another Coast Salish people, the Skyomish, have an etiological version of the myth of the Mountain Goats that explains why only the Skyomish use a certain kind of trap for this hunt. According to this myth, the daughter of the bird Qē'Qē (an unidentified mountain species) was offered in marriage to the victor of a footrace. The youngest of ten Mountain Goat brothers won in spite of his big belly, but he let his oldest brother have the wife. The Skagit, neighbors to the Skyomish, also knew the bird Qē'Qē and attributed to it a son who, in the form of a Dog, seduced the daughter of a chief. Abandoned with wife and son, he created another humankind, invented the game of lacrosse, and filled the woods with game and the sea with smelt while his persecutors were suffering from hunger.[16] These myths from the Coast Salish thus lead us back—the first and the third ones to the story of Lynx, and the second one to that of the dentalia thieves (through the motif of the marriage race)—thus confirming that in North America, as I had postulated, these myths and those of the Mountain Goats are part of one transformation.

I have noted (see p. 68 above) that in comparison with the other versions of the Goat hunt, the Shuswap narratives exhibit some anomalies. In one version, the young hero is replaced by an old man whose instructions are to shoot only at old Goats, never at young ones.[17] Another version inverts the sexes: it is a He-Goat who pays a visit to the Indians, marries a human woman, and takes her back with him. They have a son; the wife returns to her parents with the child. She brings back meat and goatskins in a compressed form that magically grow back to their original volume upon her return. Then the woman and child, permanently transformed into Goats, leave forever.[18] It is likely that these changes stem at least in part from the geographical location of the Shuswap: they lived in a plateau area lying between the Coast Mountains range and the Canadian Rockies of British Columbia, where goats were rare or even absent (fig. 8). The Kwakiutl of Vancouver Island and the Tlingit, inhabitants of the Alaskan

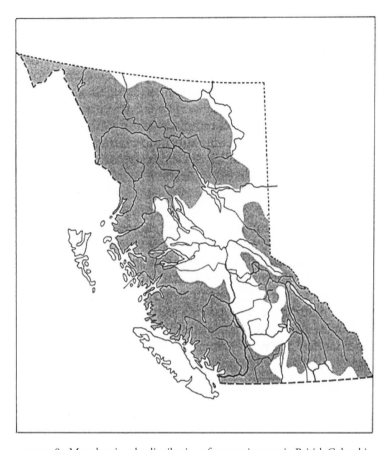

FIGURE 8. Map showing the distribution of mountain goats in British Columbia

shoreline, both experienced similar difficulties: to hunt goats, the Tlingit, like their Tsimshian neighbors,[19] had to venture into the mountains, whose dangers they feared. One can observe in these peoples' myths changes comparable (in relation to inland versions) to those found in the Shuswap narratives.

A Kwakiutl myth inverts the motif of the sexual union (or even that of promiscuity) with the Goats: to succeed in the hunt, the hero, by order of the Goats, is to observe sexual continence for four years. He succumbs one day to the advances of his girlfriend, loses his power, and disappears into the interior, transformed into a Grizzly Bear.[20]

The Tlingit version narrates the circumstances in which a hunter became a great shaman. The villagers hunted excessively and disregarded rites. To punish them, the Mountain Sheep (who replace the Goats here) captured one of them. They taught him how to show respect to the remains of killed animals without sticking their heads on the end of sticks, a treatment reserved solely for Grizzly Bears. They then freed the Indian, who, upon his return and following the instructions he had been given, ordered that the Mountain Sheep skins resulting from the carnage perpetrated by his companions should not be touched. The skins then filled up with pieces of meat, each in the required spot; the Mountain Sheep came back to life and went back to the mountain:

> But they had been so long among the Indians that just before they reached the highest mountain, where they belonged, they lost their way and became scattered over all the mountains. Because the Mountain Sheep once saved (or captured) a man, they have beards and look in other respects like human beings.

In exchange, the Mountain Sheep had given their special smell to the hero.[21] (The Inland Salish believed instead that the great ungulates, such as Elk and Goats, are disgusted by human smells.[22]) The versions that for convenience' sake I have called anomalous thus differentiate themselves from the others through a series of oppositions: the hero is young or old; either only old Goats or only young brother-in-law Goats can be killed; human spouse or Goat spouse; acceptable promiscuity with female animals or required continence with human women. And while the Thompson versions, for instance, evoke the metamorphosis (though temporary) of a human woman into an animal, it is striking that the Tlingit version explains why the Mountain Sheep resemble human beings.

❧

I have shown in *The Raw and the Cooked* (pp. 91–92) and in *From Honey to Ashes* (pp. 20–21) that one could draw a simplified representation of the set comprising the Gê myths on the origin of cooking and their myths on the origin of meat. Jaguar, a brother-in-law wife taker (he married an Indian woman), who shows his benevolence toward the hero (standing for the human species) in giving him cooking fire and cooked food, is the counterpart to brother-in-law wife givers, who behave malevolently in refusing to give food to the hero, in bartering it, or in giving it to him insultingly. These last brothers-in-law are changed into Wild Pigs—in other words, into raw meat on hoof, into the matter to be cooked with fire as the means.

The preceding allows us to simplify in the same manner the set formed by the North American myths on the origin of body ornaments and the origin of meat. These myths can be consolidated into the following schema:

This reduced model calls for several remarks.

1. In this region of North America, the nature of the line of descent, which we had to take into account in interpreting the South American transformations, loses much of its pertinence. Indeed, Salish-speaking peoples in general—and, more particularly, those of the interior from whom the myths I have discussed come—had an undifferentiated mode of descent. This makes the sociological armature subject to fewer constraints, and myths can play around it more freely. But even though it has become less rigid (but is it ever really so, except in idea?), the sociological armature is in no danger of collapsing: regardless of the nature of

the mode of descent, fundamental distinctions, such as that between kin and affines, remain. In between these two, the myths conceive and eventually juxtapose different types of relations so as to vary the content of the messages and provide contrasting significations.

2. Thus the group [story of Lynx + dentalia thieves] is made up of two variants that appear to be antithetical. The story of Lynx has as its heroine a girl who is rebellious against marriage: $\triangle \neq \bigcirc$; in the story of the dentalia thieves, her role is held by an indiscreet girl whose father or brother decides to separate from her: $\triangle^{\prime\prime} \bigcirc$. Thus in both cases there is disjunction formulated in terms of affinity or of degree of kinship.

3. The model is just as ambiguous when looked at from the other side. The hero, specify the myths, has two wives, whom he leaves for the two Goat wives, who later send him away. The motif of the disjunction of spouses thus can be read in two opposite ways, according to whether the hero separates himself from his human spouses or his Goat spouses separate themselves from him.

4. Yet more striking is the chiasma that, in relation to the South American myths, develops symmetrically at the edges of the model. On the left, the Goats—benevolent brothers-in-law like the Jaguar of the Gê myths, but wife givers instead of takers—can be likened to the Wild Pigs (the malevolent brothers-in-law in these same South American myths) in the sense that they, too, are flesh destined for food. On the right, the malevolent brothers-in-law (Coyote the trickster, Lynx starving his fellows) behave like the future Pigs of the Gê myths; but they are wife takers instead of givers, each winning a spouse at this game just as Jaguar does in the South American myths.

5. Both in the story of Lynx and in that of the dentalia thieves, the fog plays a part: in bringing on the fog, Lynx deprives his fellows of meat, and through this same means grandmother Doe or Mountain Sheep deprives her people of a spouse. To this fog, a natural meteorological phenomenon, corresponds the artificial fog in the South American myths on the origin of meat: the smoke of

burned feathers or of tobacco, which causes the transformation of nasty brothers-in-law into Pigs.[23]

6. Finally, it must be noted that from one end of the diagram to the other, the theme of the great ungulates functions as a continuous bass (in the musical sense of the term): while on the left the hero goes to the Goats and becomes one of them, on the right the heroine, a rebellious girl or indiscreet sister, goes to her grandmother, who, like her, belongs to the family of Elk or Mountain Sheep (see pp. 17, 22, 27 above). The preceding discussion indirectly shows the continuity of the set as well as the homology of the two great North and South American mythical sets.

It is possible to give additional proofs of this homology.

In South America, the Tenetehara, members of the linguistic family Tupi–Guarani, were telling fifty years ago (and perhaps still tell today) their origin myth with the same elements as those collected by Thevet four centuries previously. According to the myth of the origin of Wild Pigs (indexed M_{15} in *The Raw and the Cooked,* pp. 84–85), the "godson" and maternal nephew of the demiurge Tupan, called Marana-ywa, becomes the master of the forest, protector of the game against hunters' excesses. The Indians depict him as a very short man with a shaggy head of hair and enormous testicles. The Tenetehara also believe that in cases of twin birth, one of the children was fathered by Marana-Ywa, who has secretly copulated with the mother.[24] This is like Opossum in the Tupinamba myth and like Coyote, father of a child to whom the fateful sentence gives a dual nature as long as it is not yet born, among the Salish (see pp. 57–64 above). Thus the beliefs of a South American people who remained faithful to an archaic tradition provide us with the confirmation of the unity of the system that in North America also includes the respect for hunting rites and the problem of twinness.

We can as well draw a second argument from the fact that in North America the Salish have a myth on the origin of Salmon, a myth very close to the one the Bororo, neighbors of the Gê, use to explain the origin of Wild Pigs (in a way, however, that differs from the Gê myth). This Bororo myth has been indexed M_{21} in *The Raw and the Cooked* (pp. 94–95). Day after day, the men would come back from fishing empty-handed. The women declared that they would go fishing themselves. In fact, they only called upon the Otters, to whom they prostituted themselves in exchange for the fish. The men, who still didn't catch anything, became suspicious and had the women spied upon by a Bird. Following this, they surprised the Otters and strangled them. To avenge themselves, the wives gave their husbands a magical potion that transformed them into Pigs.

Now, in the estuary of the Fraser River, there is a small Salish group, the Tcilqéuk (a name usually transcribed as Chilliwack), that has a myth whose resemblance to the Bororo one is immediately evident in spite of some obscurities and missing parts.

In olden days there was once a famine. The men went far away from the village and succeeded in catching a few salmon. Instead of bringing them back to their wives and children, they decided to eat them by themselves and to abandon their families. A boy who accompanied the fishermen warned his mother. Furious, the wives performed some magic on the beds, blankets, and other possessions of their husbands, causing these men to be transformed into Birds. They flew away, and their group landed farther away on the river. Beaver, who was there, revealed to them the location of salmon country and helped them reconcile with their spouses.[25]

I have already noted (*The Naked Man,* pp. 53–54, 542–43) the usefulness of the Bororo myth on the origin of Wild Pigs in understanding the relation of homology between the myths of central Brazil and those of the Northwest of North America. Also, in *The Raw and the Cooked* (pp. 92–95), I used the same myth to show that in passing from the Gê to the Bororo, in the case of an invariant message, the armature becomes deformed: a conflict between kin replaces one between affines.

One can observe the same phenomenon in North America when passing from the Inland Salish to a Coast Salish group and from a myth on the origin of the goat hunt to a myth on the origin of salmon fishing. A complicated armature involving interventions by human spouses, animal spouses, and brothers-in-law becomes thinner and takes on the simpler aspect of a conflict between spouses. But mostly, the Tcilqéuk myth and the Bororo myth reveal themselves to be closely akin to each other. Otters or Beavers, animals mediating between earth and water, provide fish, in one instance to the women and in the other to the men. In one case, their brutal elimination leads to a definitive rupture between men and women; in the other case, their benevolent apparition makes the reconciliation of the sexes possible. The following graph shows the symmetry of the North and South American myths:

TCILQÉUK   BORORO

The men catch little fish, ———————— Men are not catching any fish,

they deprive the women   The women fish for them-
of food.   selves alone,

The men abandon   The men deprive the women
the women   of their Otter lovers,

The women use magic,   Otters which were providing
                                       them with fish.

which transforms the men   The murder of the Otters
into birds.   causes the break up of
                                       the spouses

Beaver provides fish for   The women use magic,
the men.

Beaver's help reconciles   which transforms the men
the spouses.   into pigs.

    I have emphasized on several occasions that, like the Wild Pigs of central Brazil, in the North American Northwest, where there were no buffalo (except in the eastern part, but even there they were very rare), Mountain Goats connoted the category of large game (a role held on the coast by Salmon). The reduced model on page 75 gives us a glimpse of a second difference between this choice game and all others: on the left of the model, the Goat people constitute a single animal family (also the case for the Elk or Mountain Sheep people, which are used as substitutes in certain variants); each of these people thus makes up a closed group. In contrast, the right part of the model features a heroine showing an affinity with the big game. This is because as she goes to her grandmother, who is either Doe or Mountain Sheep, this latter pretends to offer her granddaughter's hand in marriage to an indefinite series of aspirants of various animal species, of which none is to succeed in marrying her. This group of aspirants thus forms an open set. The myths in their consolidated form manifest the characteristics of a semiconductor body: though marriage is possible in one direction, it is impossible in the other:

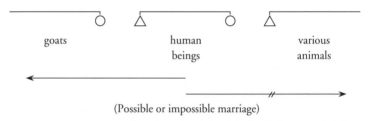

goats   human   various
               beings   animals

(Possible or impossible marriage)

It must be remembered here that a southern version of the story of Lynx claims to explain the origin of badly matched marriages (see p. 7 above). In the central part of the area of diffusion of the myth of the Mountain Goats, a part where these animals are rarer (see p. 72 above), the Shuswap have a myth that is symmetrical from the standpoint of etiology. Ram's two wives, one a Goat and the other a Mountain Sheep, are jealous of each other; they have a fight. Mountain Sheep wins, and Goat wife leaves. First she lives alone; then she remarries someone of her own species. In olden days, Mountain Sheep and Goats lived together and married one another; now they are encountered in the same territories but lead separate existences.[26] Marriages between animals contrast with the sometimes-mismatched marriages between human beings: animal spouses are well matched as long as the zoological families or genera agree to live on their own. The response to this endless endeavour to overcome the opposition between the similar and the different (in which either one is the price paid for the other) is a dream of an impossible twinness that haunts the myths in both South and North America (see pp. 62–63 above) and of which the right part of the preceding schema shows the theoretical location.

In proposing this syncretic vision, I am not trying to prove the diffusion of one myth or an ensemble of myths from one hemisphere to the other. When the mind is relatively free from external constraints, as is the case in the elaboration of myths, after being given the first motif and regardless of this motif's origins, the mind gives itself over to an automatism through which it executes, one after another, all of the motif's transformations. All that is required are a few like seeds scattered here and there for mythical contents to come out of them. Though the contents of these myths might appear very different on the surface, analysis reveals the presence of invariant relations between their structures.

ᚵ

There is one last aspect of the myth of the Mountain Goats that needs to be discussed. The myth's explicit function is to explain the origin of the rites on which the hunter's success depends. The myth thus involves a theory of ritual, even though it leaves it in an implicit state. Can we give it form? This theory appears to boil down to the affirmation that ritual has as origin and as condition a return of man to nature. In order to come into possession of the hunting rites on behalf of all his people, a hero was required to give up the human condition. He had to learn to live more like an animal, and this in two ways. On the one hand, he could have sex with his Goat wives only during the rutting season—thus, in the natural, asocial mode (see pp. 68–69 above): "Our season comes but once a year and lasts about a month. During the rest of the year we have no sexual connections."[27] In contrast, when the rutting season did come, promiscuity was the rule: "He [the hero] rutted with all the female goats, both young and old, including his wife and mother-in-law."[28] (The Inland Salish observed a very strict taboo regarding the mother-in-law.) "You can," said the Goat wives to the hero, "choose and pair with any of the women now, and when the rutting season is over and we return, we shall be your wives again."[29] However, the hero didn't like "the young males having sex with his wife; it made him sad."[30] It is amusing, in this regard, to note the following anecdote. The Western Shuswap were neighbors to the Chilcotin and the Carrier, for whom they had borrowed the practice of organizing themselves into societies or confraternities, most of these groups bearing the names of animals. In their dances, the Shuswap imitated the rut of their eponymous animals with such realism that, in the course of a visit they paid to the Thompson, the latter marveled at their dances but begged them to censor parts of their next performance so as not to shock their wives.[31]

"They were beautiful and charming," say the myths of the Goat people, who were not in the least concerned about the rules through which human societies control their reproduction. In contrast, the Goats could show themselves incredibly punctilious when it came to the rules on which depended their own survival. The hunter had to pick up the game's bones one by one and submerge them in water to enable the animal to come back to life. If the hunter could not do this, he had to burn the bones. The animal would then die for good, but it would not bear him a grudge. These are only the rudiments; let us listen to the Goats giving their instructions to the hero:

> Tell your people to paint their faces before they begin to skin and cut up a goat, and to place the sacred down upon the tongue and lungs and heart, and hang the whole up to dry in the house over the fire, for that is good medicine for us. They must also carefully gather up the bones and other offal, and put them in the water, as you have seen us do. In cooking the meat, first roast the liver on a spit, after putting down upon it; that is good medicine for us. When the liver is cooked, take some fresh cypress branches and place the liver upon them, and cut it up into small bits and give a portion to each person. If you should make use of and cook the head, mark the face first with red paint, sprinkle down upon

it, and place it before the fire nose foremost. Let it remain there a little while, and then skin it. The man who does this must paint his face and put down upon his head, and all who are near and watching him must be silent and make no noise of any kind. When the head is skinned, then place it before the fire again, carefully turning the right side toward the flame. All the time the head is thus roasting, the people must keep silent; not even a cough or sneeze must be heard or the spirit of the goat will be frightened away, and you would have no more luck in hunting goats. Let the head remain before the fire until the right eye bursts under the heat with a splutter; then turn the left side to the fire. Now the spirit cannot see the people misbehave, and it does not matter if they talk and make a noise. If the spirit should ask the cook what that noise is, he can answer, "That is your people's noise, not mine." When the head is cooked, give a little of it to each of the elders; the women and young men must not touch it. This must always be done at sunset on the day of killing.[32]

This list of prescriptions and interdictions, which I have cited at length to show its punctiliousness, is nonetheless of interest. It might be bringing back into question a distinction I made in *The Naked Man* (pp. 668–69) between two mythological modes: one was explicit mythology, consisting of narratives whose importance and internal organization make of them oeuvres in their own rights, and the other implicit mythology, which limits itself to accompanying the unfolding of a ritual so as to comment on or explain its aspects.

The text we have just discussed has two faces. It unfolds parallel to two series—one mythological, the other ritual, and both explicit. It is thus within a myth very rich by itself that we find a carefully spelled-out list of rites. But except for this fact, we find no other correspondence between the story the myth tells and the ritual acts the myth prescribes. The details of each prescription remain unmotivated. Nothing in the mythical narrative explains why any of the ritual gestures are required, why such or such a substance must be used, why a certain sequence must be followed, and so on. The myth and the rite progress at the same pace, but they keep their distances and do not communicate with each other.

Consequently, even in a case that appears to be exceptionally promising for understanding the link between mythology and ritual, this latter remains external to the narrative, without any perceptible relation to the narrated events. The ritual consists in words (or in the absence of words: silence), in gestures, and in the handling of objects or substances, and these exist outside of any sort of exegesis that might be required or even allowed by these three kinds of activities.

The link between mythology and ritual nevertheless exists, but it must be sought at a deeper level. This gratuitous work of parcelling and repetition, in which rites indulge with a punctiliousness exemplified by the text cited above, offers itself, so to speak, as compensation for the return to the state of nature imposed on the myth's hero, a state in which he is immersed in a fluid environment where clear and distinct ideas and the rules of social life are dissolved.

No matter how detailed they already are, the rites of the hunt and the cooking of goats could still be multiplied. And yet these rites, like the images of a cinematographic film examined one by one, could not reconstitute the experience, unlivable except in thought, of a man becoming a goat—unless, like the images of the film, a pious zeal produces rites in such a great number and makes them go by so fast that, thanks to this very jamming, they engender the illusion of an impossible lived experience, since no real experience ever has or will correspond to it.

PART TWO

Breaks through the Clouds

7

The Child Taken by the Owl

L et us agree to call "cell" an ensemble of incidents forming a whole that is separable from the particular mythical context in which it was first noticed and that can be transported as a block into other contexts. At the very beginning of our investigation, the most developed Nez Percé version of the story of Lynx included such an ensemble: in this version Bear suddenly appears at the end of the narrative; he is a new protagonist who suffers several misadventures, though nothing in the previous episodes announced him (see p. 5 above).

This "bear cell" posed a problem. It seemed all the more difficult to integrate into the story of Lynx in that the other versions of the myth do not include it and in that we can find it again in entirely different myths. Thus I had temporarily set it aside. But as the investigation progressed, this bear cell revealed itself as superimposable on an "owl cell" that also appeared unexpectedly in several versions of the story of Lynx (Okanagan, Coeur d'Alene, Kutenai). This owl cell appeared along with the occurrence of a triple transition: from the rebellious girl to the indiscreet sister (a transformation that marks the passage from the story of Lynx to that of the dentalia thieves); from the rejected father to the child joyfully accepted; from the abandoned couple to the kidnapped child.

The sequence of the child that is first stolen and then found again and that ends with his metamorphosis into a Waterbird, usually a Loon, links up with a large mythological cycle called "The Loon Woman," to which all of the second part as well as a segment of the third part of *The Naked Man* were devoted. This set has as its central motif the transformation of an incestuous sister into a Loon. In the versions of the myth of the dentalia thieves that we are now going to look at, it is, as we shall see, through equivocal behavior bordering on incest that the sister of the hero, who has been transformed into a Loon, lies down next to him and holds him in her arms to give him back his human form. He then marries a young woman, local or foreign according to different versions, but in fact a double of the sister, or in some versions her accomplice (see pp. 89–90, 93 below).

At the same time as the motif of the stolen-and-found-again child emerges in the mythical series, we observe as well a transformation whose nature is etiological. The story of Lynx is directly or indirectly linked to the origin of the fog. The versions of the dentalia thieves in which the hero changes into a Waterbird send back to the wind that these Birds usually announce (see p. 33 above; *The Naked Man,* pp. 205–6); they thus fill a function tied to seasonal periodicity.

Another bird plays a major role in the same myths: Owl. All of North American mythology associates Owls with periodic phenomena: the alternation of day and night on the one hand, the measured duration of human life on the other. There is a close relationship between these phenomena since souls, reincarnated into nocturnal birds of prey, inhabit the world of the dead during the day and come back at night to the world of the living. It is not always easy to know which genus or species the texts refer to. There was a belief in California that, after death, good persons would turn into Eared Owls while bad ones would become Earless Owls. A myth from the Quinault, a Coast Salish group of Washington state, tells that a young girl who had gone off to marry the son of Great Horned Owl got lost and ended up with Screech Owl, who was a ne'er-do-well. According to a Kwakiutl version of a Salish myth of the lower Fraser (see pp. 92–93 below), the abductor of bad little girls is White Owl (perhaps species *nyctea,* an Arctic owl that spends the winters in the area).[1]

The Inland Salish attributed to Screech Owl (*Otus asio*) a primary role in announcing a coming death. The Great Horned Owl (*Bubo virginianus*) appears in their myths mostly as a thief of children. The name of the Great Horned Owl—*skelula* in Thompson and in Lilloet, and *snina* in Shuswap and in Okanagan*— resembles the name of the human hero of these myths, called Snánaz, Ntsaâz, and Tsa'au'z in different versions. The version I will start with has been titled by Boas "Owl and Ntsaâz" and comes from the Thompson Indians. Boas notes that, according to some informants, the name Ntsaâz would be related to Snánaz, the name of the hero in a short variant of the same myth and a name also encountered among the Shuswap.[2] I will come back to this point later (see p. 169 below).

A little boy was crying all the time. To make him stop, he was threatened with Owl, so much so that this latter took him away. Owl made him grow magically, and in a few days the child became an adult. Owl took him along hunting, but he barely fed him. Luckily, the hero made the acquaintance of Crow and his wife, who showed themselves more hospitable. And since Owl not only starved him but also offended him by calling him his slave, the hero decided to kill him: he burned Owl's heart, which the latter always left hanging in his cabin before going out. Crow inquired whether the hero had a family and if, as a child, he had "toy dried salmon, toy dried berries, toy salmon oil, toy deer fat" (what we might call a play meal)[†] and offered to go get them. Crow flew off, arrived at the village, and told the hero's mother and sister that he was still alive. He then told them to observe his flight and to locate smoke puffs that would show them where they had to go. Only one villager had a gaze strong enough to succeed, even though he fainted from the effort.

The two women arrived at their destination, let themselves be known, and took the road back, accompanied by the hero. A little while later, the hero, feeling too hot, decided to bathe in spite of the contrary advice of his mother and sister. He jumped into a

---

*I thank Dorothy I. D. Kennedy from the *British Columbia Indian Language Project* for kindly verifying and confirming these terms. On Canadian owls and their distribution, see Godfrey.

†TN: Lévi-Strauss uses the term *dinette,* "a child's or doll's meal" or "play utensils."

FIGURE 9. The American great horned owl (*Bubo virginianus*)

lake and turned into a Loon. He said to his sister, "I am going to stay here. If you long for me, come here and call me"—which she did a while later. The hero appeared, gave her precious shells and his own dentalia necklace (cf. *The Naked Man,* p. 203), and told her not to show them to anyone. But a young woman from the village saw them and understood where these jewels came from. (The informant at this point says that there is a gap in his memory.) She asked the hero's sister for permission to go with her. When the sister called her brother, he appeared in all his splendor, his body covered with sumptuous shells. His sister invited him to sit very near her and threw her arms around him while the other young woman threw magic herbs on him, which gave him back his human form.

All three then left and passed near the cabin of an individual called Ntsaâz. The hero (who had been too hot in a previous episode) now complained of the cold. He wanted to enter to warm himself, even though his companions tried to talk him out of it: "No one ever goes in there; Ntsaâz has a bad smell." The women continued their journey; the hero remained behind, grabbed hold of Ntsaâz's nose, and shook him so hard that his body escaped from his skin, which the hero then put on himself: he became Ntsaâz.

Meanwhile the young woman with the magical herbs was rejecting all her suitors. Her parents shamed her: "You refuse everyone. Go marry Ntsaâz!" She then went to the old, smelly, crippled man's cabin, wrapped him in a mat, and brought him home without listening to all the villagers' sneers. To further humiliate their daughter, her parents told her to send her husband to cut wood. She took him to the forest, where the hero came out of his skin. With one kick of his foot, he brought down four dry trees that split by themselves into logs, whose volume contracted so that the woman was able to carry them without any difficulty.

When she returned home, she unloaded her logs, and they grew back to their original volume and filled up four cabins to the roof. One of these cabins was that of Moon, who, too slow to get out of the way, got wounded in his enormous testicles. The hero then succeeded in catching lots of game despite the snow, while the other hunters, among them Lynx, came home empty-handed. The hero's wife took advantage of his going off to pursue some game to burn the old skin, which he had temporarily taken off. The hero was then forced to remain young and handsome, as he was in reality. Everyone envied his wife, the more so that he became a great hunter and supplied the whole village with meat.[3]

While in this story Moon has enormous testicles (like the master of the animals in the Tenetehara myths—see p. 77 above—and Tanuki in Japanese folklore), Moon is elsewhere a cannibal, eater of testicles. I will discuss this motif later (see chap. 12 below); for the time being, on the topic of the lunar connections of characters with large testicles, I will limit myself to referring the reader to *The Origin of Table Manners* (pp. 82–83); *The Naked Man* (p. 567); and *The Jealous Potter* (pp. 167–168). Of more immediate interest is another Thompson version, but this time originating downstream. Teit collected it and published it under the title "Owl and Tsa'au'z." Teit specifies that this is a given name found in the Lytton band belonging to some famous shamans and warriors of old.

This version starts out like the other. Owl feeds his prisoner insects (and, in one variant, snakes). The hero doesn't complain to Crow that he is being starved but that Owl only gives him meat and insects and not, as he would like, roots. Crow goes to fetch some in the hero's native village. The only inhabitant able to follow Crow's flight with his eyes is, as in the other version, called Sha'kuk ("small owl whose eyes do not run"). According to myths of the same origin, this would be the Screech Owl.[4] Instead of Owl's external heart, the hero burns his house. Owl changes into a Bird henceforth incapable of stealing small children.

Once married, Tsa'au'z takes off his diseased skin every night and shows himself to his wife as he really is: young, handsome, adorned with dentalia. Another difference from the first version: it is not the hero's wife but his brothers-in-law who discover the skin he has taken off in the course of hunting. They do not succeed in burning it completely but do succeed in transforming it into fog by blowing on it:

> That is the reason why fog can be smelled at the present day: it is the smell of the sores and of the burnt skin. When Tsa'au'z returned to get his skin, he found out it had been turned into fog. He tried in vain to collect it, for the fog moved up and down on the distant mountains. Therefore he had to remain as he was, in his natural shape—that of a handsome young man.[5]

There is a detail in this version that needs to be noted. When getting up each morning, the hero leaves behind a supply of dentalia in the bed he shares with his wife. His parents-in-law collect them and thus become very wealthy. The episode is in perfect symmetry with the one that opens up the myth of the dentalia thieves, in which a sister (instead of a spouse) benefits from the shells that her brother produces in circumstances that forbid the proximity of the sexes (see chap. 3 above). Here it is the opposite, since the shells are formed in the marriage bed.

The symmetry is even more marked in a version from the Chehalis of the lower Fraser. The stolen child was a naughty little girl of whom Owl made his spouse. Later she wanted to escape, so she walked some distance away under the pretext of an urgent need and then told her urine to fool Owl: as she fled, it screamed that she was not through yet. She came back to her village, but her parents found their daughter still too unruly; they sent her back to her husband. One day her brother came to visit and liked it there so much that he settled with his brother-in-law Owl and invited his other sister to join them. This latter came accompanied by a nice-looking friend, whom she hoped her brother would fall in love with and who then would convince him to return home. This did indeed happen. The brother tricked Owl into going away. He, his sisters, and the pretty girl burned Owl's house. Owl's child died in the fire.

Next came the episode of the lake, from which the brother wanted to drink; he fell into the water and changed into a Loon. Later, a beautiful lonely woman gave him back his human form—because, explains the myth,

> he had not been drowned or carried off by an aquatic monster as his sisters and wife had supposed. As the waters closed over his head, this diver-woman had come to him and offered him a diver's skin and persuaded him to live with her in the lake. He had complied and had stayed with her ever since.

The hero accompanied his liberator. Arriving at his village and wishing not to be recognized, he took a leper's skin and put it on. The girl had up to then rejected all of her suitors; she was mocked to have picked this disgusting husband. They lived away from the others. The hero went to wash himself secretly in a neighboring stream,

> using the tips of spruce and balsam branches to scrub himself with; and as the needles fell off the branches they became transformed into *ts'ākwes*. He brought back some and told his wife to go get the rest from the bottom of the water and to give some to her younger sister for their parents. The father admired the gifts and told his wife, "You had better go and bring our daughter and her husband home here."[6]

It can be seen that this version's final episode respects in all the details the symmetry with the first episode of the dentalia thieves.

However, the *ts'ākwes* seem to be a different kind of jewel. According to Hill-Tout, who has collected this myth, these were "some kind of valuable treasure, which is only to be got ordinarily from the coast and which was very valuable, one being worth many blankets. I could not understand what this treasure was; only that it was 'something white with a hole in it' but not a shell of any kind."[7]

8

Jewels and Wounds

Beyond the Thompson, the Shuswap, the northernmost members of the Salish ensemble, change the myth of the stolen child in two ways. On the one hand, they take a part away from it, which they incorporate in another context (the myth indexed M_{738} in *The Naked Man,* pp. 471–73); on the other hand, they impoverish the original by reducing it to the episodes of the hero's kidnapping and liberation. Transformed into a Bird, Owl is to fill the function usually given to nocturnal birds of prey: that of announcing an upcoming death. And instead of acting like a tyrant as in the Thompson myth, or like an ogre as in the Kutenai one, Owl in the Shuswap version is a wise and powerful magician; he does not enslave the hero but imparts his knowledge to him and even makes him superior to himself.

The Chilcotin, the Shuswap's neighbors, belong to the Athapaskan linguistic family. In their midst, the myth of the stolen child regains all of its richness while also undergoing important transformations. I have noted many times this double phenomenon, observable when crossing either together or singly a linguistic and a cultural boundary or again an ecological one (see p. 10 above).[1]

Here is the Chilcotin version.

Under the pretext of offering him some treats, Owl led a naughty boy outside. He captured him, raised him, made him grow through magical means, and gave him lots of presents, among them a dentalia necklace. The parents set off looking for their son. When they found him, he was in no hurry to leave Owl's place, where he enjoyed himself. His parents succeeded in convincing him and, taking advantage of Owl's absence, they burned his cabin down. Owl chased after them, and they hid in ambush at the end of a small bridge. When Owl was on the bridge, the hero appeared on the other shore brandishing his fingers, each covered with a goat horn. The terrified Owl fell into the water, swam to the shore, and gave up the pursuit. Upon the hero's return to his village, a feast was given in his honor. He presented himself adorned with the shells he had brought along, and he distributed them to everyone. "And that is where the Indians first got dentalia shells."

One day, the hero's mother found him dirty and sent him to bathe. He first refused, but she insisted. He dived in and disappeared. The disconsolate mother remained at the edge of the lake, from which she refused to move.

Winter came soon after. The women of the village went to the lake to make holes in the ice to draw water. The hero, who lived at the bottom of the lake, had fun breaking their buckets. Two sisters succeeded in attracting him to the shore by getting him to grab onto a richly decorated bucket. The hero was covered with mud, his skin was all loose, and his aquatic stay had made him so weak that he could not walk anymore. The two women tried in vain to scratch off the mud; they carried him to their cabin to warm him up, and they nursed him.

It got colder; snow covered the ground. It was not even possible to find wood to make the snowshoes necessary for hunting. The hero dragged himself outside, where he discovered just enough wood to make one pair of snowshoes. He told one of the women to bring in this wood and to shake it when she was halfway down the ladder through which one entered the cabin in winter. (These cabins were half-buried; they were entered through the smoke hole and by going down a ladder made out of a notched tree trunk; see fig. 10.) When the wood was shaken, it multiplied and filled the cabin so it was possible to make snowshoes. And yet the hunters returned empty-handed day after day. There was nothing left to eat.

Even though still weak and covered with mud, the hero announced he would go hunt Caribou if each man gave him an ar-

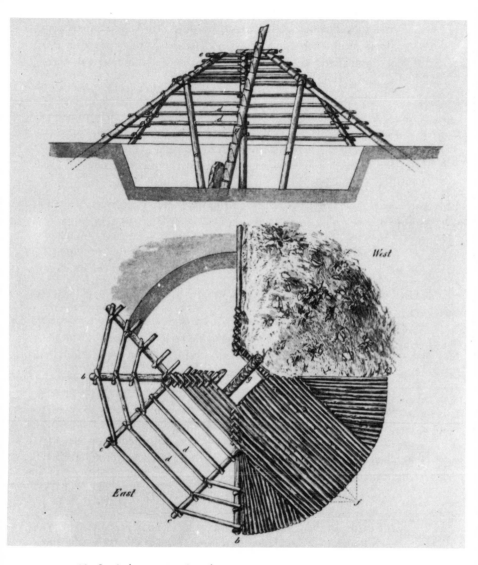

FIGURE 10. Semisubterranean winter house

row. The one he received from Raven was made out of leather and thus soft. The hero left, took off his mud skin "like a shirt," and hid it. With each good arrow he killed a Caribou, and with the bad one a Coyote. He put his mud skin back on and sent each man to get the animal he had coming.

The hero was now hunting successfully every day. Raven spied on him and discovered the mud shirt hanging between two adjacent tree trunks. Raven ripped it apart and spread the pieces about, but the hero succeeded in mending it. The next time, Raven succeeded in surprising the hero without his skin on; he saw him young, handsome, strong, adorned with shells. From then on, the hero kept his natural appearance and married the two sisters.[2]

I have discussed at length in *Structural Anthropology,* volume 2 (p. 262) and in *The View from Afar* (pp. 105–8) the specific reasons the Chilcotin had for surrounding the origin of dentalia shells with mystery. Now it is other aspects of the Chilcotin myth that need to be discussed. Because of the constraints I have just alluded to, though the theme of the dentalia thieves is echoed among the Chilcotin, it could only be so in a disguised form: instead of the women *taking out* of the water the shells produced by their *brother* as *he bathes,* here the women pull out of the water a nonkinsman, a future *spouse,* who *had not wanted* to bathe, and they pull him out by *immersing into* the water a richly decorated bucket. This bucket tempts him, and he gives in to covetousness, just like the dentalia thieves, who too were incapable of resisting the covetousness that shells, these other precious objects, aroused in them.

The Thompson myth explained the origin of fog (see p. 92 above), a meteorological phenomenon that mixes up the sky and the earth. In the Chilcotin version, the "fog skin" is replaced with a "mud skin"—mud being a mixture of water and earth. The fog originates from the sick skin of an old man and is thus a symptom of an internal pathological state. The Chilcotin hero's mud skin has an external origin: the aquatic milieu in which the hero lived, as stressed by the fruitless efforts of the women to scrape it off—which, incidentally, shows well that, in a mythological narrative, the smallest detail can have a meaning and fill a function.

The most remarkable transformation is that affecting the relationship of the hero and his mother (or the woman who returns him to the human condition) with water. I have given five versions of the myth. Four come from peoples belonging to the Salish linguistic family—that is, Coeur d'Alene, Thompson, and Chehalis—while one comes from the Chilcotin, who are Athapaskan.

In a Coeur d'Alene version, the hero's mother is thirsty. She asks her son for water, which he is slow to bring her or, in an Okanagan version, even refuses to bring her.[3] A Thompson version replaces this motif with a bath that the overheated hero wants to take but his mother tries to talk him out of. The Chehalis version from the lower Fraser basin includes an extra constraint in that the child stolen by Owl is a girl. It is thus necessary to introduce a male character into the story and to give him a spouse who tries to talk her husband out of going to the lake to drink: she prefers to bring him herself what he needs to quench his thirst.

In all three cases, the protagonists are thus a man and a woman close to him, mother or spouse. One of the two protagonists—sometimes the man, sometimes the woman—puts up obstacles to the fulfillment of the desire for water expressed by the other. Finally, this desire can take two forms: either for a drink (thus, water contained in the body), or for a bath (that is, for water that contains the body).

In addition to the three permutations illustrated respectively by the Coeur d'Alene, Thompson, and Chehalis versions:

Drink desired by the woman; obstacle raised by the man

—   —   — man,   —   —   — woman

Bath   —   —   —   —   —   —   —

it is clear that we would expect a fourth one:

Bath desired by the woman; obstacle raised by the man.

There are no grounds to think that this formula did not exist in the versions remaining unknown to the researchers. We cannot forget that we know only a small part of the mythological corpus in this as in all other areas of America. At the time when the major part of the research was done—roughly in the second half of the nineteenth century and the first half of the twentieth—the native cultures were already dying. Older informants were becoming rare, and the memory of certain myths or versions had probably gone.

It is nonetheless striking that we do not encounter the expected permutation when crossing the linguistic boundary separating the Thompson and the Chehalis from the Chilcotin. Instead, we come across another one that the versions discussed above did not lead us to foresee. Instead of the woman desiring a bath for herself, she wants to impose one on her son (using the pretext that he is dirty, a reproach that nothing in the narrative explains, which he refuses to accept. From the role of subject, the woman passes to that of agent, and the refusal by the other is not anymore aimed at a need felt by oneself; it translates an absence of need felt by the other. Indeed, a bath desired by oneself for oneself, in spite of the other, is the contradictory of a bath wanted not by and for oneself, but for the other, who does not want it.

If, for the reasons I have explained, we can set aside as not pertinent the change in the identity of the woman in the Chehalis version, the double twist that one observes when passing from the Salish versions to the Athapaskan one can be written up as follows:

$$
F_{man} \atop \text{(wanted bath)} \quad : \quad F_{woman} \atop \text{(wanted drink)} \quad :: \quad F_{man} \atop \text{(wanted drink)} \quad : \quad F_{\text{wanted both}} \atop (woman)
$$

in which the four terms correspond (from left to right respectively) to the Thompson, Coeur d'Alene, Chehalis, and Chilcotin versions.

This mythical set does not disappear beyond its major area of diffusion. Toward the northwest it is transformed into legendary tradition by the Tsimshian and gravitates toward the fictional genre among the Carrier, while to the east the Cree have incorporated it into their recent history. I have used this as an example in my study of "How Myths Die" (*Structural Anthropology*, vol. 2, chap. 14) and need not come back to it here.

૨૬

Anyone doubting that myths do come out of the same mold in North and South America should look to myths M_{245} and M_{273} and page 378 and following in *From Honey to Ashes*. Of course mythology is universally full of werewolves who steal children. But even if we limit ourselves to a single example—M_{273}, a Guyan myth—it exhibits, along with those I have just summarized, analogies that are too specific to be fortuitous. Thus there are the expeditions of the kidnapper to his prisoner's village to bring to her everything that she is missing: clothing, household utensils, vegetables (because he feeds her only with meat); and, in the North American myths, the journey of a helpful character to the village of a starving captive to get the food which he was fed since his childhood, or, in another version, to fetch roots so as to vary a diet made up exclusively of insects.

Two sequences of the North American myths are clearly seasonal in nature. After having run away from his kidnapper, and on the way to his village, the hero is too hot; he feels the pressing need to bathe in a lake or to drink of its water. There, he transforms himself into a Loon and thus becomes the master of dentalia shells, the natural adornment of this bird.* It is during the summer that these Loons live on inland lakes; they winter on the coast, as the lakes are then frozen. In contrast, when the hero arrives at his young wife's village, he complains of the cold and enters the cabin of an old man to warm himself. It is there that he puts on a skin covered with wounds and sores, forming a pair of opposition with the healthy skin adorned with precious shells that

---

*"The loon was a great shaman, and used to kill and eat his friends. He made his body spotted with white by touching it with his finger-tips during his period of training. Some of the Uta'mqt say the spots on his body were originally dentalia." (Teit, *Mythology of the Thompson Indians,* p. 336)

is really his. All the rest of the myth occurs in a winter climate: lack of wood for heating, snow making hunting difficult, and so on. The Loon that makes up the hero's first avatar announces the wind. His second avatar, the sick skin, gives birth to the fog. The myth thus implicitly or explicitly elaborates a series of oppositions: summer/winter; water/fire; wind/fog; jewels/wounds. And these oppositions, when laid out next to each other, reproduce an armature with which we are already familiar.

In *The Raw and the Cooked,* this armature resulted from the transformative relation of certain Bororo myths. As we have seen regarding the problem of twinness (see chap. 4 above), North and South American myths often send back to each other. In the present case, the recourse to the Bororo should not be surprising since, as I wrote in 1964 (*The Raw and the Cooked,* pp. 141–42):

> the Bororo way of thinking was greatly influenced by Tupi my-
> thology. In both groups the same myth—the one about the ja-
> guar's human wife, who is the mother of the two civilizing
> heroes—occupies an essential position. And the modern Bororo
> versions remain astonishingly close to the one that Thevet re-
> corded as existing among the Tupinamba in the sixteenth century.

Let us now look at two other Bororo myths, pertaining respectively to the origin of water and adornments (M_2, pp. 49–50) and to the origin of illness (M_5, pp. 59–60). I have shown that these myths partake of the same single transformation. Both have for protagonist a character, male or female, whose name Biri-moddo means "pretty skin." (This name brings us already quite close to the North American hero, who hides his beautiful skin, "as smooth and soft as that of his wife,"[4] underneath that of an old man covered with pus.) In the Bororo myth M_5, a woman named Pretty Skin exudes illnesses, and later she changes into a rainbow—rainbows being seen as the cause of illnesses according to a belief found in South America from Guyana all the way to the Chaco (*The Raw and the Cooked,* pp. 246–50).

Amerindian thought, which often compares fever to a warm garment, sets in correlation and in opposition, on the one hand, wounds and skin diseases, which are natural coverings, and on the other, adornments, which likewise are visible from the outside but are a cultural covering.* These latter have magical properties that heighten the vitality of the wearer while, on the contrary, the natural coverings weaken him. But even though these coverings act in opposite ways, both are intermediaries between life and death. They thus occupy a median position, comparable from a formal viewpoint to that of the rainbow and the fog existing between the sky and the earth.

However, we need to note a difference between the myths of the two hemispheres. In order to pass from adornments to illness (or the inverse), the South American transformation needs two distinct myths, at least in appearance. In North America, the homologous transformation requires only a single myth, which incorporates wounds and jewels into a single framework. It is this ambiguity that enables us to understand why the personality of the heroine—or of the two heroines—oscillates all through the mythical ensemble that is the object of the present book. A young girl, shy and rebellious against marriage, changes into a shameless sister, whose lack of reserve borders on incest. The myths in which these two types of heroines appear associate them respectively with wounds and adornments. Married against her will to Lynx, the rebellious young girl nurses him and cures him of the wounds he

---

*Our popular language does likewise. Under the heading *rubis* ["ruby"] the dictionary Littré gives as its meaning "red bumps or rash that appear on the nose and the face." And under the heading *perle* ["pearl"]: "one of the common names for albugo or white spot in the cornea." Medical vocabulary is full of metaphors borrowed from the jeweler's art: *vesicule perlée* ["pearled blister"], *douleur en bracelet* ["braceleted pain"], *lesion en medaillon* ["lesion in the form of a medallion"], *eruption en collier* ["necklace rash"], and so on. The surgeon "sets a wound."

A version of the Thompson myth summarized earlier (see pp. 92–93) well brings out this equivalency: Tsa'au'z took off his sores or spotted covering, and became clothed in dentalia instead. On the following morning the dentalia fell off, and, by the time the people awoke he was clothed in sores again. This happened four nights, so Tsa'au'z' parents-in-law became rich in dentalia" (Teit, *Mythology of the Thompson Indians*, pp. 241, 265–68).

has received. As for the indiscreet sister, she takes away from the hero the adornments he has produced.

The dialectic of the myths does not stop there: at a later stage of the transformation, one sister, by using gestures that are too free, gives back to the hero the human form he has lost, or alternatively she makes it possible for her double to do so. In this sense she cures him. Likewise, by becoming her own inverse, a young girl who first rejects all of her suitors chooses the most wretched and repulsive one, thanks to whom she obtains rich adornments not for her own use and against the will of her parents but for their benefit and without them being aware of it:*

$$
\frac{F_{wounds}}{(\text{rebellious daughter})} : \frac{F_{adornments}}{(\text{indiscreet sisters})} :: \frac{F_{wounds}}{(\text{indiscreet sisters})} : \frac{F_{\text{rebellious daughter-1}}}{(\textit{adornments})}
$$

⸮⟓

The transformation at which we have just arrived consolidates a mythical set that the needs of the analysis had required us to section into successive stages. Let us thus attempt a bird's-eye view. The set has the aspect of a network whose segments are all explored by mythical imagination. It must be noted that the segment leading to Coyote fades away. The reason for this will soon

*When I proposed this formula for the first time in 1955 (*Structural Anthropology*, p. 224) it was shrugged off, but during these last few years, it has been met with interest and used in various applications ranging from rural architecture to the *Cogito*. See R. Bucaille et al., *Pigeons de Limagne*, Université Populaire de Clermont-Ferrand, 1987, p. 140; J. F. Bordron, *Descartes. Recherches sur les contraintes sémiotiques de la pensée discursive*, Paris, P.U.F., 1987, pp. 80–82; J. Petitot, "Approche morphodynamique de la formule canonique du mythe," *l'Homme*, 106–7, 1988, pp. 24–50; Mark S. Mosko, *Quadripartite Structures*, Cambridge University Press, 1985, pp. 3–7; "The Canonic Formula of Myth and Non-Myth," *American Ethnologist*, 18/1, 1991, pp. 126–51; A. Coté, "L'Instauration sociale. Du schème canonique à la formule canonique," *Anthropologie et sociétés*, vol. 13, no. 3, 1989, pp. 25–36.

For other uses of the formula in this work (in instances in which I have not always found it necessary to transcribe it with symbols), cf. pp. 108, 132–33, 140–41.

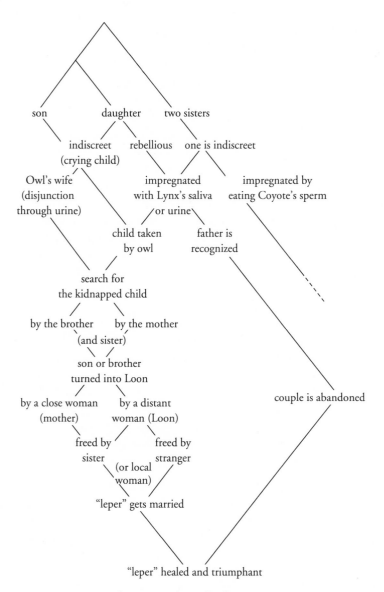

FIGURE 11. Network structure of a mythical set

become clear: all of the network is ordered around the character of Lynx, whether it be under his appearance as a crippled old man or as that of a disguised hero. Coyote elsewhere holds the main role in a parallel series on the conquest of the wind (instead of the origin of the fog, which up to now was our main focus).

Starting with a very simple story, that of Lynx, we have seen it progressively grow richer as if, at each stage, mythological imagination was trying to create new motifs to fill the blank spots of an incomplete canvas. The story of Lynx is first transformed into that of Lynx and Coyote. Then two types of possible developments appear, depending on whether the heroine or the two heroines are rebellious girls or indiscreet sisters. The resulting set is inserted into yet another larger network: the myth of the child stolen by Owl. The schema in figure 11 shows how complex forms are, so to speak, grafted onto the simpler one. This latter occupies the right part, while the others occupy the segments in the left part of the network.

Finally, it must be noted that the network, drawn here in two dimensions, would require more dimensions, as the use of the canonic formula has shown. On the left of the schema, the dentalia shells have a positive function as a factor of conjunction. On the right side, where the indiscreet sisters are featured, dentalia shells fill a negative function: they cause the disjunction of the thieves from their parents. By analyzing the schema, one would easily come across other dimensions that graphic constraints do not allow us to represent.

9

The Son of the Root

In the densest part of the network, the hero undergoes two transformations that respond to each other. First he changes himself or is changed into a Loon, a bird prized for its beauty and whose neck feathers resemble a dentalia necklace. This incident explains why he is later to become the master and the giver of adornments. However, before getting to that point, he transforms himself into an old and crippled man covered with wounds— wounds that, as we have seen, form a pair in opposition to and correlation with adornments.

Let us focus on the first transformation. In the myths, it can occur in only two ways: either when a woman who is close to the hero—that is, his mother—distances him by causing his meta-morphosis into an aquatic bird (while she herself changes into a land bird); or, on the contrary, when a distant woman—in this case, a Loon—brings the hero closer to her by turning him into a member of the same species.

These two formulas, inverse of each other, belong in fact to a triangular system, and at this point we need to remember the reasons for this. A famous myth found south of our area, from northern California to southern Oregon, features a sister driven by incestuous passion who in the end changes into a Loon. In that case, a woman who is close distances herself from the hero instead of distancing him from her, and her position as incestuous sister, agent of her own transformation, yields a triple contrast with that of a disjunctive mother and a conjunctive stranger, both agents of the transformation of somebody else.

Studied at length in *The Naked Man* (pp. 48–150), this myth of Loon Woman has extensions all the way to the Thompson and the Lilloet. One of their myths, whose protagonists are at the outset Loons (instead of one of them becoming a Loon in the end), reproduces and inverts the myth of Loon Woman. This myth features a daughter rather than a son kept away from view (the son is called Lynx in most of the versions); there is then the running away of the incestuous siblings, thus replacing the escape of the family to heaven; there is the suicide of the guilty parties, who throw themselves on a fire instead of the guilty character making his whole family perish in a fire; and so forth.[1] We will come back to this myth later (see pp. 159–163 below).

One of the most widespread myths in both Americas* has as its heroine a woman who distances herself under various pretexts and goes to meet a seducing animal. In the South American version it is Serpent or Tapir, while in versions found in North America and as well in Siberia the seducer can be Serpent, Bear, Water Monster, and so on. The husband finds out the truth, puts on his wife's clothing, calls up the animal as she used to do, and kills him. Numerous versions specify that he cooked the sex organs and forced his wife to eat them. I refer the reader back to *The Raw and the Cooked* (pp. 266–68) and *From Honey to Ashes* (pp. 296–307) for more on this important group of myths. The peoples of the Salish linguistic family knew this myth well.[2] The Lilloet, neighbors to the Thompson, gave the role of seducing animal to the Loon and made him intervene in very odd circumstances, to say the least. A woman went every day to the shore to collect *skemtc* roots (*Erythronium grandiflorum*). One day, these plants to which she was drawn inspired erotic thoughts in her. She lay down on a rocky platform that jutted into the lake and sent out calls for an inhabitant of the water to come satisfy her. Loon offered his services.[3]

Represented by only one species in Europe and about fifteen in the New World, the genus *Erythronium* belongs to the family

*The pages that follow take up and develop a text written for a volume in honor of Professor E. Meletinsky.

of lilliaceous plants. The French and English names—*dent-de-chien* and dog-tooth violet (also adder tongue and deer tongue)—can be explained by the shape and the white coloration of these bulbs.* *Erythronium grandiflorum* grows abundantly in the open forests and grassy meadows of British Columbia and Oregon. Even though these bulbs are said to be very small, the Indians sought them out because of their earliness. They ate them boiled or raw and, according to the Kwakiutl, they were particularly appreciated raw on a hot day because of their refreshing and milky taste.[4]

In the Lilloet myth, a plant exerts on a woman a seductive power, power that is then embodied in a Waterbird. How are we to interpret this notion, not very intelligible at first sight, of a seductive plant? We would of course like to be able to put in a relation of equivalency the *Erythronium* bulbs and the dentalia shells, which they resemble in their shape, size, and color. Though mute regarding *Erythronium,* the ethnographic literature mentions this resemblance when it comes to another root, which is known as bitterroot in English on account of the taste of its skin: *Lewisia rediviva,* a member of the portulacaceae family, gathered in the spring and reputed for its nutritive qualities. According to the Nez Percé, "a single ounce in the dried state is sufficient for a meal."[5] This was not its sole quality:

> Bitterroot contains a part that has the shape of a heart and the Flathead [the easternmost members of the Salish linguistic family]

*"The bulbs . . . too small for the Whites to use . . . barely bigger than a peanut," writes Teit; but sometimes they are "the size of a thumb," according to Turner's Thompson informants. The freshly dug bulbs were perhaps toxic; according to some accounts, they had to be set aside for several days, the time required for the inulin they contained to be converted to fructose. Thompson children called them "candies." Bouchard and Kennedy mention the ancient existence of a first harvest ceremony for *Erythronium* among the Shuswap (Teit, *Ethnobotany of the Thompson Indians of British Columbia,* p. 481; Turner, Thompson, Thompson, and York, pp. 122–23; Abrams, vol. 1, pp. 426–30; Turner, p. 82; Bouchard and Kennedy [*Shuswap Stories,* p. 268). Dr. Dorothy Kennedy has kindly sent me photocopies of recent or not easily accessible sources on the genus *Erythronium.* I thank her again for them.

believed that this heart put bitterroot above all other plants, and that it perhaps had a soul and feelings.[6]

Queen of all the roots according to the Okanagan, "she resembled, when dried up, dentalia shells in shape and size."[7]

Let us come back to the *Erythronium,* a plant on which we do not have the same kind of information. At any rate, it is clear that through the motif of the seductive plant, the Lilloet myth forms a juncture between the Pan-American group of the seductive animal and a smaller group of myths—proper, in fact, to the Salish-speaking peoples—to which North American mythographers have given the code name of "The Child of the Root."

Found in numerous versions among the Lilloet, Thompson, Shuswap, and Coeur d'Alene, this myth tells of a young girl who refused all suitors and had to content herself with a Root when she wanted to marry; or, alternatively, that a woman busy collecting Roots experienced the desire to copulate with one of them; or, again, that lost in the woods and leading a solitary life, she resigned herself to such a union. A son was born to her and grew up under her care. Surprised that he did not have a father, he asked his mother about it, and she at first told him various lies. Finally, having found out the truth (through a dream, or through the teasing of other children), he drowned his mother in a lake, or changed her into stone, or simply left her: "Henceforth women may not have intercourse with roots, nor bear children to them."[8] At first alone and then in the company of great Transformers like himself, the son of the Root helped to put the world in order and to give to beings and things their present-day appearance. Among other feats, he stopped the Sun in its course, almost triggering a cosmic conflagration; then he put the celestial body back in motion and the weather became temperate again. He could also make a water source spring forth by hitting the ground with his foot. In some versions, he became the Moon after a Frog jumped in his face, thus disfiguring him forever.

There are two comments to be made regarding these exploits. The power to make a source appear so as to quench the thirst of his companions is reminiscent of that of Coyote's son, who in a myth also originating from the Thompson makes fire appear to warm up his companions by kicking tree stumps (see p. 19 above). In other words, these are two inverted sequences, one belonging to summer while the other belongs to winter and sends back to Coyote: this would place the son of the Root on the side of Lynx.

The other episode in the myth goes in the same direction. The son of the Root becomes the Moon after Coyote has failed in this role because of his indiscretion. The Kutenai versions (see p. 61 above) end on an analogous episode: Coyote is not accepted as the Sun, in part because of his indiscretion, while according to one version Lynx's twin sons become the Moon and the Sun.[9]

The myths often refer to the hero by the name of the paternal plant, Lomatium (*Peucedanum* L. = *Lomatium* Raf., *Lomatium* coming from a Greek word meaning "border," alluding to the shape of the seed). This umbelliferous genus was of great importance to the people of the area, first as a food plant, called *kouse* in the old texts (after *kowish,* the name of the plant in Nez Percé and other related languages). In English it was called biscuit root because the Nez Percé ground the roots in a mortar to make long and thin wafers, cooked slowly above the hearth. Gathered from March to May, these roots were one of the main vegetable foods before the *camas* season (a bulbous liliaceous plant).

A whole variety of medicinal properties was attributed to Lomatium: it worked against sterility, cough, migraine, insomnia of very young children, and so on.* But the plant's major properties

---

*In versions of the myth, the plant is more specifically *Peucedanum macrocarpum* = *Lomatium macrocarpum,* whose popular name, hog fennel, corresponds to those of Lomatium in French: *Fenouil de Porc* ["hog fennel"], *Queue de Pourceau* ["hog's tail"], and so on. Even though this taproot was also a major food resource for the Thompson, they believed that its overuse, just like that of *Balsamorhiza sagittata,* could cause drowsiness (Turner, Thompson, Thompson, and York, pp. 155).

Lomatium appears to have held a place in the beliefs of Old Europe as large as that among the Indians. The index of the translation of Pliny's works by A. du

were magical. According to a Thompson myth, the person who ate only this plant and nothing else would get miraculous powers and become immortal.[10] The root chewed and spat out could make wind and storm disappear.[11] Lomatium was used in other ways in the rites of the people of the lower Fraser and of Vancouver Island. The Songish, close neighbors to the Thompson and the Lilloet, burned it as an offering to the first salmon of the year. It was also one of the most powerful magical charms: it could be burned to chase away ghosts.[12] The Kwakiutl of the north of Vancouver Island used Lomatium for several pharmaceutical purposes and addressed to it prayers appropriate for each of its uses. They also chewed and spat out the seeds to make sea monsters run away.[13]

The Sanpoil and the Nespelem appear to have been the farthest inland of the Salish-speaking peoples to celebrate the first salmon rites. Probably because of the rarity or the absence of Lomatium in their territory, they substituted another plant for it—a Helianthus plant, identified by a researcher as *Helianthus annuus,* but incorrectly, it would seem. The plant would instead be of a genus close to the same family, *Balsamorhiza*—that is, balsam root.[14]

This genus was of great import to the Indians as a food plant gathered from March on. It also had medicinal and magical properties. Among the Thompson,

> women, while digging this root, must abstain from sexual intercourse. A man must not come near the oven when the women are

---

Pinet (1584) includes almost thirty entries, to the point that one wonders if there was anything that oil of Lomatium could not do!

I shorten the main text: "pig's tail . . . slim stalk, long and resembling that of fennel . . . black root, fat, massive, full of juice and bad smells. [When extracting it] one must perfume and rub oneself with rose oil . . . to prevent the strength of the juice and of the root from causing a fainting spell . . ." (Pliny the Elder, *L'Histoire du monde,* vol. 1, pt. 25, p. 9.

Certain American species of *Lomatium* are also toxic, notably *Lomatium dissectum,* which was used as poison to stun fish by the Indians of the middle Columbia River (Hunn, p. 113).

cooking the root. The women, when going out to dig the root, often painted their whole face red, or they painted a large black or red spot on each cheek. . . . . It was sometimes said, when [the roots] had been cooked successfully, that the coyote had caused the success by urinating on them.

The Thompson looked upon *Balsamorhiza,* which the Sanpoil called salmon plant, as the "greatest of all mysteries." When adolescents tasted for the first time of a new fruit or a root, they addressed their prayers to *Balsamorhiza.*[15]

Here are thus two plant species to which these beliefs gave prime value, to which magical powers were attributed, that were the objects of worship, and that could be substituted for each other in the first salmon rites.* Do they have something in common, and, if so, what?

The name *Peucedanum* comes from the Greek *peukédanos,* "bitter," derived from *peuké,* "pine," "resin." Indeed, these are the odors and the tastes of this root, which are so well described in Diderot and d'Alembert's *Encyclopédie:* "the root is fat, long, hairy, black inside, full of sap; when cut it gives a yellow liquid having a virulent smell of pitch . . . the seeds . . . have a sour and somewhat bitter taste." At the end of the nineteenth century, a missionary with the Puget Sound Indians remarked on the strong and, according to him, peppery taste of the seeds.[16] An observer among the Shuswap attributed a taste of licorice to the plant when green.[17] The American species of Lomatium thus resembles in

---

*In his work *The Squamish Language* (The Hague-Paris, Mouton & Co., 1967), A. E. Kuipers notes (p. 356) that the same word *q'ex.mi'n* is used in Squamish to designate a plant resembling a sunflower as in Cowichan to designate a Lomatium (cf. in Thompson language *q'aqme? = Lomatium leiocarpum*). When questioned during a recent investigation, a Thompson informant considered balsam root (*Balsamorhiza sagittata*) to be related to *Lomatium dissectum,* which also has a fat taproot and a bitter taste and is used as a remedy for coughs.

Also regarding *Balsamorhiza sagittata* she remarked: "She is the boss. She's got lots of relatives that look like her." Another informant, who did not know *Lomatium dissectum,* thought that the native name for this species designated sunflower root (Turner, Thompson, Thompson, and York, pp. 154, 156, 176).

this the Old World *Peucedanum officinale* L. And the scientific name of Helianthus (*Balsamorhiza*)—whose English name, balsam root, is the literal translation—also denotes a characteristic smell and taste.

Let us now introduce another plant that too has a strong and bitter taste and that native thought associates, as it does bitterroot (*Lewisia rediviva*), with dentalia shells, and that, like Lomatium and Helianthus, holds an essential place in first salmon rites. I have already mentioned (see p. 35 above) the value of comparing the beliefs and rituals of the Salish-language peoples with those of the Yurok, a northern Californian coastal tribe. In this I was only following Kroeber's illustrious example.[18]

The Yurok attached great importance to wild Angelica (species *angelica*) in their beliefs and rites. When burned, the plant let out a smoke that had a special property: that of enriching the Indians with dentalia shells, for which they had an immoderate passion. A shaman evoked professional memories:

> I put Angelica root at the four corners of the fireplace and also threw it into the blaze. I would say: "This Angelica comes from the middle of the sky. There the dentalia and woodpecker scalps eat its leaves. That is why it is so withered." Then I inhaled the smoke of the burning root. Thus the dentalia would come to the house in which I was.[19]

While a Thompson myth promises supernatural powers to the one who would eat nothing but Lomatium (see p. 112 above), a Yurok myth attributes the same powers to the person who would eat nothing but Angelica roots.[20]

The Yurok compare large dentalia, which they hold to be the most precious of treasures, to fish that are caught. The first salmon rites involve cooking the fish on a bed of Angelica roots; as well, Angelica brings big winnings in gambling. There is thus a link between dentalia shells, fish, and Angelica (a trout that exudes a smell of Angelica presages events of supernatural origin[21]). And yet mixing the Angelica roots with the charcoal on which the fish were being cooked gave the fish a horrible taste that transformed its eating into a test.[22] According to one informant who remembers her childhood,

> it is said that if one eats his piece in three swallows he will become wealthy. . . . But my father failed to swallow more than one bite. He could hardly get that down. It was very strong because it was cooked without firewood, on Angelica only; and I suppose it is difficult to swallow much just because succeeding would help one so much.[23]

❧

Let us backtrack quite a ways here. It is the presence of a "bear cell" in one of our very first myths that led to a botanical discussion, and it would be a mistake to see it as a digression. In accordance with the myth, I emphasized that it was obligatory to cook bear meat in an earthen oven, fired with pine wood, which gave the meat a resinous taste that, according to old travelers' accounts, most Whites found distasteful (see p. 7 above). This custom appears to have been the rule in all of the northern regions of North America. Father Le Jeune, writing in 1634 about the Montagnais, a people of the Algonkin linguistic family established in the east of Canada, noted: "Making a feast out of bear meat, the one who had killed it roasted its innards on pine branches."[24] In the western area that is of interest here, numerous myths attribute the first cooking of bear meat and the spelling out of its rules to an old man called Bake-on-Hot-Rocks.[25] Other myths invert this motif: the bear is killed by making him swallow boiling resin and red-hot stones[26]—thus by treating him as if he were an earthen oven whose heat, stored by the stones put in it, came from a resinous wood fire.

Similar rules have been also noted in Siberia. During the bear feast, pine and pine branches were used in many rites among the Nivx of Sakhalin. The Ghiliak fed the "oven of the bear" with pine branches—thus from a tree whose needles always remained green and connoted a vitality that, it was hoped, would be communicated to the animal species. The Ket cooked bear meat on "mountain fire," likewise fed with pine branches.[27]

In America itself, a Nez Percé myth helps us to the path of a possible interpretation. In olden days, when animals and trees were talking, only Conifers had fire; they refused it to all living beings except their own kind. A very cold winter came to pass, and all the living beings were in danger of dying for lack of heat. While the Conifers were gathered around a warm fire, Beaver stole an ember and gave the fire to the other trees. This is why at present fire can be made with two pieces of wood rubbed against each other.[28]

Fire from coniferous trees is thus a primordial fire.* This explains why it is the only one allowed on an occasion as solemn as the cooking of bear meat, for everywhere the sacrifice of this animal or simply its consuming holds a central place in ritual and religious beliefs.[†] In the Northwest of North America, first salmon rites provide the only ground for comparison, though both rites did coexist. The recourse to primordial fire to ritually cook bear meat would thus be analogous to the rites of first salmon, which prescribed the use of precultural utensils—a mussel shell

---

*The Aztec would put pine branches in Tezcatlipoca's sanctuaries, which were located at crossroads, during the last five days of each month. Under other circumstances, the ritual offerings of pine branches could be replaced with the richer one of quetzal feathers or the more modest one of cane (Sahagún, book 3, chap. 2; book 7, chap. 2). In Korean folklore, the brother and the sister called upon to generate the new humankind unite in imitation of the smoke of two distant pine trees that they have themselves set on fire (In-hak Choi, *A Type Index of Korean Folktales,* Seoul, Myong Ji University, 1979, no. 725). And Plutarch wonders why in Apollo's temple in Delphi "only pine wood is burnt there to maintain the eternal fire" (*Que signifiait ce mot Ei,* etc.) in *Les Oeuvres Meslées* (vol. 1, appendix, p. 162).

†It is remarkable that in the Southeast of the United States—thus, far away from the area of diffusion of the bear feast—the paternity of the first fire is attributed to the plantigrades. In olden days, only Bears possessed fire. They always carried it with them. One day they put it down and left to eat acorns. The fire almost died out and called for help. Human beings saw it and fed it. The fire came back to life. When the Bears came back to get it, it told them it had nothing in common with them anymore. Since then, the fire belongs to human beings (Swanton, *Myths and Tales of the Southeastern Indians,* p. 122).

instead of a human-made knife—and a vocabulary made up of archaic words.

But while the cooking of bear meat on conifer wood can be explained, why do roots of Lomatium, Helianthus, or Angelica replace this wood for the cooking of the first salmon? I have noted that these plants have in common a resinous taste, which they impart to meat cooked on them; this is their pertinent trait. In the first salmon rites, they thus play the same role as conifer branches, which, from Siberia to eastern America, are the required fuel to ritually cook bear meat. The three plants have a metaphorical relation with conifer branches. But if we do see Lomatium, Helianthus, and Angelica as images of pine wood,* two consequences must follow.

First, the first salmon rites themselves appear as a metaphorical transposition of the bear rites: they would constitute their equivalent or substitute among some of the peoples whose economies rest mainly on fishing. Though the two rites exist side by side in the Northwest of North America, first salmon rites themselves occupy only a very small part of the area where salmon fishing is primary in the economy. To explain the simultaneous presence of the two rites in a limited territory, Gunther hypothesized that there, and only there, did two sets of beliefs found separately in the other cultures of the area come to blend. These were the belief that killed game comes back to life and the belief that animals willingly serve as food for human beings.[29] And yet the particularities of the geographical distribution of the two rites would rather lead us to recognize the logical and probably as well the historical priority of bear rites.

*However, among the Lilloet, the literal rendition prevailed. The first salmon had to be cooked on a bed of fresh red pine boughs (*Abies magnifica* Murr.), which Hill-Tout called the "mystical pine" because of its place in the ritual (Hill-Tout, "Report on the Ethnology of the Stlatlumh of British Columbia," pp. 137–38, 295–97).

On the presumed archaism of the rites for bear meat cooking, cf. Rémi Mathieu, "La Patte de l'ours" (*l'Homme,* 24(1), 1984, pp. 5–42).

Second, botanical considerations have led us to bring together salmon and bear rites. This, as we shall see, brings us right back to concerns with twins, which held such a large place in the first part of this book (chap. 4 and 5). We now need to come back to this concern from the standpoint of the cultures of the Northwest and surrounding areas.

10

Twins: Salmon, Bears, and Wolves

I n many parts of the world there is, or was, a belief that twins
and meteorological phenomena are linked: twins predict the
weather and even command it; they cause or stop the rain, the
wind, and storms. This raises the question of whether the belief
in this connection stands alone or is rather part of an ensemble,
from which it would be arbitrary to separate it. The birth of twins
is a relatively rare phenomenon in the human species; it is (or used
to be) unpredictable as well. Popular imagination thus linked it to
other unpredictable phenomena, not all of which were necessarily
meteorological in nature. Thus twins were thought to have the gift
of divination: they could throw spells, transform themselves into
supernatural beasts, and make epidemics and other ills that befall
livestock and gardens go away; they could cure certain illnesses;
they were immune to bites of venomous animals; and they could
give success in hunting, fishing, and so on.

However, it does appear that in the American Northwest, the
link between twins and meteorological phenomena is more pronounced than everywhere else; the connection is so clear and is
manifested in beliefs and ritual practices that are so detailed that
they give one the feeling that a problem exists and cannot be
avoided. This was, moreover, the opinion of the old authors, as is
shown by the place this region of the world was given by Frazer in
The Golden Bough (pt. 1, p. 262ff) and by Sydney Hartland, author of the entry "Twins" in *Hastings' Encyclopaedia of Religion
and Ethics.* But while these authors mostly made use of information originating from the American Northwest to bring out the
link between twins and meteorological phenomena, they limited

themselves to writing these facts down without wondering about the cause and nature of their connection.

Twins' special powers over the weather (which they sometimes shared with their parents) applied to rain, wind, and fog. When the Kwakiutl wanted to have good weather, they painted the bodies of twins red, had them dressed in their best clothes, and made them parade in public. If they wanted rain (to make the rivers swell so that salmon could swim up more easily), they washed the twins, put oil in their hair, and painted their bodies red and black.[1] It was also by putting oil or fat on the hair of one or two twins that the Coast Salish made the wind blow, while to calm the sea they washed a twin's hair that they had previously oiled.[2] The Kwakiutl believed that the influence of twins over the weather grew as they aged. "When it is foggy," they also said,

> one of the twins may act as though he gathered the fog in his hat, which he then presses against his chest. It is believed that by doing so he puts the fog inside his body, and that it will clear up.*

Twins could also call up winds from any direction by talking to them through the stem of a hollow seaweed used as an acoustic tube. A twin needed only to let his hair hang into the water for salmon to be caught, as if it were fished with a line.[3]

Countless customs and beliefs found in Alaska and from the north to the south of British Columbia, inland as well as on its coast, confirm this mastery attributed to twins over good and bad weather, fog, clear sky, and wind and storms.

In contrast, it does not appear that all the peoples occupying this vast territory greeted the birth of twins in the same manner. The Tlingit of Alaska feared them so much that a man could leave

---

*The father and the mother of twins have the same powers. The Tsimshian and the Tlingit have a myth in which the brother of the demiurge caused the fog by taking off his hat and putting it upside down in the canoe that they were both in (Boas, *Tsimshian Texts,* p. 17; Krause, p. 178). In the register of clothing, the hat is both a mediator and a separator between up and down, just as, in the meteorological register, fog is between the sky and earth (see p. 8).

his wife if she gave birth to twins; they were immediately put to death.[4]

The same attitude existed to the south. The Skagit of the present-day state of Washington

saw in twin births a terrifying sign of the anger of supernatural powers. The mother of twins was seen as a sort of wild beast ["a worrisome creature" according to the Tlingit].[5] The best thing to do was to abandon the twins and let them die. If they were of different sexes, the boy was even more feared than the girl.[6]

Thus the same horror for twins prevailed at both ends of this geographical area. But in between, very variable attitudes were observed: twins were welcomed by the Squamish because their birth added to their father's hunting ability;[7] the birth of twins was feared by the Alsea,[8] while some tribes of the Puget Sound even looked upon twins as monsters and put them to death.[9] In contrast, right next door, the Lummi attributed to twins the power to enrich their fellows because, whether hunting or fishing, twins knew how to control the elements and cause the wind to blow in the right direction. Parents of twins of the same sex could expect to see all their wishes fulfilled.[10] Finally, some of the peoples of the interior (and, moreover, contiguous peoples such as the Okanagan and the Coeur d'Alene) appear to have looked upon twin births fairly indifferently, as if, in relation to their neighbors' positive or negative attitudes, theirs was the most weakly marked.[11]

A nineteenth-century observer already expressed surprise at these divergences: Myron Eells, who lived as a missionary with the Puget Sound Indians during the last fourth of the century, noted their fear (the inverse, as we have seen, of beliefs widespread elsewhere) that twin births cause the fish to disappear. They expelled the parents of twins from the village, forbade them to fish, and reduced them to feed themselves from shells gathered on the beach. In olden days, parents of twins were even forced to live in the forest, and they were forbidden to come back to the coastal area as long as one of the twins was not dead. Eells adds as a comment: "Other tribes on the Pacific coast had somewhat similar customs, while others honored the twins greatly." [12]

⅔

How should we interpret these discordances? They were certainly real, but they pertained mostly to the complexity of the beliefs regarding twins and the ambiguous behavior resulting from these beliefs. Attitudes that are contradictory on the surface or that are given greatly differing weight give the impression that there was more contrast between these societies than there was in reality. As Barnett has rightly noted,[13] twin births were held everywhere to be a supernatural event, but his remark does not inform us on the specific way each society treated these births. The observers' own personalities led them to emphasize one aspect of the customs and overlook others instead of considering the whole, as should always be done.

The Kwakiutl case illustrates well these difficulties. The Kwakiutl saw twin births as "a wonderful event" (as Boas put it).[14] However, they put the father and the mother through all sorts of prescriptions and interdictions, so numerous and so complicated that their description by George Hunt, Boas's incomparable informant, occupies no less than twenty-two densely typeset pages of a large in-quarto volume.[15] For four years, the parents had to submit to these rules and live cut off from their community. It was impossible for them to engage in any productive activity and even to see to their own needs. Their relatives helped them. During all of this period, they gave the parents material and moral support because the families of the wife and the husband were proud to have in their midst these beings with supernatural powers: twins who, among other gifts, could cure the sick, raise favorable winds, and command the rain and the fog. They knew that the immense prestige of the twins would reflect on all those with whom they related. These were not the sole motives, as Hunt tells us:

> All the relatives will die if they do not follow our customs;
> . . . although the father of twins and his wife may not want to

follow the rules, all the relatives beg them to do so. . . . When the minds of the married couple who are the parents of twins are really strong, they do not do any work for four years; that is, when there are many to look after them to get firewood and food.[16]

Thus, being able to raise twins required having the means to do so. Only those families who belonged to what we might call the wealthy class could afford it. What happened with people of modest means? On this, too, Hunt is explicit: "This is the way of those who have twin-children and who have no relatives [to help them], those who do work [meaning with their hands] before they have twin-children." Right away after giving birth, the mother orders the midwife, whom custom forces to obey, to strangle the children so "that they may go back home to where they came from." The father announces everywhere that his wife has given birth to stillborn twins. Their funerals are then held. Three days later, in front of the assembled people, an orator starts to speak in lieu and place of the chiefs—"for the chiefs are afraid of the parents of twins, because nobody ever succeeds in anything if the parents of twins wish ill to him"—and the orator solemnly asks the parents if they plan to observe the taboos. The mother answers no: "We are going to dress in our work clothes in the morning." The dawn having come, all of the men assemble; they beat rapidly on planks with sticks that have been distributed to everyone. The father first appears out of his house carrying his work tools (wedge to split wood, stone mallet, paddle, mat); then comes his wife with her clam-digging basket, another for wild berries, her paddle, her digging stick, her mat, and her shovel. They take a few steps and stop, putting an end to the charivari.* The orator then proclaims that the parents of the twins will not observe the taboos and for this reason are wearing their work clothes. After this, they are free to follow their usual routine.[17]

*This is comparable to the practice in the French countryside, which, I wrote in *The Raw and the Cooked* (pp. 288–89, 336–38), signifies "the rupture of a chain, the apparition of a social discontinuity," exemplified in that case by the difference in the ages of the spouses, the marriage of a pregnant woman, the remarriage of a widow, and so on.

Consequently, among the Kwakiutl, and probably elsewhere as well, it was possible for opposite attitudes toward twins to coexist. Twins are prized to the point that to keep them their parents and families assume heavy sacrifices; or they are killed for lack of means. In short, and as we have noted for South America regarding the Tupi (see pp. 61–64 above), there are two different types of twins in both areas—one beneficial and the other harmful. In South America, this distinction is the result of nature: true twins are harmful, while those sired by different fathers fulfill functions necessary to the proper functioning of the world. Among the Kwakiutl and their neighbors, the difference stems from socioeconomic causes. (But for the peoples of the Northwest Coast, did social rank not constitute a second nature, one that was probably the more important of the two?) Good twins are born of the rich, who can spend as much as necessary to neutralize the dangers inherent to this kind of birth and to draw, at a later date, enormous benefits from them. The poor do not have this option; thus twins born of a poor family are a curse not only for the family but for the whole of society.

On the western coast of Vancouver Island, the Nootka had prescriptions and prohibitions as rigid and long-lasting as those of the Kwakiutl. South of the Kwakiutl, the small Salish-speaking groups occupying the eastern coast of the island and the continent facing it had a more democratic social organization; the distinction between rich and poor was less marked. But they, too, saw in twin births an extraordinary event carrying advantages and risks. Thus, the existence of a slight disequilibrium between these opposite representations is enough to make the practices sway to one or the other side.

❧

How does this discussion of the way twins were treated connect to that in the preceding chapter pertaining to the bear feast and first salmon rites? The link is direct since, for most of the peoples of the area, twins have a close affinity with either bears or salmon. When killed, the Kwakiutl twins "go back to the dwelling whence they came"—that is, to the country of the Salmon. Before being born, twins of the same sex were indeed Salmon, and this is why they have power over these fish. Twins were given special names corresponding to the particular species of Salmon they were thought to be issued from. If twins were of different sexes or if they had very small hands, they were usually seen as Eulachons or Candlefish (species *thaleitchtys*). Family legends tell how the marriage of an ancestor with a female twin caused the fish to go up the rivers for the first time; or, again, how the ancestors learned what twins really were when they caught one of them as they would a fish.[18] In various forms, which I will not discuss in detail here, the tie uniting salmon and twins (sometimes also the parents of twins) is clearly extant throughout a continuous territory encompassing the Kwakiutl, the Tsimshian, the Nootka, the Makah, and the Klallam.[19]

Inland Salish peoples attributed another animal nature to twins. Thus a pregnant Thompson woman who often dreamt of a grizzly bear would know that she was going to have twins. The Thompson called twins by names meaning "grizzly-bear children" or "hairy feet." They believed that they were under the special protection of this animal. Like the Kwakiutl, but in an apparently less rigorous manner, they submitted the parents to various obligations and interdictions for four years.[20] The Lilloet, contiguous neighbors to the Thompson and the Shuswap, carried these beliefs even further. They held Grizzlies to be the real genitors of the twins: in their eyes, the mother's husband was not the father. In other words, they looked upon the twins as Grizzlies in a human form.[21] Finally, among the Shuswap, the link with the grizzly bear becomes less clear, even though still evidenced by the word designating twins, meaning "young grizzly."[22] According to these Indians, the fetus split and formed two distinct individuals because of the influence of the Grizzly, the Black Bear, or the Deer.* The

*In North America, *deer* is a generic term referring to two species, respectively *Odocoileus hemionus* and *Odocoileus virginianus*, the first being "black-tailed deer" and the second "white-tailed deer." The sources seldom specify which one they are referring to.

responsible animal became the protector of the twins, who later on would hunt this species with much success.[23]

The Twana of the Puget Sound had a horror of twin births: "a disaster for the parents and, to a lesser extent, their entire community." However, twins were not killed but were simply considered dangerous to oneself and others. Twins were called "wolves." This association of twins with a third animal poses a problem. Perhaps this other animal was only replacing the second one among a people to whom wolves were less foreign than bears? However, the black bear was trapped all the way to the coast. It is also possible that the label "wolf" was an everyday application of the native idea according to which "bearing twins is not human; it is animal-like."[24]

It is possible, however, that there were more profound reasons for the equivalency. A Salish-language group, the Quinault, who settled on the coast of the state of Washington, "never referred to twins by the proper word but instead called them wolves so as not to humiliate them."[25] The equivalency "twins = wolves" also appears to have existed in Siberia among the Kamchadale and farther west among the Ket. In the whole of the North American Northwest, there are numerous mentions of a special place reserved for wolves. Among the Kwakiutl, hunting rituals for wolves had to be observed or else the hunter would be "unlucky, particularly unable to kill any more game."[26] Among the Nootka, wolves had a considerable place in religious rites.[27] The Nootka of Vancouver Island and the Lummi of the coast believed that human beings and wolves had something in common. The Lummi saw the wolves as psychopomps,[28] and a Nootka narrator concluded a myth by saying: "Now you know what happens to the dead: we turn them into wolves."[29]

We should also pay attention to myths of the area that set wolves in relation to the splitting-in-two theme (the cause of twin births, according to the Indians). If there are still Wolves today, it is because a hero did not succeed in killing them all; he could only split the last one in two, half of which escaped him and went to live in the mountains.[30] Through this we are rejoining the motif of Hare's split nose in the group of myths about the dentalia thieves (see pp. 18, 29 above) because, as I have shown in *The View from Afar* (chap. 15), in Amerindian thought, a harelip is the beginning of a body splitting in two. Through this anatomical particularity, the Hare appears as a potential pair of twins, whence the importance of the role the myths give to it. Symmetrically, the Coast Salish explain the present existence of Wolves by the fact that one of them managed to escape from the extermination of his species because he had four eyes—two in front and two in back—which enabled him to get away from his attacker.[31] This Wolf is thus split in the form "two in one," unlike his fellow Wolf in the other myth, which was split in the form of "one in two."

In spite of the lack of more explicit customs or beliefs, the myth contains enough indications of a link between wolves on the one hand and splitting in two or twinness on the other to enable us to draw the triangle:

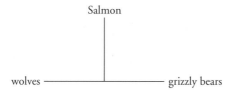

Let us look at the main opposition: that between fish and terrestrial animals. The Inland Salish are not the only people who see twins as Bears. In Siberia, the Ghiliak believed that twins were Bears who had taken this appearance in order to be born among human beings. At their death, twins were buried in a Bear cage in the forest.[32] The Ket saw in twin births mysterious events. They laid the twins and their mother on a bed made of pine branches, they dressed them with clothes made from fresh bark, and they gave the twins animal names. Upon their death, the twins rejoined the Bears. Bear cubs whose mothers had been killed were to be nursed by a woman who was already the mother of twins.[33]

The belief identifying twins with bears is thus extant over a very large area. This fact supports the temporary conclusions I sketched out at the end of the preceding chapter (see pp. 117–18 above). I proposed to see the three different plants used to cook the first salmon in different regions as botanical metaphors replacing the pine branches that were the prescribed fuel for the ritual cooking of bear meat. We can now go further and extend the metaphorical relation to representations of twins. The relation likening them to salmon has only been found in a limited part of the area where first salmon rites are celebrated, and this area itself occupies only a small part of the larger one where salmon fishing constitutes the main economic activity. On account of its very limited spread, the identification of twins with salmon could thus be just a metaphor for the identification of twins with bears. From a rhetorical and probably as well a historical standpoint, the bear metaphor might have been prior to the one involving salmon.

This interpretation would contradict the thesis that the first occupants of the Pacific coast arrived there already in full possession of a river and maritime fishing economy.[34] Instead, my interpretation would accord better with the thesis of Borden, who saw in the cultures of the coast—notably those of the Haida and the Tlingit—the evolved product of a northern tradition several millennia old whose origin should be sought inland.[35]

11

Meteorology at Home

The marriage of a woman and a Root is an even greater mismatch than that of a young and pretty woman with a sickly old man covered with sores (see pp. 109–10 above). This match reaches the boundaries of exogamy and even goes beyond them. In this respect, the story of the son of the Root is in total opposition to another myth, told by a few coastal peoples, which focuses on mother-and-son incest: a form of endogamy this time, but likewise an extreme one.

This myth is told at the tip of Cape Flattery, in a small territory where the Klallam, a group from the Salish family, live side by side with the Quileute, who belong to a linguistic isolate. Here is the Quileute version, whose intense poetic charm unfortunately could not be preserved in the following summary.

A graceful young woman had an old and ugly husband. Their only son, who lived with them, was extremely handsome. One day when he and his father were duck hunting on the sea, they became lost. The wind that was blowing calmed down and a thick fog fell, through which they made out the shore. They landed and the old man sent his son to reconnoiter. The boy arrived at a cabin inhabited by a pretty woman with long hair and rich ornaments. She invited him to stay with her, along with his father, until the fog lifted and she proposed to the young man to marry him. They thus lived all three together. This lasted a very long time.

The father used to go gather wood for the fire daily. One day, he left his usual path and found a wooden wedge with a stone hammer and a wedge that strangely resembled the ones he had used at home. This incident occurred again elsewhere, and the man wondered if the cabin where he lived was not his own and if the hostess was not his wife.

When he came back, his son was in bed with his wife. They loved each other dearly. The father sent them to bathe, and he lit a big fire next to which, upon her return, the woman lay down with her legs spread open to warm herself after her bath. The old man pointed a burning stick toward the woman as if he wanted to burn her; she was startled and spread her legs even more, thus letting the old man see her vulva, which he recognized as that of his wife. Filled with resentment against the two incestuous lovers, he sat in a corner in silence, his eyes fixed on the ground. After a while, the wife looked at him and said:

> "Go south because you are bad. Hence you will be called South-
> wind by the people. But my son will go north, because he is good,
> and he will be called Northwind."*

Before leaving, the old man ordered his wife to go deep into the forest and told her that she would be called Hemlock-Knot— *Tsuga canadensis,* a conifer with knotty branches. Since then, Southwind brings storms, Northwind brings fair weather, and hemlock knots make a fine fire.[1]

The Klallam version is shorter. It sends away the former spouses, the husband to the east and the wife to the west. The incestuous son goes north and his younger brother (there are several brothers in this version) goes south. It was agreed that if Northern Wind blew too hard it would not be too harmful, as Southern Wind would quickly make it stop.[2]

---

*The wind from the south that predominates on the coast in winter brings rain. "It makes land animals miserable and chases away the fish from waters rich in food towards deep waters where the breakers often throw them in great number on the shore where they die" (Swan, *The Indians of Cape Flattery,* p. 92).

A more recent version of the myth distinguishes four winds coming from the south, each personified by a brother of the heroine: the coldest southern wind; a southern wind that is lukewarm and begins to make the ice and snow melt in the spring; the real southern wind; and finally the "chinook," a warm spring wind (see pp. 233–34; Elliot, p. 166). For other variants, see Boas, *Tsimshian Mythology,* pp. 732–33.

This myth from groups close to the ocean attributes a different value to the winds from that of their neighbors, who are better protected inside fjords or inland. These peoples have a myth that inverts those of the Klallam and the Quileute. In olden days, they say, Northern Wind and Southern Wind competed to be stronger than each other, and the Indians suffered much from this conflict. They finally ensured that the adversaries made peace, sealed by the marriage of a southern daughter with a northern son. Unable to stand the cold, the young woman called for help from her brother, or brothers, who brought her back to her own country. Since then, the Wind has behaved in a less brutal manner.[3]

An act of incest resulting in opposing winds is thus symmetrical to a myth featuring an exogamous marriage that maintains the winds distinct but reconciled. The equivalent of the fog of the first myth is, in a version of the second myth, a fire of wet wood (the only one allowed his wife by Northern Wind because it does not give out any heat), "which smokes so much that [the wife] could not see."[4] This wet fire is in opposition to the big and beautiful fire of hemlock knots of the other myth.

The second myth includes a bizarre episode. Without her brothers' knowing it, the woman tries to bring back the son of Ice she has had from Northern Wind. To hide him, she ties him under her clothes against her thighs (this is the reason why the backs of women's thighs are colder than those of men). But the child, poorly hidden under her dress, makes a lump, which betrays his presence. Could we not see in this lump a transposed image of the protuberances that form knots on a branch? These knots, as we have seen, make the best fuel. The son of Ice, in contrast, is thrown into the fire, where he melts. Or else, like knots separated from the branch, he becomes the prototype of the lumps of ice floating on the water when the weather warms up.[5]

We would even be tempted to go further and put the Quileute and Klallam myths in a relation of transformation with the one that has the son of the Root as a hero. This is because the metamorphosis of the Quileute woman into tree knots would seem incomprehensible if it were not for the remark that a piece of

wood that has lost its knots presents holes that, in the plant register, are the female counterpart of the male root that a woman
uses as a husband. This perspective is thus yet another confirmation that the last stage of a mythic transformation presents
a double twist: the woman does not change, as we might expect, into a wood with holes; rather, she changes directly into the
knots, whose loss is that which makes a piece of wood become
"female."

If I might be allowed a somewhat risky image here, I would
venture that the transformation gathers itself up so as to jump
over, to bypass, its opposite, contrary form so as to land feet first
into the contradictory that lies beyond it.* In spite of this, however, the contrary is present not as a transformation but as a local
elaboration of the myth of the beginning—that of the son of the
Root. This elaboration is told by the very same peoples from
whom came the main versions of the son of the Root myth. The
Shuswap tell that the demiurge taught human beings sexual relations at a time when women knew how to copulate only with
roots of Lomatium and men with branches that had holes because
they had lost their knots.[6]

A Lilloet myth develops this motif:

> Once a man lived alone in an underground house. . . . He longed
> to have a wife, but did not know where to obtain one. At last he
> made up his mind to make a tree branch his wife. He traveled
> around many days, breaking branches from trees, until at last he
> found a suitable one, which broke off, leaving a hole through the
> part that had been next to the tree. He carried it home and treated
> it as his wife. He talked to it, and, changing his voice, talked again
> as if it were answering him. He slept with it; and when he went
> out, he covered it over with a blanket and left food and water
> beside it.[7]

---

*TN: I have added some redundancy to the English translation of this sen-
tence so as to render the meaning of the French text. The Lévi-Strauss original
French reads: *Si l'on me passe une image risquée, je dirai que, prenant son élan, la
transformation saute par-dessus le contraire et retombe à pieds joints sur le contrad-
ictoire au-delà.*

We can thus write:

$$\frac{F_{male}}{(hollow)} : \frac{F_{female}}{(protuberance)} :: \frac{F_{male}}{(protuberance)} : \frac{F_{hollow}}{(\textit{female})}$$

in which the third term corresponds to the child forming a lump over his mother's body (see pp. 131–32 above) and the fourth term to the woman becoming the personified knots of tree limbs.

Other factors enable us to connect these myths to the ensemble of those we have been looking at. Whether it be in filigree or in a more visible form, they all have a meteorological or seasonal connotation, and they pertain to the origin either of the fog or of the regime of the wind. This was already clear with Loon's first appearance in our myths, as the Loon, through his travels, keeps, so to speak, the beat of the alternation of the seasons and of good and bad weather. I have noted that in summer the Loon dwells in inland lakes, and he moves to the seashore when they freeze over (see p. 101 above). The Loon reacts similarly when there are more abrupt changes in the weather. The myths stress these habits:

> Now Thunder is Loon's grandfather. When it storms, Loon goes on the lakes where it is calm. In April he comes down to salt water. Loon is chief of the saltwater people.[8]

The Quileute and Klallam myth has the originality of bringing together the motifs of the fog and of the winds. At the beginning, the fog, which is disjunctive, separates the hero and his father from ordinary existence. Persisting all along the narrative, the fog isolates them in a dream world that mixes up the elements and makes possible the union of mother and son. Enter the winds at the end of the narrative: they are the antagonists of the fog, since they cause it to dissipate and they make the sky and the sea distinct again. The winds are also the form in which the son and the father separate themselves from each other. Respectively beneficial and harmful, they will thenceforth be in opposition (Quileute version) or, again, in spite of their periodical conflict, they will neutralize each other (Klallam version). It is thus mostly the regime of the winds that the peoples of the coast, most exposed to changes in the weather, talk about. Inland peoples prefer to focus on the alternation of the seasons. In the myths examined previously, the emphasis was more on the fog than on the wind. Here both meteorological phenomena take on equal import and receive the same attention.

12

Jewels and Food

In chapter 7 we made the acquaintance of a character who was named either Ntsaâz, Tsa'au'z, or Snánaz (who had been stolen by an Owl when he was a child), and I had to temporarily set aside an episode of that myth. This episode figures in only one of the versions coming from the Thompson (see p. 91 above). Though of little import on the surface, it deserves special treatment because, as we shall see, the whole of the interpretation of this group of myths depends on it.

A shy young woman had moved in with the hero, even though he had the appearance of a smelly old man covered with sores. To mock them, the young woman's parents sent their "son-in-law" to fetch wood. The small quantity of wood he gathered and gave to his wife magically multiplied when she unloaded it: there was enough to fill four cabins. Let us listen to the myth:

> His wife carried the pieces [one piece of wood for each underground house] and lowered them down with a line; but in lowering a piece down in one of the houses, it turned over, and, sliding quickly, it ran a splinter through the testicles of the moon, who was sitting underneath. [The logs multiplied] until each house was so full of split wood that there was no room left for the people.[1]

The presence of Moon in one of the cabins, the accident of which he is the victim, and his enormous testicles will never be mentioned again. Must we nonetheless attribute a meaning to the episode, and, if so, which one?

To answer this type of question, structural analysis always follows the same procedure: the search in the same geographical area for the possible existence of a myth containing a motif with a recognizable inverted image of the one that posed a problem when encountered in an isolated state. From the fact of their opposition, the two motifs make it possible to map a semantic field. Taken separately, each instance seems to say nothing; the meaning comes to light through the relations we detect between them.

In the present case, we do not need to look very far to discover such a motif: it is typical of the mythology of the Nez Percé, who are members of the Sahaptian* linguistic family. This family forms a block that is contiguous on its northern side to the one formed by the Salish linguistic family (fig. 12).

In olden days, tell the Nez Percé, Moon lived in the East and shone during the day as the Sun does now. But his heat was too intense: it consumed the earth and killed all living things. Moreover, Moon had cannibalistic appetites; his son hunted for him and each day brought him back human corpses, of which Moon ate the testicles. (According to another version, Moon cooked the cadavers after having cut off their testicles, which he ate raw.)

Coyote, who lived in the West, wanted to put a stop to these criminal activities. Under the pretext of old ties of friendship or of kinship, he went to talk to Moon's son and offered to hold his club for him while he drank from a very cold spring. Then Coyote killed him. Coyote donned the clothes and took on the appearance of the dead person; thus disguised, he brought to Moon his son's corpse. As was his habit, Moon quickly ate the testicles, which he found too strong in taste and even a bit bitter.

Moon was a fat old man. He lived in a tent filled with magnificent adornments. Coyote decided to steal them. During the night he took them and left, but at dawn he woke up in front of Moon's tent and, according to one version, "he had not even passed through the ring around the moon." He failed in this manner several times in a row.† Surprised to find Coyote asleep every day

---

*The Sahaptian linguistic family includes the Nez Percé language along with languages, called Sahaptin, of various neighboring peoples (cf. Hunn, pp. 58–88).

†The Okanagan, a Salish-speaking group, have a very different version of the myth in which Coyote, who was the guest of a giant for the night, decided to

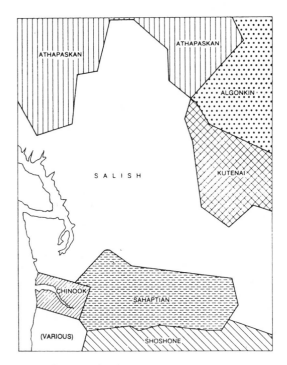

FIGURE 12. Main linguistic families

at his doorstep, Moon understood that he was not his son. According to different versions, the two characters came to an explanation, and in some cases they reconciled; in others, Coyote decapitated Moon before the latter could discover he was an imposter. But the conclusion is the same everywhere: "After this,"

---

run away with the two marvelous fire-making flint stones possessed by his host. But in spite of his efforts, Coyote did not succeed in leaving the site of the cabin. Amazed by this mystery, Coyote made one last try while mentally taking note of all his gestures: "Now I am getting up; now I am beginning to walk; now I am taking the flint stones; now I am at the foot of the ladder; now I am outside; now I begin to run . . ." He continued in this manner, and, as he knew the territory well, he kept on muttering: "I am here; I am there . . ." The whole night long he talked to himself, believing he was getting away with his ill-gotten gain. At dawn,

said Coyote to Moon, "you will kill no longer, but will give light for travel at nighttime."[2]

A myth summarized in the preceding chapter occurs in a time when the Winds were persecuting human beings (see p. 131 above), and in the Nez Percé myth we are discussing here, Moon (who was then the Sun) was also cruel. In both cases, either the Winds or the Moon end up forced to be restrained and orderly: the Winds are forced to blow with moderation; the Moon is limited to the role of providing night light, which it fills today. However, one case pertains to the alternation of the seasons and changes in the weather, while the other is concerned with daily periodicity.

The Shuswap have a myth that bridges both formulas. In olden days, Moon lived in a faraway land covered with snow and ice.* He married a woman from a warm country and locked her up in an icy cave, where she died of cold. Under pretext of replacing her, he caused the deaths of two of her sisters one after another. Only the youngest, who had a limp, managed to best her spouse: she warmed the country up. The seasonal role given to a limping

---

when the giant's household woke up, Coyote was seen running round and round the hearth, continuing his monologue and covered with sweat, so much his efforts had exhausted him (Hill-Tout, "Report on the Ethnology of the Okanak.ēn of British Columbia," pp. 144–45).

When a myth crosses a linguistic boundary, two types of changes can occur: either the central motif of the myth alone survives but changes or becomes inverted (as I will demonstrate for the Thompson), or else, as in the present case, the framework of the myth remains intact but it is emptied of its content and only serves as a pretext for a brilliant literary piece.

For another example of the first phenomenon, cf. the Snohomish myth indexed M_{677} in *The Naked Man* and p. 382, n. 10, in which I began the discussion that will follow here.

*Moon is thus a murderer in both myths either through the cold or through an unbearable heat, as in the Nez Percé myth. But even in this myth, the Moon family still has an affinity to the cold, since it is by showing Moon's son an "extremely cold" spring or else the place where the "water was the coldest" that Coyote persuades him to take a drink. Even this detail, which appears to be insignificant on the surface of the syntagmatic chain, reveals itself pertinent when put in a paradigmatic ensemble.

woman was discussed in *From Honey to Ashes,* pages 459–65, in regard to the myth indexed M_{347}. I will only bring out here that this story of Moon reproduces that of the marriage of Northern Wind (see pp. 131–32 above). Informants, moreover, specify that Moon belonged to the Cold Wind or Northern Wind people, but he wanted to impose his rule over all the inhabitants of the earth.[3]

The Nez Percé myth and its Okanagan variant develop an intriguing motif that could be called "the impossible departure." In spite of all his efforts, Coyote does not succeed in leaving the immediate vicinity of Moon's house. He thinks he has traveled all night, but he wakes up in front of the door. We encounter this motif in a parallel myth from the Kutenai, in which Coyote becomes separated from his family because of a famine (which is a kind of inverted cannibalism: to be eaten → having nothing to eat anymore; one dies in either case). He finds his lost wife with Sun, of whom she is the daughter. But Coyote does not know the customs of the house, and the food dishes go by without his being able to touch them. His wife explains to him that, if he enters Sun's tent in the evening, he will have nothing to eat; to get his share, he must enter in the morning. Like the Nez Percé Moon, Sun (who, we must not forget, is Coyote's father-in-law) possesses a treasure (according to different versions it is a torch, or perhaps a frame to stretch skins, probably in both cases symbols of the sun). Coyote steals it and walks all night. At dawn he falls asleep, exhausted, and he wakes up right where he started from. Sun explains to Coyote that he has to run a whole day, then a whole night, and then until the next midday (another version has three days and three nights) if he really wants to escape from him.[4]

A Coeur d'Alene myth about a fight between Coyote and Sun sheds light on this motif. "Why do you go around in the daytime when Sun is out?" asks Coyote of a bird to whom he is giving advice. "He can see you walking around. Don't walk anymore in the daytime but only at night. At daylight, lie down in a hole in the ground and sleep. About sunset get up and walk."[5] In short, one cannot travel at night if there is no Moon; thus Moon must switch from diurnal to nocturnal. And one cannot escape Sun by traveling during the day; he sees us. It is also not possible to escape by traveling early in the morning since Sun will catch up with you as soon as he has risen. One must either go more quickly than he or only stop at noon, at the moment when Sun turns his back and begins his descent.

꙰

But it is mostly the relation between Moon and testicles that is of interest (already discussed in *The Naked Man,* p. 567). It is clear that from the Nez Percé to the Thompson, this relation is maintained only thanks to two inversions: a *fat* Moon, eater of testicles, is transformed into Moon, wearer of *fat* testicles. Moreover, in the Nez Percé myth, Moon is the *agent* of a wound inflicted to the testicles of his victims; these testicles are a choice meat, which he cuts up and eats first. In the Thompson myth he is the *patient,* the victim of an accidental wounding of his own testicles. Unmotivated in the Thompson myth, the episode can only be an inverted reflection of the Nez Percé myth.*

The question that then arises is, why is Moon featured as a testicle-eating cannibal in the Nez Percé myth?

*However, this transformation is in no way arbitrary. Another Thompson myth features an old woman with a toothed vagina (a penis-eater through a lower part of the body, as the Nez Percé Moon is a testicle-eater through an upper part) who sharpens her legs and uses them to stab people, whose hearts she then eats. (The heart is here an internal round organ, in opposition to and correlation with the testicles, which are external round organs.) She tries out her sharp legs first on small trees, which she runs through, and then on a large tree, in which her legs get stuck. After a night of struggle, she succeeds in freeing herself. Other versions replace the woman with a man—very fat according to one version, in which he is thus reminiscent of the Nez Percé Moon—who does not succeed in freeing himself (Boas, *Folk-Tales of Salishan and Sahaptin Tribes,* p. 46; Teit, *Mythology of the Thompson Indians,* pp. 269, 365–67).

Instead of a protagonist being pierced with a wood splinter, here a "splinter" from a protagonist (her legs sharpened into stakes) pierces the wood. Thus, while the episode of Moon appears to be nonmotivated in the syntagmatic chain of the Thompson myth considered alone, it finds its place again in a paradigmatic ensemble as a permutation when related to other myths of these same Indians.

A myth from the Takelma—a small, isolated linguistic group in the present state of Oregon who are located about five hundred kilometers southwest of the Thompson—could provide a simple answer. The myth has to do with very old Grizzly Bears who only eat human intestines, penises, and testicles, "the soft food that is brought home for them to eat, being without teeth."[6] The Nez Percé myth features Moon as an old man. The Takelma narrative is based on an important distinction in Amerindian thought: that between the hard and the soft parts of the body. The ears, nose, and sexual organs are held to be weak and exposed unless adornments of bones, teeth, wood, and so on give them the strength they are lacking.

However, the Nez Percé myth cannot be understood in this way since, after he has eaten the testicles, Moon cooks and consumes whole bodies and Coyote partakes of the meal. In fact, the episode of the testicles is part of a vast transformation whose stages can be mapped from the Salish on the coast to the Kutenai in the Rocky Mountains. Only a careful study of all the stages of this transformation would make it possible to interpret the set on the basis of its invariant characteristics. Some Coast Salish myths tell that Coyote, while cleaning a male salmon to eat it, pulled out of it two white and round milts, which were so pretty that he could not bring himself to cook them with the rest. He set them aside, and they were transformed into two young women, who at first lived with him and then left when he made sexual advances. They set out, stole a baby, raised him, and later on took him as a husband. He was none other than Moon. When his family found him again, Moon separated from his spouses and began a long journey, in the course of which he created fish and trees and put the universe in order. According to several versions, he finally decided to go up to the sky. He tried to be Sun but was too hot and made the rivers boil over. He thus gave his place to his brother, while he himself became Moon.[7]

I already mentioned (in *The Naked Man,* M_{615}, and in the present book in regard to Bear, see p. 115 above) a myth from the Klikitat, a Sahaptin-speaking neighbor to the Coast Salish. This myth tells of a deadly fight between two Bear women, and then between their daughters. Only one of them survived. She ran away and got lost among a people of cannibals, who wore the testicles of their victims as earrings. They forced her to follow this fashion. Helpful young ladies freed her and got rid of her hideous adornments. Instead, they put their own ornaments, of deer hunters and trout fishers, in her ears. The heroine married her liberators' brother, but a cannibalistic Salmon soon took her away. The husband pursued the captor and succeeded in killing him by using the same trick as that used by Coyote against Moon's son in the Nez Percé myth (taking advantage of the moment when he bent down to drink from a stream; see p. 138 above). The two spouses were reunited.[8]

This is not the sole detail that sends us back to the Nez Percé myth (and through this we can already guess that it illustrates a stage of the same transformation). Cannibals for whom testicles serve as food (but a luxury food) are replaced here by cannibals who use testicles differently: they wear them as adornments.

Arrived at this stage, we can already take as given three equivalences:

Thompson myth: one's own testicles   =   wounding;

Nez Percé myth: testicles of another   =   food;

Klikitat myth: testicles of another   =   adornments.

A Kutenai myth, some of whose elements I have used earlier (see pp. 30–31, 61, 111, 139 above), illustrates another stage of the transformation. Separated from his wife because of a famine, Coyote wanders with his young son. He sees Beavers building their dam, catches two young ones, and ties them to his son's ear as ornaments. But the other Beavers, who pretend to be dead, jump into the water as soon as Coyote's back is turned, and they are followed by the "earrings" of the young boy. These throw themselves into a water hole, and Coyote's son thus is in danger of being torn apart. He calls for help. Coyote comes back and pulls his son from the water along with the two Beavers. He cooks them, gives the fat to his son because it is tender, and prepares to eat the meat, but then he changes his mind and trades dishes in spite of the boy's cries.[9]

Thus we have lined up on two axes, one geographical and the other logical, a series of myths between which we can see affinities. There is affinity from a geographical standpoint since the peoples from whom these myths come occupy a line going from the west eastward: from the maritime coast to the territory of the Kutenai on the Rockies and beyond. There is affinity from the logical viewpoint, as well, and this in several ways.

It must first be noted that the group of myths considered as a whole sets up a correlation between adornments and food. In the myths from the coast, Coyote found salmon milts too pretty to eat. He asked himself, "What can I make from them?" and he carefully put each of these round things between two leaves, one on top of the other.

> Whatever you turn into, I shall be very pleased. I wish for the very best thing I can think of, the best thing I have ever seen.

The next day the milts have changed into gorgeous women

> wearing very pretty blankets. They were small, very fair, and had hair that was almost red. He was so proud of them that he nearly died.

He let the young women believe that they were his daughters, born before the time he became a widower.* Several months went by. Coyote became ill and almost blind, which did not stop him

---

*In passing from the Coast Salish to their Sahaptin-speaking neighbors, these frivolous milt girls whom Coyote wants to make his spouses are triply inverted into Feces-Sisters, givers of good advice, whom Coyote expels from his body and reincorporates at will—a transformation so radical that it does not continue beyond this point. I analyzed it in detail in another context (*The Naked Man*, pp. 309–11, and indexed under "Milt girls"). Inland Salish groups provide intermediary states: there are some reasons for supposing that among the Coeur d'Alene, Coyote's "powers," which he calls by a special kinship term, are his excrement, his penis, and his testicles. According to the Thompson and the Okanagan, Coyote's feces help and advise him but they are not his "sisters."

from showing his lust. The young women got mad and put him in a canoe, which the current took away.[10]

There is no need to invoke physiology to understand the passage from milts to testicles; anatomy suffices to explain it. Both milts and testicles are pairs of round glands, relatively independent from the body, the first lying inside and the second outside. As much appreciated by the Indians as fish eggs, milts have an appearance as pretty and delicate as ornaments. As for testicles, which are seen as adornments in one of the stages of the transformation,* and as food in another, they too partake of this double nature. From the testicles we pass to the pair of Beavers, who when young resemble small round organs. The Beavers, which are good game, are a food that Coyote pretends to treat like adornments. He makes earrings out of them, sending us back to the testicles used the same way by cannibals in another myth. In a third myth, an old man, also a cannibal, prefers to eat testicles because they are a soft food. Finally, in the myth under discussion, a child is deprived of the fat of the little Beavers—an appropriate soft food for children of his age, as the myth takes care to specify. It is thus clear that milts, testicles, and the small Beavers are permutations of an invariant function and represent stages of a single transformation.

One fact stands out in these narratives: they feature adornments even when there are no obligatory reasons for this. The Milt Girls are richly dressed; in one version of the myth, the hero, the future Moon, leaves them and carries away a coffer filled with dentalia shells (which only a sick and smelly woman, covered with sores, will be capable of opening so as to distribute the shells to all comers;[11] this shortcut sends us back to the story of Snánaz and would deserve a separate study). As for the liberators in the Klikitat myth, they not only get rid of the hideous earrings of the heroine, they insist on replacing them with their own. Finally, Moon,

---

*French popular language also makes this identification through various metaphors. Moreover, Old World folklore is cognizant of the transformation of food into body ornaments; cf. M. Djeribi, "De la nourriture aux parures," in *Cendrillon* (*Cahiers de Littérature Orale,* 25, 1989, pp. 55–70).

the old cannibal of the Nez Percé myth, is a collector of precious objects.

The analysis of the myths on the origin of fog laid bare an armature reducible to a relation of correlation and opposition between wounds and adornments (see pp. 102–6 above). The armature of the mythical transformation that we have just looked at sets adornments and food in relation of correlation and opposition. In this transformation, testicles, so to speak, function at times as adornments and at times as food. It is thus in the Thompson myth (from which we started at the beginning of this chapter and which directly sets into relation testicles and wounds) that the two armatures join. We now need to come back to it.

13

From the Moon to the Sun

In fact, the Thompson transform the testicles motif in not just one but two ways. We have seen the first one: Moon—at the time he was still human [1]—was wounded in the testicles. A myth illustrates the other transformation. An Indian who was ugly and was seeking solace in games of chance was ruined by them and then took to the road. He arrived at the dwelling of Sun, who was then a cannibal. Sun's son protected him, made him a gift of a large bag, and sent him back to his village. The hero was not supposed to touch this bag before he got home, even if the cord stretched and the bag, which he carried on his shoulder, slipped to the small of his back.

Upon his arrival at his village, the hero opened the bag, which he found filled with precious clothing, which he distributed to everyone. Thankful, Loon and Goose offered him their daughters; the hero took them back to Sun and his son to marry. Thenceforth, Sun would not kill and eat human beings.[2] There are variants in which a rebellious young woman replaced the unlucky gambler and became herself the wife of Sun, who, it is specified, had never seen a woman before.[3]

With this myth, two loops come to a close. Instead of the son of Moon—the master of rich adornments—killing human beings so that his father could eat their testicles, here the son of Sun protects a human being and gives him a bag (an inverted metaphor of the testicles; it is carried on the back) filled with adornments. This confirms the postulated equivalency between adornments and food.

We find in this myth an equivalency between women and adornments that had appeared already in the first stage of the transformation. Too pretty for Coyote to eat, the milts change themselves into women; thus: food → adornments → women. The ethnography of the Coast Salish (the peoples from whom we got the myth of the Milt Girls) accounts for this, at least the Twana of Puget Sound, in the eyes of whom

> polygyny reflected the wealth and prestige of the husband and of his family. The plural wives were themselves a form of wealth article, conspicuously displayed by very rich men. . . . Wives were regarded . . . as valuable articles in themselves. A shaman who effected a particularly spectacular cure . . . might be given a marriageable girl in payment. . . . Girls were also, although rarely, given in payment of debts.[4]

So it can be seen that in the final stage of the transformation, women are given in return for riches; the loop is thus joined here as well.

We have seen that the Thompson myth, which substitutes a metaphorical object (the bag that slides down to the small of the back of the bearer), also replaces Moon with Sun as main protagonist. This is as well the case in the Kutenai myth, in which, after the episode of the small Beavers (the metaphorical equivalent of testicles), Coyote continues his adventure in the home of Sun, who, like Moon elsewhere and like Sun in the Thompson myth, is the owner of a treasure (see p. 139 above).

As it happens, in this region, the myths in which Moon is the most prominent fit in with others that make of Sun not a lover of testicles, like Moon in the Nez Percé myth, but at any rate a cannibal. Close to the Nez Percé, and members of the same linguistic family, the Klikitat knew the geste of the demiurge Moon either directly or through the intermediary of their Coast Salish neighbors, whose daughters they sometimes married.[5] And they tell with much detail how a young man, humiliated by the young woman he loved, left his village and went eastward. He traveled for a long time and arrived at Sun's house, where Sun's daughter welcomed him as the husband she had waited for. Sun was a ferocious cannibal who ate human bodies. His daughter talked him into sparing the young man. To exempt him from cannibalistic meals, she made him fishing and hunting implements, and they both convinced Sun to eat salmon and deer in the manner of human beings.*

The young couple had children and, with Sun's permission, they decided to go to the husband's country. Moon, Sun's younger brother, brought them in a canoe. During the trip they marked the place where thenceforth the sun would set. When they arrived at the village, the young woman who had rejected the hero received her comeuppance: humiliated in turn, she could not find a husband; this is the origin of celibacy. Thenceforth, the Sun, the Moon, and the Stars were to regularly follow their course.[6] This cannibal Sun also possessed great wealth. When his daughter left, he gave her "a little something" sufficient to enrich those who had supported her husband's cause. The family and partisans of the too-proud woman received nothing. More clearly yet, a myth coming from the Chinook sets in opposition a young lady Moon, cannibalistic and "adorned with human bones up to her hair," with a young lady Sun, covered with dentalia shells.[7]

A Thompson myth (indexed M_{598h} in *The Naked Man*) inverses these roles: the marriage of the hero to Sun's daughter ends in failure; he finds her too hot and cannot stand her.[8] But the aim of that narrative is to explain the origin of the parhelions, which announce changes in the weather (cf. *The Naked Man,* pp. 235–48), instead of the proper distancing of the sun or its periodicity.†

At this point, we need to open up a parenthesis. The Skagit, a Coast Salish group, have a version of the myth in which Sun—dangerous because he is too hot, though he is not in the least

---

*It is salmon fishers and deer hunters who help a young lady Bear get rid of the human testicles that cannibals have put on her (see p. 142). The two mythical series, one lunar and one solar, closely parallel each other.

†According to other Thompson cosmological myths, which appear to belong to a distinct tradition, Earth woman couldn't stand her husband Sun, whom she reproached for being mean, ugly, and too hot. He left her, followed by the other celestial bodies. This is the origin of the separation of the sky and the earth (Teit, *Mythology of the Thompson Indians,* p. 341, and *Traditions of the Thompson Indians,* pp. 50, 109).

the east in contact with the Blackfoot, a Plains tribe through their culture and their language, a branch of the Algonkin linguistic family. The Kutenai are the only ones among the peoples of the plateau to have borrowed the sun dance from the Blackfoot.* Their Salish-speaking neighbors—the Flathead, Coeur d'Alene, and Okanagan—knew of the existence of the dance but had not adopted it.

It is probable that the name of this great Plains Indians ceremony (a ceremony that had the unusual aspect of involving the whole tribe while other dances involved only religious fraternities, age classes, or associations) made the sun and its cult appear to be more important than they were. But even though this name exaggerates solar inspiration, one should not for that underestimate it (cf. on this point *The Origin of Table Manners,* pp. 210–13). Sun worship did exist, at least among the Blackfoot, who held the Sun to be the master of the world and saw it as a beneficent divinity, full of wisdom and kindness and to whom daily prayers were addressed, particularly in the course of the sun dance ceremony.[11] The Kutenai myth in which Coyote is Sun's son-in-law is permeated with Blackfoot mythology, to the point that certain incidents become intelligible only when referred to it. Thus the myth tells how Coyote, while visiting Sun, had a successful hunt by encircling the game with a brushfire, which he lit everywhere he ran thanks to the woodpecker feathers attached to his moccasins. Several versions of a Blackfoot myth attribute to Sun hunting leggings embroidered with porcupine quills and decorated with brightly colored feathers. The one who wore them needed only to walk to light brushfires, which started the game. In the Blackfoot myth, it is precisely these leggings that the trickster tries to steal several times without ever being able to leave Sun's dwelling. The Blackfoot myth comments on this last episode in a much more coherent manner than the Kutenai version: "He [the trickster] did not know that the whole world is Sun's hut and that, no matter how far he ran, he would always remain within sight of Sun."[12] A

*"The Kutenai claim to have received the sun dance from beyond the eastern ocean where Sun Dance Spirit dwells" (Turney-High, pp. 178, 184).

wise Blackfoot elder explains: "Sun keeps the earth and the sky together in one room." [13] In all the versions of the myth, the owner of the leggings—whether he be Sun or a friend or brother-in-law of the trickster—seeing his obstinate efforts to take it, ends up by giving them to him and teaches him how to use them; but the trickster uses them carelessly and triggers an enormous fire. [14] Sun has thus shown himself to be conciliatory, even generous—a nature that the Blackfoot versions explicate better. They also lead us to attribute to him the same qualities in the Kutenai versions, derived from the Blackfoot ones, in which Sun, without resentment toward his thieving son-in-law, teaches him in detail how to successfully leave his hut and apparently doesn't even try to take back his property (see p. 139 above).

14

The Dog Husband

I n the mind of the native audience, the story of Moon
wounded in the testicles could not fail to evoke a little rite
of neighborliness with which they were quite familiar.

The Thompson Indians and their Lilloet neighbors indeed had
a custom called "letting down." When the people had settled into
their winter quarters in their semisubterranean cabins, a neighbor
sometimes paid a visit to one of them. He announced himself by
lowering through the smoke hole a bucket filled with food attached to the end of a rope. Among the Lilloet, the visitors would
begin by throwing water on the hearth while yelling "Thunder!"
The inhabitants thus knew they were about to receive guests and
hurriedly relit the fire. The guests then went down through the
inner ladder (fig. 10), each carrying a gift of food. Fun and a party
followed. However, the most common practice involved lowering
the presents at the end of a rope or a long branch sculpted with
animal motifs and a representation of the thunder.

To carry these gifts, the Thompson used a kettle (a stone in
earlier times) decorated with feathers and cordons painted in
bright colors. They filled it with food, clothing, or tanned hides
and tied to it pieces of burning bark, which gave it the appearance
of a ball of fire. The visitors would shake it vigorously and make
it go up and down while the inhabitants of the cabin tried to
grab it.

The cosmological allusions are clear. Other allusions pertain to
a deeply buried cabin in which dwell the *xaxa,* a mysterious and
fearsome people with whom one could trade only by lowering and
raising merchandise at the end of a rope. This was because the
person who came too close would fall into the chthonian world

and never come back. The xaxa had the power of setting cut sticks on fire by talking to them with their backs turned.[1]

It is thus no accident that, in the myth, the chief's daughter is above, on the roof of the cabin; that she lowers the logs at the end of a rope through the smoke hole; and that Moon, then human, is below, near the hearth. Indeed, in those versions reduced to the story of Lynx—that is, to what we could call the metamyth, which has concerned us since the beginning of this book—the heroine is absolutely or relatively below in relation to Lynx. This latter impregnates her by making go down to her the saliva or the urine, which penetrates her body just as the wood splinter penetrated Moon's body. There's more: the heroine, *passively impregnated* in one case, becomes, when exchanging her position with that of the partner, *actively sterilizing* in the other case. This can be represented by a chiasma:

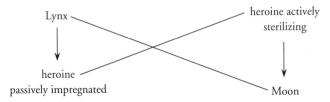

It must be hypothesized that the heroine is equivalent to herself in both cases, and thus it results that we must see Lynx as being equivalent to Moon.*

*I have dealt with Moon's sexuality in *Mythologiques,* so I will limit myself to a brief reminder here. At times a man with a long penis (which Lynx actually is: old and feeble, he impregnates a young woman from afar but with small means), at times hermaphroditic and impotent (the likely fate of Moon wounded in the testicles), Moon inspires a mythology of ambiguity. Too close, the union of Moon and Sun would be incestuous. That of Moon (male or female) with a human being would entail all sorts of dangers because it is too distant. A human being seeking a mate runs the risk of stopping too close or going too far. Celestial bodies that come back periodically each day, each month, or each year provide a means of representing the fluctuating values of endogamy and exogamy. Moon's ambiguity is linked to monthly periodicity, which is specific to it and which puts

ॐ

Another group of myths extant in the whole of the Northwest of North America[2] gives support to this deduction. There, too, the heroine is a shy young girl who refuses all of her suitors. She finds herself impregnated against her will (except in one version, in which the act is voluntary)[3] by a Dog who has the appearance of a man, or by a jilted lover who transforms himself into a Dog to humiliate her. She wants to identify her night visitor, marks him with red ocher while he embraces her, and discovers the next day that he is a Dog. As in the story of Lynx, the culprit is beaten close to death, and he is abandoned with his victim. Soon she gives birth to Puppies, who get rid of their animal skins and take on a human form when they think they are alone. She comes upon them unexpectedly and burns their skins (like the pus-covered skin burned in the story of Snánaz, a story that is a development of the narrative of Lynx, who too recovers his handsomeness). The Puppies then stay human, except for a daughter who remains a Dog or becomes only half-human. Again, as in the story of Lynx, the Man-dog or Dog-man, cured of his wounds, hunts for his family and accumulates or has his children accumulate provisions of food. His starved persecutors ask for forgiveness and receive it with food supplies.[4]

It is clear that native thought was conscious of the parallels between this myth and that of Lynx: "A pregnant woman," the Thompson say, "must eat neither lynx nor dog meat because of the role played by these animals in mythical traditions."[5] What, then, does differentiate these two groups of myths? Not only are

---

it at equal distance between the seasonal periodicity of the constellations and the daily periodicity specific to Sun (because there are nights without moon but no days without light). The phases of the moon have an equivocal nature, straddling the longest and the shortest periodicities. On all these points, see *The Origin of Table Manners* (pp. 109–10, 195, 224–25, 299–304) and *The Naked Man* (pp. 448–54).

the Lynx and the Dog opposed as a wild and a domestic animal,* but I have brought out in *The Naked Man,* in which the myth of the woman with the Dog has its place (cf. pp. 471–73, 482–84), that contrary to what is observed in the other regions of America, the peoples of the Northwest coast and their inland neighbors see dogs as quasi-human (*The Naked Man,* p. 523).

In the form that concerns us here, the myth of the woman and the Dog contains explicit references to the great Pan-American mythical ensemble on the incest of siblings (the unknown nocturnal visitor whose body is marked so that it can be identified the next day, and so on). According to one version from the Puget Sound area, the hero—who, transformed into a Dog, seduced a "shining" princess—was born of an incestuous couple of siblings.[6] A version from the lower Fraser sends back to the incest theme at the end: having become tall and beautiful, the ten Dog children marry one another.[7] In the far north of British Columbia, the Kaska, speakers of an Athapaskan language, tell that the mother of the Dog children suspected one of her sons of sleeping with his sister. She covered the bed of the young girl with resin and, the next day, discovered black spots from the body of her youngest son. Out of sadness, she transformed her children and herself into rocks.[†] The Dene Flanc-de-chien, who also speak an Athapaskan language and are neighbors of the Kaska, think of themselves as the descendants—whence their name—of an incestuous union, a polyandrous one to boot, which was entered into by two of the sons and the daughter of the woman and the Dog.[8]

*The Thompson gave their dogs descriptive names. The peoples of the Puget Sound named them as they named people. But Puget Sound tribes had slaves who, like small children, received descriptive names; the Thompson did not practice slavery. On the comparative onomastic of human beings and animals, cf. *The Savage Mind,* pp. 204–8, and *The View from Afar,* pp. 152–56.

†According to Tlingit and Haida versions, the family was changed into rocks because the young girl had broken the taboos (puberty or other) to which her brothers had subjected her. In *The Way of the Masks* (pp. 197–98) I proposed to see this failure in following prescribed behavior among siblings of opposite sexes as a combinative variant of incest (as in the myth of the dentalia thieves; see chap. 3). The Kaska version confirms this interpretation.

However, things are more complicated than this, as several versions of the myth broaden the family circle. In the particularly significant Polar Eskimo version, the woman divided her ten children—five boys and five girls—into couples, which, though incestuous, were to give birth to different peoples. The first couple gave birth to the Europeans, the second to "savages," the third to wolves, the fourth to a supernatural race of giants, and the fifth to a supernatural race of dwarfs.[9] It would be hard to imagine a more eclectic assortment!

Living on the northwest coast of Greenland, the Polar Eskimo are far away from the rivers of the Pacific shore. I have, however, made a point of citing their version of the myth because there are narratives from British Columbia that lean toward the same meaning and in which either one or several incests tend to institute the norm of exogamous marriage. According to the Thompson and the Lilloet, the Dog children married either women from the village, once it was reconstituted,[10] or women belonging to a people their mother had created with wood shavings, the leftovers of her sons' woodworking.[11] The Lilloet myth concludes that since these shavings came from essences of various colors, people ended up with white, red, yellow, or brown skin: "This is the reason these shades are to be found among the Indians at the present day."[12]

There is the same conclusion in a Thompson myth, which will be discussed later (see p. 165 below). Working together to steal a copper ball (sometimes identified with the visible sun), Coyote and Antelope each had four sons and four daughters who married one another. Their children had different skin tones: white, yellow, red, and brown, because Coyote's children were themselves born of their father's two wives, Alder and Poplar, woods that do not have the same colors.[13] The nature of these marriages between Coyote's and Antelope's children is highly exogamous: Antelope, specifies the myth, was a migrant from the south, and he later settled in Montana. This is why antelopes are abundant in this area and are not found among the Thompson. *Antilocapra americana* indeed lives on the eastern slopes of the Rocky Mountains. One should note, however, that the difference in skin color stems exclusively from Coyote's spouses. This is an endogenous diversity that owes nothing to the fact that Antelope is of foreign origin; thus, we find on another plane the same wavering we have uncovered in the myth of the Dog husband. It is obvious that all of these myths form a joint between exogamy and endogamy. As we have seen, Dogs are quasi-human beings: close enough to humans that the sons of a woman and a Dog could definitively become human (but not the daughter, who becomes only halfway human or retains her canine nature),* yet far away enough that the union of a woman and a Dog introduces anatomical differences in the human species, differences that had not existed up to that point and that were made visible by skins of various colors.

The Kutenai myth on the origin of the sun and the moon tends toward the same meaning, and it is the more interesting in that, in a very original manner, it combines through a sort of shortcut the myth of Lynx and that of the incest of siblings. The Kutenai myth unfolds in three acts. In the first act, Hare is abandoned by his wife, a Bird, who follows her lover Red Hawk. Second act: Hare falls in love with Doe, learns that she is his sister, hides her, and lives with her secretly. In the third act, Lynx, who has discovered Doe's presence in Hare's house, impregnates her by leaving some of his hair on the spot where she goes to urinate. Lynx is then beaten up, the couple is abandoned, and their children are to

*It seems clear that native thought compares the intimacy, in some sort against nature, that occurs between the hunter and his dog with the intimacy bordering on or leading to incest that occurs between siblings. The version from the Carrier Indians explains one through the other:

> The boys grew very rapidly during the winter and played continuously with their little dog-sister Upits, which explains why dogs now prefer to accompany human beings. In the earliest days dogs were wild like other animals; but because Upits always stayed with her brothers and warned them of the approach of animals and strangers, dogs have accompanied man to this day.

As for the Lilloet and the Thompson, they saw woman and dog as beings dangerously close to each other. They forbade bear meat to both women and dogs. If a dog urinated at the same spot where a woman did, he was killed, out of fear that he had a sexual desire for women (Jenness, pp. 139; Teit, *Traditions of the Thompson Indians*, p. 113 n. 208, and *The Lilloet Indians*, pp. 267, 279, 291).

become the Sun and the Moon.[14] The myth thus tells of three successive unions. The first, which is too exogamous, and the second, which is too endogamous, fail. The third union constitutes a middle term and is crowned with success since it produces children who, one being not too hot and the other not too cold, alone show themselves capable of performing the functions of the two celestial bodies.

⁂

The Dog husband myth is not specific to the New World. Numerous versions have been collected in Siberia and as far away as China. In Japan, still in the nineteenth century, it provided the theme for the popular novel *Hakkenden,* written by Bakin and first published in 106 episodes from 1814 to 1841. In America, it flourished among the Eskimo along with the myth of the siblings' incest. Among the Salish, though this latter myth appears to be eclipsed by the one of the Dog husband, the siblings' incest is nonetheless present in a particular form that we need to discuss.

After being surprised, the incestuous siblings did not run away to the heavens to become the Sun and the Moon, engaged in an endless pursuit. Rather, according to the Salish versions, they went far away but took the precaution of marking their trail with bits of wool and pieces of embroidery that the young woman pulled from her dress and tied to branches. She soon gave birth to a son (a son and a daughter according to one version) who one day became curious about the resemblance between his parents. They confessed the truth (or it appeared to him in a dream) and sent him back to the village, where he arrived by following the path marked by his parents. As soon as he was gone, they killed themselves on a pyre.

Several versions end here,[15] while others continue the story. The Thompson narrative tells that the boy, making himself invisible thanks to the magical powers his mother has given him, first reveals himself to his uncle, a small, elderly man with only one eye, to whom he gives back his sight. He then goes to his grandmother, who sequesters him (she had done the same with her daughter, the hero's mother). Intrigued by the mystery, two female witches make beautiful birds with their excrement. The uncle tries in vain to shoot them; he asks and obtains permission for his nephew to go out with him. The boy kills the birds, puts them under his shirt, and becomes dirtied and smelly from them.

Ashamed of this mishap, he decides to go far away with his uncle. Together, they spend several years in the deep woods. Having become an adult, the hero one day decides to go up to heaven to marry the two inhabitants of the country of the clouds. He kills an Eagle, puts its skin on, and agrees to bring his uncle along. But the uncle cannot keep his eyes closed during the flight, and each time he opens them he and his nephew fall heavily onto the ground. The separation is thus unavoidable. Upon his request, the hero transforms his uncle into a small, red-eyed Duck* and tells him that he will be about to return when his uncle sees the clouds turning red.

The hero thus arrives alone in the country of the clouds where the two sisters live. He marries them, and each gives him a son. He and his wives decide to go down to the earth. Dressed in his Eagle clothes, he flies off with a woman under each arm after having tied each of his sons to one of his legs.

The uncle welcomes them with joy but understands that he is now in the way. He will remain a small, red-eyed Duck, the ancestor of the whole of the species. As for the hero, he settles with his family with his grandparents, who are still alive. He is the ancestor of a great and powerful tribe.[16]

I have reluctantly much abbreviated this narrative, which, in

---

*This Duck uncle occupies the same position as the brother of the incestuous couple in a Kutenai myth already cited several times (see pp. 30–31, 61, 111, 139, 158–9). Hare, betrayed by his wife, gave Duck the mission of getting his rival Red Hawk to choose a deer stomach filled with blood during the cutting up and sharing of the animal. Hawk loaded it on the back of his wife. Hare caused her to trip, she fell, and the blood covered her and congealed; she died of cold. Could we see in this episode a last state, barely recognizable, of what we could call the "testicles transformation," the topic of our chapters 12 and 13? Compare this with the bag carried on the back in the Thompson version (see p. 146), which from beneficial becomes harmful here.

its complete text, has a great dramatic force. The narrator even mentions that this story makes women and young girls cry each time it is told,[17] a comment that I have never encountered in the whole mythological corpus of the two Americas.*

The Sanpoil version, even more moving, expounds on the passion the brother and the sister felt for each other (contrary to what I would call the vulgate, in which the sister is not aware of the identity of her seducer). Their mother spied on them—alone at first; then she had her husband accompany her.

> After coming back quite upset to the camp, the chief asked his wife what he should do. "It's up to you," she answered. "You are the chief. I love my children, but it's up to you to decide." After a while he said: "All right; I know what I have to do. I am going to kill my son. We would be laughed at if it were known."

The chief executed his plan, discreetly informed the village of the death of his son, and forbade that his daughter be told. But this latter got her younger sister to tell her the truth. She put on her most beautiful clothes, ran to the ravine where lay the body of her brother, and threw herself in. United in death, the two lovers triumphed: "We wanted to be together, and now we are united for-

---

*A version collected lower on the Fraser River is different. Having come back to the village, the hero voluntarily hides from all gazes. To force him to show himself, a curious village woman draws him out with a beautiful Bird made from her excrement. A cousin of the hero—thus taking here the place of the uncle— agrees to run away with him and even to serve as bloody bait to capture an Eagle, whose skin the hero puts on before flying off.

In heaven (where the cousin had not been asked to accompany him), the hero meets two blind old women. He gives them back their sight in thanks for the help they give him in marrying Sun's daughter (on the motif of the blind old women, cf. *The Naked Man,* pp. 392–421). The hero passes the tests imposed on him by Sun, but Moon persecutes him for having refused his own ugly and hunchbacked daughters.

Sun's daughter gives the hero two children, who demand to know their paternal family. Sun agrees to the departure, but the return to the earth brings some difficulties: Sun's daughter shines so brightly that it is impossible to look at her face to face without burning one's eyes. She herself cannot stand the smell of human beings. Everything works out in the end (Boas, *Indianische Sagen von der Nord-Pacifischen Küste Amerikas,* pp. 37–40).

ever."[18] The American myth reaches here the tragic greatness of kabuki.

The etiological function of the group to which this myth belongs is quite clear. The murderous chief felt remorse and tried to resuscitate his children: "Thus, from now on, people will be able to die and come back to life." Another shaman opposed this. When he in turn lost a child and wanted him to come back to life, he was given his own argument back: "One day the world will be civilized and people will have to be buried. People will die for real. When one dies, it is forever."[19] Remarkably, yet another etiological function is added to this major one: it is thought that the people to which this myth belongs (or, narrators say also, a neighboring or a distantly related people) is descended from the incestuous couple.[20] Consequently, the human condition, conceived here as both temporal and spatial, results from events that occurred once and for all and that cannot be undone. In contrast, the myth of the Dog husband preserves some indeterminacy to the human condition, at least in its physical aspect: skin color.

In the Northwest of North America, the myth of the Dog husband would thus be a double of that of the incest between siblings. If our analysis is correct, these myths differ only as to the type of closeness between the culprits. This is because, through a trick culture plays (in the sense we speak of, a trick history plays),* the Dog can appear simultaneously as an unacceptable spouse on account of its animal nature and as a sibling on account of its nature as domestic animal (see p. 158n above)—"a lower brother," as we ourselves sometimes call him.† In that case, the astronomical encoding explicit in the myth of incestuous siblings should be present at least in a latent state in the other myth. We know that the incestuous siblings ran away to heaven, where the woman became the Sun and the brother the Moon. The Dog being homologous to the brother, this animal should also be congruent with the Moon—thereby matching the lunar equivalency we have found

*TN: In French, *au sens où l'on parle de ruse de l'histoire.*
†TN: In French, *frère inférieur,* the equivalent to the English "man's best friend."

in Lynx—in myths that parallel that of the Dog husband in other aspects as well.

⁊

Let us develop this hypothesis. If Lynx and his avatar, the hero who as a child was stolen by Owl, have a lunar congruency, and if there are myths in which their roles are inverted, we then need to ascertain that these myths give center stage to the Sun. A version of the story of Lynx I discussed at the very start of this book contains the beginning of this transformation. The Coeur d'Alene tell that, in order to forgive those who had abandoned her along with her husband and her children, the heroine demands "the blue coat" or the "blue necklace" of Bluebird (see p. 10 above). It is striking that this transformation takes on its definitive aspect not in the other versions of the story of Lynx but in a version of the myth of the Dog husband. This version comes from the Slaiamun (or Sliammon), who are Salish speakers like the Coeur d'Alene. But the two peoples are in opposition through their geographical location on far ends of the Salish linguistic area, one on the coast and the other inland.

According to this version, the woman gave birth to seven Puppies who, once their animal skin had been burned, became one girl and six boys. The girl, a good seamstress, was making coats for her brothers. The eldest brother's coat was made of Bird feathers. Sun, who wanted it, came down to earth. He offered to exchange the boy's coat for his own, with which one could catch fish simply by dipping its edge in the water.[21]

Sun's magical coat often appears in myths. According to the Squamish, another small, Salish-speaking people of the coast, Sun's coat was made of Striped Squirrel skins (species *tamia*). They tell that the hero exchanged his own for it, thanks to which he made miraculous catches of fish. This coat gave those who wore it "the radiant and resplendent appearance of the noonday sun."[22] It is possible that in Squamish, as in Thompson—both languages belonging to the same family—the cry of the Striped Squirrel was expressed by onomatopoeia resembling the word for "light."[23]

The motif of the miraculous coat extends far to the south, all the way to the Chinook.[24] I will limit myself, as I did before, to the versions coming from the Salish speakers. According to the Lilloet, a local chief had a son who was lazy and a glutton and whom he decided to abandon. The chief and all his people left. Only the boy's grandmother remained with him. She made him a tunic with Bird feathers (from Magpies, specifies a version). Sun offered to exchange it for his own, which would make a great fisherman of the boy:

> Before Sun obtained the boy's robe, he was pale; and his light was faint, like that of the moon. But thenceforth he became bright and dazzling because he wore the boy's bright and many-colored robe.[25]

Another version tells us that in olden days, Sun, who was invisible, emitted an unbearable heat all year long. He proposed to exchange his coat for that of the hero. This latter hesitated:

> "If I give you my robe, you will be hotter than ever and the people will all die."—"No," answered Sun, "it will make me bright, so that you can see me every day; but my heat will not be able to come out so much as through the robe I am wearing, therefore the people will be cooler." The lad said, "Very well, if you promise to be brighter and cooler, getting only moderately hot during the summer and remaining cool during the rest of the year, you may take two of my robes [one made from Blue Jay and the other from Magpie feathers] in exchange for your one [made from Mountain-Goat wool]."*

*In a version from the lower Fraser, Sun's coat is also made of mountain-goat wool. In it the celestial body says: "I am Sun; Moon is my brother and the star that shines next to him is his wife." Later on, Qals, the Transformer, changes the hero and his dog into rocks while they are hunting a moose, which, after being thrown to the heavens, becomes the four main stars of the Big Dipper (Boas, *Indianische Sagen von der Nord-Pacifischen Küste Amerikas,* pp. 19–20). The Dog Husband's children are also changed into stars, according to the Carrier (see p. 158n).

The exchange took place, and the Sun taught the hero the art of fishing, which the Indians still did not know at the time. In summer, Sun wears only the robe made of Magpie feathers, and he is thus clearly visible; in winter he wears the two robes over each other, and this cools his heat. Since then, summers are moderately warm and winters are bearably cool.[26]

According to Thompson versions, Sun, who traveled naked by day and only covered himself up to sleep, acquired the four robes of the hero in exchange for numerous objects. His heat, which had been very high, became less uncomfortable to human beings.[27]

In one case, Sun, even though invisible, emitted an unbearable heat, while in other cases his light was too weak; in both cases, thanks to his new coat, he became luminous and bearable. In order to be convinced that this coat is an inversion of Snánaz's sickly skin, from which fog originated (this skin being itself a transformation of Lynx's sickly skin at the very beginning of the mythical series), we need only encompass the ensemble of our myths into a single glance. From a simple ornament obtained by the heroine in the Coeur d'Alene versions of the story of Lynx, the coat, sometimes even the necklace, of Bluebird is transformed at the end into rich clothing, which the hero agrees to give up. In exchange he obtains fish, the ideal food of human beings who live from fishing (while testicles, another transformation of adornments, are the food of an inhuman people, the cannibals).

The inversion of the coat, which makes the sun visible, into its opposite, the fog, which hides the sun, becomes literal in a myth from the Bella Coola, a Salish people located to the north and separated from their linguistic family. In the beginning, they say, there was no sun. A cloth stretched between heaven and earth kept this latter in darkness. (We, too, use the image of "a curtain" of fog,* another textile metaphor.) Crow gave Heron the mission of ripping it apart, but Sun's light barely came through, as if through a thick fog (*dichten Nebel* in Boas's German transcription). Crow

*TN: The French expression the author uses is *nappe de brouillard.*

went looking for the good Sun, stole it from the Master of Dawn (who kept it locked up in a box), and transported it to heaven.[28] Parallel to the myths we have just discussed, other Salish narratives have as protagonists two partners and their children, who together steal a sparkling object: a hoop, a disk, or a ball, according to different versions. This object is at times identified with the sun and at times with the rainbow, which will thenceforth be seen shining in the sky.* Almost all the versions specify that the thief or thieves escape their pursuers by causing a thick fog.[29] Fog thus fills a double function: either it keeps the sun from lighting up the earth, or it constitutes the means with which the sun (or the rainbow) delights the gaze of human beings. Disjunctive in one case, fog becomes conjunctive in the other. It is conjunctive as well in a myth already mentioned (see p. 146 above), in which a cloud "that went up and down like fog" is used by the hero as a pathway to Sun's dwelling.

*I have to mention a later version from the Skagit for its picturesque quality. At the time when night ruled on earth and the moon was the only heavenly light, Mink, the trickster, stole from the people of the East a machine that made the sun work. It was like a clock; three keys were needed to wind it up. Mink, who had carefully observed how to make it work, wound up the springs with the three keys. As soon as he had given the last turn with the third key, the sun rose. Mink, who had been a slave up to then, was made chief of the village (Haeberlin, pp. 392–93).

PART THREE

On the Side of the Wind

15

The Capture of the Wind

I have written (see p. 89 above) that the Thompson hero of the myth of the child stolen by Owl is called in various versions Ntsaâz, Tsa'au'z, or Snánaz. This latter name, also found among the Shuswap, is the object of a remark by Teit: "The name Snánaz could mean 'small robe,' but some Indians seem to think that it is a variant of the word 'Owl.'" In Shuswap, the great horned owl is indeed called *snina*. According to Thompson informants there is a relationship between the names Snánaz and Ntsaâz, and the meaning of the first name would be "little blanket."[1]

Two remarks are called for here. On the one hand, the Indians perceive a semantic link between names that, moreover, resemble each other phonetically. On the other hand, they say that one of these names, Snánaz, could have two meanings, one of which sends back to Owl and the other to a piece of clothing. The myths we already know set in close relationship the bearer of any of these names and Owl. We are now going to see that the small robe or blanket plays an essential role in a group of myths that partially intersects the other group and in which perhaps the same hero (or at any rate a hero also called Snánaz) distinguishes himself by capturing and domesticating the wind, precisely by using his blanket or another piece of his clothing.

That the name Snánaz could also mean "owl" reminds us indirectly of the role given this bird in the myth. The relation is thus of a metaphorical order. In the continuation of the same myth, the hero puts on a sickly skin that, when burned, gives birth to the fog. Fog and wind form a couple of correlated and opposed terms: both are meteorological phenomena, but they are mutually exclusive. Moreover, the other meaning of the name Snánaz, "little robe," designates the material means of the capture of the wind; it thus belongs to the metonymical order. Finally, this blanket or garment is the equivalent of the sickly skin that is the hero's clothing in the group of myths in which it is the origin of the fog.

Having thus schematically sketched out the relations of symmetry occurring between two mythical series, one of which was the object of the second part of this book, we can now broach the other series. The Thompson version is titled "The Story of the Lad Who Caught the Wind."

In olden days, the Wind blew violently, causing death and destruction. A man lived near Spence Bridge with his three sons. The youngest dreamed of glory. One day he announced he was going to snare the Wind. He was told this was impossible: "The Wind is unseen." The boy nevertheless set his traps several times in a row, though without success because the snare was too big. Night after night he made it narrower, and one morning he found the Wind had been caught. He had a lot of trouble getting it into his blanket and bringing it back to the village. He was laughed at when he announced he had captured the Wind. To prove he was telling the truth, he opened the blanket: the Wind blew furiously and almost demolished the lodge. The hero was begged to put it back in his blanket. Finally, he freed the Wind on the condition that it promised to stop tormenting human beings, a promise that the Wind has always respected since then.

Inspired by a dream that presaged riches and a good marriage, the hero departed southward. He traveled for so long that he wore out all of his spare moccasins. He was continuing his journey in spite of his wounded feet when he met Coyote, who offered him his help in exchange for his life (because the hero was about to kill him). Coyote took him on his back; he first went slowly, then more and more quickly as the hero killed animals of bigger and bigger sizes, which Coyote immediately cooked and ate. Coyote finally ran like the wind, arrived at the house of a chief, and explained to the hero how to get admitted inside.

The hero passed in front of armed guards. He was received coldly but then succeeded in making himself liked. One night he ran away with the chief's daughter using the chief's two best horses and his most beautiful saddles. They were pursued. At the moment they were about to be overtaken, they changed their saddles and horses into *stsûq*, which they hid under their shirts. They hid in the brush and were not found. They continued their journey and met the hero's brothers, who had accompanied him at the beginning of the journey but who, quickly discouraged, had given up following him and were hunting in the area.

On the return journey, the hero's brothers, who wanted his wife, threw him in a chasm. Although he was not killed, the young man was unable to find a way out. He called on all the animals to help him, but they all failed. The hero then thought of old Coyote, who had his home near his village. Coyote came in answer to his summons. As the other animals had done, he let his tail hang over the cliff, and this time he succeeded in drawing the hero out. The young man then changed his stsûq back into a horse, with which he ran and won a race in a nearby village. He sold the horse for many valuable goods, but then he turned the horse into a stsûq again and then the latter into a canoe, with which he went home. He found his wife, whom his father had protected from his two mean brothers in his father's lodge. After this, he was considered a great man in magic. The Coyote was his friend.[2]

According to James Alexander Teit (1864–1922)—a native of the Shetland Islands who emigrated while still very young to Canada and lived among the Thompson, whose language he learned and about whom, at Boas's suggestion and with his help, he published numerous works—the word *stsûq* probably designates a mark or drawing of any kind:

> Some Indians say that the stsûq in this story was probably a mark or picture on birch bark. Such, when made by a person gifted in magic, has supernatural powers. Some rock paintings are also "mysterious," and have not been made in any ordinary way. Some of them have not been made by the hand of man. The Indians at

the present day call the white man's writing and pictures stsûq. They also call paper stsûq.[3]

I will come back to this important comment.

Spence Bridge is located on the Thompson River about twenty kilometers from its junction with the Fraser River.

The Thompson say that when the hero captured the Wind, the latter had the appearance of a man with a very large head above a body that was so thin and light that he was hovering from right to left without touching the ground. According to another text, Wind-Man had a round body, hollow and boneless; he was bouncing like a ball. The head, the mouth, and the eyes were enormous, while the arms and legs were atrophied.[4]

After these few clarifications, needed to understand the text, we now come to the essential points. We are not dealing anymore with the fog but with the wind, and, as the myth shifts interest from one meteorological phenomenon to another, it brings to the forefront of the scene the character of Coyote, a character who had been eclipsed by Lynx in the myths we previously discussed. I have shown that in the myth of the child stolen by Owl, Snánaz (or the bearer of a similar name) is a double for the character of Lynx: like him, he is covered with a sickly skin of which he will later be either cured or freed, and, like him, he is the master or the creator of the fog. Here Snánaz (or the hero of this name) has Coyote as double or even as alter ego. This is emphasized in the last words of the myth, "Coyote was his friend," a conclusion that might have seemed abrupt if we had not recognized Coyote's function.

However, this parallel must be qualified. The relation of the stolen child to Lynx is metaphorical in nature: on several points, their stories resemble each other. In contrast, the relation of the boy who caught the Wind and Coyote is metonymical: Coyote is physically present to twice play a key role as the plot unfolds. And it is not relevant whether Coyote here is one or two distinct individuals.

All this is all the more true in that several versions coming from the Coeur d'Alene attribute to Coyote the capture of the Wind by means of a snare and the Wind's pacification. Neighboring both the Thompson and the Coeur d'Alene, the Sanpoil tell how Coyote fought with his bare hands against Blizzard and vanquished him; since then, snow storms only last two or three days. We are not sure of the origins of a short myth (it might be either Salish or Sahaptin) in which Coyote also captures the Wind but with the opposite result: there would have been no more wind at all if Coyote had not freed it.[5]

In crossing the linguistic boundary separating the Coeur d'Alene from their southern neighbors the Nez Percé, the system that I have sketched out (see pp. 169–70 above) turns over. We have indeed seen at the very beginning of this book (see p. 5 above) that there it is Coyote who disguises himself with the sanious skin of an old man, just like the boy stolen by Owl—a boy who is Lynx's double—but in that case *to escape from* Bear, who is pursuing him, contrary to the hero of the other myth, who disguises himself under a sanious skin *after* Owl, *from whom he has escaped,* gives up the chase. A loop that we had left open thus comes to a close with a mythic series that is an alternate to the series in which the presence of the motif posed a problem. This presence now takes on a differential meaning, confirming that the two series are in relation of inverted symmetry.

Let us come back to the myth of the capture of the Wind. The Thompson version (see pp. 170–71 above) is surprising on account of its incongruous details. Armed guards in front of the chief's house and saddle horses do have a European flavor. And even though the concept of stsûq belongs to native tradition, we have seen that it had been broadened to include the paper and the writing of the Whites. In the present myth, it functions less in what we might call "Indian style"* than as a commonplace element abundantly represented in the folklore of the Old World.

---

*TN: In the original, *à l'indienne.*

This European folklore coloration comes out even more strongly in the Shuswap version, one constructed in two acts sometimes told as separate stories. A man lived with his four sons not far from a large village that included Coyote among its inhabitants. The youngest one of the brothers, called Snánaz, was ugly and had big eyes; he was not respected. At that time Wind was causing damages. One after the other, the brothers tried unsuccessfully to snare it. In spite of being mocked, Snánaz tried it, using gradually narrower snares. On the morning of the fourth day, he found Wind a prisoner. Wind was a very small man with a very thin body and limbs but an enormous head; he had an unruly head of hair and protruding eyes.

Snánaz imprisoned Wind in his robe and consented to free him only in exchange for the promise of thenceforth blowing with moderation. However, Coyote, who refused to trust Wind, was taken by him to a swamp, where he sank. Snánaz rescued Coyote and brought him back to the village.

It was the beginning of spring. Waterbirds were beginning to come back to frozen lakes, but there was nothing left to eat. Snánaz succeeded through magic in numbing the Wild Swans; he was thus able to kill them with a blow over the head to feed the people. When the food situation became critical once more, Snánaz was the only one capable of breaking the layer of ice by kicking it. Water burst out from the breach ice, spreading a large quantity of fish on the surface. Good weather finally returned; the people left the winter village to go hunting.

According to some informants, the following would constitute a distinct myth. Night after night, the four boys' father noticed that potatoes were disappearing from his garden. The brothers took turns watching, but only Snánaz was able to resist falling asleep. He noticed a dark shadow, fired in that direction, and, along with his brothers, set out chasing the intruder. The trail ended at the edge of a chasm. With difficulty, Snánaz managed to go down at the end of a rope. He landed in the lower world, tied the end of the rope to a rock, and went reconnoitering. He found the thief in a hut made of twigs and covered with soot. It was an old man, wounded, black from soot, who advised him to visit a nearby chief, father, or uncle of two pretty young women (in some versions they are his captives, originary from the terrestrial world). Welcomed by the chief, Snánaz accepted his hospitality and learned much wisdom from him.

The chief, who had also given him his daughters (or nieces or captives) in marriage, allowed Snánaz to take them back to his country. Snánaz found the rope, pulled on it to alert his brothers (who, we must assume, had remained nearby), and first had the two women pulled up. The brothers found them to their liking; thus, when the time came to pull up Snánaz, they cut the rope when he was halfway up, counting on the fall to kill him.

He was only hurt and crawled to his father-in-law, who nursed him and gave him a roll of birch bark (or a piece of paper, according to some informants) bearing magical signs. He taught him how to change this talisman into a horse capable of galloping on the edge of a blade, even one held up vertically, and to pass through a ring without getting hurt on the needle or the awl pointing in the middle of the ring. Snánaz thus galloped vertically to the top of the chasm; he then changed his mount back into a roll of bark and changed himself into a ragged, dirty, and famished-looking person. He came back to his village and presented himself as a beggar. He was fed in exchange for doing some chores.

To explain Snánaz's absence, the brothers had invented quite a tale. But the women told the truth to the father, and they told him so many marvels about the lower world that he wanted to imitate it. He organized tests that neither Coyote nor the other men of the village succeeded in passing. In trying to gallop on the edge of a blade held vertically, Coyote even split his horse in two; in the test of the ring, he got himself run through by the needle. Invited jokingly to try his luck, Snánaz triumphed on all the tests, so much so that he was taken for an emissary of the lower world. Snánaz then went back to his normal appearance, let himself be recognized, confounded his brothers, and took back his wives.

They lived happily and had many children, all powerful magicians.[6] (This myth is indexed M$_{691}$ in *The Naked Man,* p. 409, only for the seasonal aspect.)

On the other side of the linguistic border separating the Salish from the Chilcotin, in contrast to what we have observed for the alternate series of the child stolen by Owl (see pp. 95–98 above), the myth does not invert itself but loses a part of its substance. More specifically, the inversion is of minor importance and only affects some details. The hero is already married; his father-in-law, of whom he has a talisman, thus lives like him in the terrestrial world. The rivalry between the brothers disappears; the myth only mentions their existence. Consequently, nobody helps the hero to go down to the bottom of a precipice; he enters the subterranean world alone in pursuit of the potato thief, who turns out to be a Chicken [*sic*]. The father of the hero, who believed him dead, offers his daughters-in-law to the winner of a competition he organizes. Having come back to the village under an unrecognizable disguise, the hero passes all of the tests, thanks to his talisman. His wives, who guess the truth, reveal it to the chief. There is a thorough search, and the talisman is discovered under the beggar's blanket. The chief then recognizes him as his son and gives him back his spouses.[7]

In discussing the alternate series—that of the boy captured by Owl—I noted that the Shuswap impoverish the myth and that the Chilcotin give it back its richness by inverting it. In the present series, the situation is the opposite, as the Chilcotin version is greatly impoverished and is entirely missing the plot of the brothers. As for the inversion, it already starts with the Shuswap. Indeed, the Shuswap preserve traces of the opposition between the two series: in one, the hero moves among women (mother, sister, spouse—this latter being either one of his compatriots or a foreigner); in the other, he moves among men (a family composed of a father and brothers numbering two in the Thompson version, three in the Shuswap one, and "numerous" in the Chilcotin version, in which they do not play a part). The Shuswap inversions are manifested on other planes as well. From being allied to the hero and capable of running like the wind—that is, a metaphorical relation—Coyote becomes the hero's detractor, carried away by the wind—a metonymical relation. Coyote completely disappears in the Chilcotin version (in which a character named Raven appears briefly in the same role). The episode from the Shuswap version in which the hero makes a nourishing water (full of fish) spring forth for the starving people (see p. 174 above) rejoins the episode of the hero hitting the ground with his foot and causing a refreshing water to spring forth to help the thirsty (see p. 111 above). I had shown that from this angle, the son of Root is an inversion of Coyote's son, who hits tree stumps with his foot to cause a warming fire to spring forth for his cold companions.

It must also be noted that, in a close parallel with the Shuswap version of the myth of the child taken by Owl (in which, in contrast to the other versions, the boy is happy at the home of his abductor, who educates him and imparts his knowledge to him; see p. 95 above), the Shuswap version of the myth of the capture of the Wind states that the hero voluntarily goes to a great chief of the subterranean world, settles at his home, and becomes his disciple. An even clearer parallelism comes to the fore between, on the one hand, the old man dressed in a robe and covered with soot and, on the other, the old man whose sanious skin the hero dons in c·der to hide his appearance—a ploy also practiced by the Wind's captor when he passes himself off as a beggar. We can thus say that, while the Shuswap version does not completely invert the other versions belonging to the mythic series, it nonetheless represents a curve that bends this series to the point of almost coinciding with the other one.

Even more so than the Thompson version, this Shuswap one exhibits a folkloric coloration evocative of the Old World. The potatoes whose theft sets the plot in motion are not a native product. Even though the Salish (whose first contact with Whites—Spanish and British—occurred on the coast at the end of the eighteenth century) were commonly cultivating potatoes fifty or sixty years later,[8] they were nonetheless still conscious of their exotic origin. One could say as much about the "chicken" playing the role of the thief in the Chilcotin version. The hero of the Shuswap myth wounds this thief with a gunshot, and the magical horse gallops on a knife blade, other items received from the Whites.* Finally, according to several informants, the talisman looked like a piece of paper.

Let us take one extra step. In his great work on the mythology of the Thompson, to which I have constantly referred, James Teit devotes a section to tales of European origin. He includes a narrative—the only one told by the Thompson—in which it is explicitly stated that the hero is called Snánaz as in the Shuswap version. In this story, Snánaz obtains the help of various animals to win a competition whose prize is the daughter of a powerful shaman. He marries the woman and comes back to his village with her. Then follows the episode of the brothers who covet the woman and abandon Snánaz at the bottom of an abyss (where they make him go under the pretext of looking for a gold nugget). He denounces his brothers' treason and takes back his wife.[9]

In the main, this narrative reproduces the myths that have just been discussed without bringing into question their native origin. However, among the Thompson and the Shuswap, Snánaz also appears as the killer of the monster with seven (sometimes eight) heads who was about to eat a young maiden. A disappointed rival almost succeeds in depriving the hero of his victory, but Snánaz succeeds in having justice done and marries the young lady.[10] The European origin of this tale is all the more certain in that this region of North America abounds with French folklore, known to the Indians and adopted by them. The telescoping of these disparate traditions poses a problem that should not be shunted aside.

---

*However, in the Chilcotin version, a lance replaces both the gun and the knife.

16

Indian Myths, French Folktales

In a book published in 1942, Dumézil wrote some reflections that he took up again in slightly different form in 1969 and then in 1985. They show that, until his very last days, he was troubled by a coincidence. In Indo-Iranian traditions, as well as on the northwest coast of North America, the initiation rites of young men—which were moreover very similar—involved a three-headed monster, "a similarity for which," wrote Dumézil, "we cannot find an explanation."[1] The cause could only be independent invention or diffusion going back to early times.

The resemblance between the Old and New World narratives that attracted our attention in the preceding chapter is of another nature. These narratives date from a recent period, and their origin is without mystery. In the course of the nineteenth century, the *voyageurs*, as they were then called—Canadians in the employ of the Hudson Bay Company—had very close relations with the Indians. They not only bought furs from them; they traveled, hunted, camped, and lived with them.

In the evening, around the campfires, the voyageurs told many a story from French folklore, probably in Chinook jargon.* We

*Made up of words borrowed from about twenty native languages, Chinook jargon was used for intertribal communication before the Whites spread its use from the California coast all to way to Alaska while adding to it French and English terms. Along the Pacific coast where lived small nations that, even though speaking mutually unintelligible languages (numbering several dozens), were trading with each other. As I have noted earlier in this book, dentalia shells gathered only in the Puget Sound and north of it were much in demand in California. In the other direction, the mother-of-pearl from abalone shells that came from southern California was traded all the way up to British Columbia and Alaska, where it was used in making jewelry and other precious objects. I

find the name Ti-Jean (Petit-Jean), a hero particularly popular in Canada, in versions collected later on from Indian storytellers: Butcetcā in Shuswap, Laptissán in Nez Percé, Ptciza in Kalapuya, Kicon in Cree, Ticon in Ojibwa . . .

Among Boas's many fruitful ideas was the one to get young researchers to collect in their own countryside that which had survived of a French folklore in which no one was interested locally. The harvest, which was fabulous,[2] is in no way a frozen image of French folklore in the seventeenth century. Transplanted into a new soil, this folklore received additions and underwent influences; it also evolved of its own. As well, its content remains much richer than that which existed in the memory of French storytellers of the same period. We can understand how the Indians were seduced by the liveliness, the marvelousness, the picturesque or fantastic details of these tales, which in these respects matched their own and in which they found the character of the ugly and despised hero with whom they were familiar. It is thus not surprising that Snánaz, after his victory over the Wind, was attributed a victory over the Seven-headed Beast. The Shuswap version attributes to Snánaz, at the time he was still obscure and mocked for his naïveté, the same blunders of a Thompson character called Jack, a name that proves his European origin.[3] The Indians were quick to grasp the resemblances between their narratives and the European ones, and they incorporated many incidents into their own traditions.

Thus two heroes from Old World folklore came to be superimposed on the character of Snánaz: one a boy whose qualities are at first ignored and who subsequently accomplishes great feats and

---

have cited in *The Naked Man* (pp. 277–79) a long text from Teit on the intertribal fairs held on the lower Columbia as well as inland, a text that draws a startling picture of commercial exchange among peoples sometimes very far removed from one another. A common language was thus required, which the French- or English-speaking fur traders readily put to use. In the middle of the nineteenth century, the Chinook jargon included more French words than English ones (Swan, *The Northwest Coast;* Eells, *The Indians of Puget Sound* and "The Chinook Jargon"; Gibbs; Jacobs, "Notes on the Structure of Chinook Jargon").

is called in French Petit-Jean; the other a stolen or found child raised by a wild animal, just as Snánaz was by Owl, and called in French Jean de l'Ours ("John the Bear"). Finally, the episode in the course of which Snánaz's brothers throw or abandon him in the bottom of a precipice so as to steal his wife or wives is practically identical to Delarue's tale type 301, "The Princesses Freed from the Subterranean World," of which several versions exist in Canada. All that is required in order to uncover them again at the back of the Indian myth is to replace the potatoes of one with the apples or pears (sometimes of gold) of the others or to replace the Chicken with a bigger fowl. According to the French, French-Canadian, and Arab versions of the tale, Eagle agrees to bring up the hero from the precipice on the condition that he give him a ration of meat (or of flesh that the hero himself cuts off his own thighs) each time he weakens. The hero of the American myth also has to feed Coyote as he carries him on his back so that he can run more and more quickly (see p. 170 above). The episode of Eagle figures unchanged in the Europeanized Thompson version. Teit, who collected it, does not hesitate, moreover, to title another version of the same origin "The Young Lad and the Wicked Brothers (John the Bear)," thereby confirming the origin—according to him French or Spanish—of this narrative.[4]

The Shuswap version replaces the old man with the sanious skin (whose identity is assumed by Snánaz) with an old man covered with soot, a thief who then shows himself to be of sound council (see p. 175 above). This substitution could be explained if we could see in this last character a reflection of the coal maker or the chimney sweep who plays an important role in French folktales.* According to a French-Canadian version of the Seven-

---

*In this case, we should admire the precision with which the Amerindian myths and the tales of the Old World can sometimes adjust to each other. In American myths and rites, soot usually stands for black clouds, bearers of rain; this might be one of the reasons for the role of the incense burner of the Maya; the Lacandon god of rain, Mensabak, is the "maker of black powder or soot." There is the same symbolism in South America with the Barasana and the Gua-

headed Beast, the imposter, who pretends to have killed the monster and demands the hand of the princess in marriage, is a coal maker. A French-Canadian version of the story of the princesses freed from the subterranean world leads the hero, lost in the forest, to the hut of a coal maker. The hero exchanges his coat for that of his host, "who had worn it for fifty years and which was black as the stove." [5]

ﻬ

But should we invoke borrowing in all these cases? The widespread diffusion of the story of Lynx—as we have seen, already extant in the sixteenth century—proves that even under the form it takes in the Northwest of North America, it belongs to the most authentic part of Amerindian patrimony. And yet this story resembles in a striking manner a folktale widespread in the Old World, titled in French "Jean le Teigneux"* ["Scurfy John"], which the Indians certainly heard from Canadian voyageurs. The hero, whose hair has turned to gold following complicated events (among which he transgresses an interdiction, as in the story of Blue Beard), changes his appearance in order to mislead his pursuers. He hides his hair under a cap of pitch or a bladder, pretending that he is scurfy, and has himself hired by a powerful person, usually a king, as a poultry-yard servant or as a gardener. One day, one of the king's daughters sees his golden hair, falls in love with the young man, and demands to have him for a husband. Her father agrees, but he is angered by this mismatch and kicks the young couple out. In several versions, the hero, at some later date,

---

yaki, as well as in North America (Tozzer, 71; Lévi-Strauss, *From Honey to Ashes,* pp. 442–43, and *The Naked Man,* pp. 490–91; Hugh-Jones, pp. 174–75, 177, 183, 191). The New and Old Worlds put in close relationship fog and blighted corn (in the first) and fog and blighted wheat (in the second), the blight having the appearance of a black powder (*Structural Anthropology,* pp. 279–80). In the American mythological corpus, the soot covering could thus in itself and without the need to have recourse to external comparisons constitute a combinatory variant of the sickly skin that, let us not forget, is at the origin of fog.

†TN: That is, suffering from *tinea capitis.*

finds out that his father-in-law is involved in a war; he runs to his help and defeats the king's enemies. The king recognizes him as his son-in-law and heir. A literary and moralizing version of this tale, the romance of Robert le Diable ("Evil Robert"), was famous in the whole of Europe from the thirteenth to the nineteenth centuries.[6]

There is no need to insist on the similarities between this tale and the story of Lynx. Both feature a hero whose sordid and sickly aspect hides grace and beauty; he is rejected along with his young wife by her parents, but, having become a great hunter or valorous warrior, saves either from famine or from defeat his father-in-law, a village chief or a king, along with the people who had been indignant at his seduction (active in one case, passive in another) of a young lady of high birth who was refusing all of her suitors.

However, the hypothesis that this would represent a straightforward borrowing is unfounded, and there are additional reasons for this besides those already discussed above. Even closer to the story of Jean le Teigneux, there exists a legend the Aztec claimed came from the Toltec, their predecessors in central Mexico. This legend, collected as it was on the morrow of the conquest, cannot be of European origin. The Aztec told that several centuries previously, the god Tezcatlipoca set out to destroy the Toltec. He persecuted their national god, Quetzalcoatl, and forced him to flee. Among other tricks, Tezcatlipoca (under the name of Titlacauan) took on the appearance of a miserable, half-naked stranger selling peppers in the marketplaces. One day, the daughter of Huemac, king of the Toltec, saw him and was bedazzled by the beauty of his virile member, which his rags poorly hid. She became sick from love. The responsible party was looked for everywhere, and he was finally found and brought to her. He had sex with her and cured her; she wanted him for her husband. Ashamed of this mismatch, the king, followed by the whole of his people, abandoned the guilty ones. He was hoping that the stranger would perish in the course of a war the Toltec were about to engage in. But the Toltec were losing and many of their people were dying until the stranger appeared at the head of all the midgets, hunchbacks, and crippled men who had been thought unworthy of conscripting. He won, and the Toltec recognized him as their leader.[7] Of course, this turned out to be a trap set by Tezcatlipoca, who took advantage of the situation to make all the Toltec perish. However, if we stick to the first part of the legend and replace the seductive hair of the false servant with the seductive penis of the false indigent, everything matches, including the military prowess of the main protagonist.

There is another case in which resemblances cannot be attributed to borrowing. The great mythological cycle titled in English "Lodge Boy and Thrown-away," which I already mentioned (see p. 61 above), could be the exact copy of the French romance "Valentin and Orson": a pair of twins, one raised by his parents while the other was lost in the wilderness, find each other and accomplish many feats together. The Pan-American diffusion of the myth precludes it from being a borrowing from the folklore of the Old World, the more so in that the romance, edited in the fifteenth century, is so cluttered with stereotypical elements from chivalric literature that the mythical matter from which it probably originated remains out of the grasp of attempts to reach and identify it.*

The problem of the relations between native and French narratives is, as can be seen, less simple than it first appeared. In some cases—seven-headed beast, freed princesses, shotgun, knife, magical horse—the borrowing is clear. But there are others that raise questions: Did the Indians borrow the whole plot or only some details? Or, again, is the parallelism between our narratives and some of theirs the result of a coincidence, as undoubtedly is the case for the Mexican legend and the tale of Jean le Teigneux? Likewise, the myth of the child in the cabin and the child thrown away cannot come from the romance of Valentin and Orson.

Let us not forget that European folktales preserve themes and

---

*However, the romance unfolds according to a scheme that offers a perfect example of mythical transformation. Valentin ends his life as a saintly man, and he is canonized after his death. As for Orson, he becomes emperor of Greece. This can be rendered *culture : supernature :: nature : society.*

motifs that are very ancient and that had lots of time to spread across the world. Many go back at least to ancient Greek and Indian periods; they are found from one end of the Old World to the other. Thus it cannot be ruled out that, in archaic times, when exchanges were occurring in the North between the shores of the Pacific Ocean, entire myths or mythical elements passed from Asia to America. They might have survived here and there, cut off from their common root, remainders of a past that the apparent isolation of the New World for millennia—until the period of discovery (which was certainly not a discovery, except from the trans-Atlantic perspective)—makes us unable to represent today. It is significant that in this respect the American myth of the child of the cabin and the child thrown away exist in the form of a trace among a Mongol people of the Siberian interior, the Buriat.[8]

We will thus look upon facts of diffusion as probable, even though we are able to reconstitute neither their itineraries nor their chronology. This being accepted, another question arises: These meetings of oral traditions so very distant from each other in time and in space, these resemblances of which I have given some examples—are they not inevitable and even in a sense necessary? They instead might stem from the inherent properties of mythical thought, from the constraints limiting and orienting its creative power.

୬ଈ

Mythical thought operates through means of oppositions and codes. However, the notion of binary opposition, which I have been accused of overusing, only intervenes in the analysis of myth as the smallest common denominator of the changing values arising from comparison and analogy. Binary oppositions thus might appear in very diverse modalities: symmetries (themselves of several types), contradictions, opposites, relative values, trope type figures of speech or of thought, and so on. These different modes of opposition belong to heterogeneous categories. Moreover, they never present themselves in an abstract form and, so to speak, in a pure state. Rather, they take on a concrete aspect within codes that are used to formulate messages, messages that themselves can be transposed into the terms of other codes and that can in turn transpose into their own system messages received through the channels of different codes. These codes are themselves heterogeneous, as they can be spatial, temporal, cosmological, sexual, social, economic, rhetorical, and so on. At least theoretically, their number is limitless, as codes are tools forged to satisfy the needs of the analysis. Only afterward can the degree to which they correspond to reality be ascertained. But we have to admit that in the first stages of the research, the selection and the definition of the axes on which are located the oppositions, and the selection and the definition of the codes to which they are applicable, owe much to the analyst's subjectivity, and thus they have an impressionistic character.

From the very beginning of *Mythologiques,* I pointed out that I was aware—more so than anyone else—of the very loose meanings I gave to certain terms: *symmetry, inversion, equivalence, homology, isomorphism* (*The Raw and the Cooked,* pp. 30–31). I could have escaped from this difficulty by taking refuge behind the notion of morphism, a notion that can be defined as "a relation—of any sort—by which two objects are comparable or opposable."[9] But then all the myths would have to have been treated through the algebra of morphisms, and the difficulty would thus simply have been shifted. In a domain so new (at least from the angle I was using), I proceeded through trials and errors. Some oppositions, even real ones, do not always have the form I gave them; others perhaps do not exist. But I will deem myself satisfied if I be granted the recognition that I have been right in a significant number of cases.

Besides, the fact of the existence of oppositions counts much more than the particular form they might take in various places. Oppositions degenerate all the time in the course of mythical transformations. An opposition of contradictories becomes an opposition of contraries, which in turn turns into a mere difference in degree. From an initial opposition between human beings and non-human beings, we might pass through transformations to one between human beings and animals, then to one, even weaker, between unequal degrees of humanness (or of animality). These latter oppositions might be connoted by terms that are heterogeneous to the preceding ones: perhaps that of big or small eaters in a society that sees moderation as a virtue. And yet it is always the same opposition that we are dealing with.

This fluidity of mythical forms has consequences. As we progressively deepen the analysis, and particularly as we enlarge its field in time and space, a more and more complicated network comes to light, and the codes and the oppositions crisscross one another, multiplying the intersections so that the network comes close to a theoretical state in which each junction would be linked to all others. The mythologist would then be faced with two alternatives: either to recognize that all paths linking one junction to another have a significative value, or not to give a value to any of them.

In the first hypothesis, mythology would become a language lacking in redundancy, in the sense used in information theory, which calls redundancy those aspects of the message predetermined by the structure of the code and, because of this, lying outside the play of the sender's free choice. Such are the predetermined aspects of syntax that the so-called telegraphic style eliminates without leading to significant loss of information. Seen from the viewpoint of phonological constraints, a language without redundancy would be one in which writing letters arbitrarily in a grid of squares would always lead to a completed crossword puzzle.

But isn't this what mythology appears to be when viewed from on high—an immense discourse men have made the effort of producing during tens of millennia, longer probably, stretching over all of the inhabited parts of the earth, leading nowhere and only succeeding in closing upon itself? From one end of the world to the other, in the course of time, this discourse has gradually taken the shape of a connex system—that is, one in which every junction is linked to all others through a chain of relations. This connexity does not render the mythologist's work invalid, but it marks its limits. It condemns general mythology to failure, as two inescapable conclusions follow from the preceding comments: of all the paths already undertaken or simply possible, general mythology can always offer a theory; and the more the field of investigation broadens, the more it becomes probable that a path chosen arbitrarily would correspond to a path that has been actually followed. The more the field of analysis is broadened, the more resemblances are uncovered, but they have less and less meaning.

Though this is the case for general mythology, it isn't so anymore when comparison is undertaken within mythological systems bounded in time and space. For these, the inverse proposition holds true: the more the field is restricted, the more differences are uncovered. It is to the relations these differences have with one another that meanings are attached. A comparative study of Indo-European, American, and African myths is valid; a mythology with universal pretensions is not.

Philosophers thus use arguments that really apply to themselves when they reproach structural analysis for turning mythology into a meaningless discourse. From the observatory point these philosophers have chosen—the highest possible, in which myths have lost all contact with ethnographic reality—myths effectively do not say anything. Structural analysis demonstrates this *a contrario* by identifying the level on which myths do say something. And yet, as structural analysis does this, it isn't blind to the consequences of its accompanying critique of mythological reason, consequences that are already readily noticeable when working on a reduced scale (cf. *From Honey to Ashes,* pp. 353–55; *The Origin of Table Manners,* p. 195; *The Naked Man,* pp. 637–39, 694). In other words, the problem this entails is ascertaining the conditions required for forms to be capable of receiving an unlimited number of contents. That everyone may find in myths what he or she is looking for simply proves that nothing of the sort is actually there.

In contrast, a limited mythical field, regardless of the manner used to define it, overflows with meanings, and we can understand why. From a theoretically conceivable network in which all lines are joined and that does not have any redundancy, each culture or group of cultures draws only a portion: a subnetwork, produced by an unconscious strategy, whereby the originality of a culture as well as its limitations manifest themselves. The meanings come out of the gaps between these subnetworks, even when they happen to partially overlap.

We thus learn from the structural analysis of myths in two ways. First, each local mythology, matched with a given history and ecological environment, teaches us a lot about the society from which it comes, exposes its inner workings, and sheds light on the functioning, the meaning, and the origin of its beliefs and customs, some of them having, sometimes already for several centuries, raised unresolvable problems. This, however, requires that structural analysis meet one condition: it must never cut itself off from the facts. Commenting on my study of the geste of Asdiwal (*Structural Anthropology*, vol. 2, chap. 10), a mathematician whom I have already cited, François Lorrain, noted that if we would limit ourselves to look upon the terms I was putting in opposition (such as sky and earth, earth and water, earth and the subterranean world, and so on) in an abstract mode, we would very soon come to see them as interchangeable within a system that would lose all of its interest. This unless—as I have done— we "come back to the myth and define with precision the qualitatively different multiple relations linking 'sky' with 'earth,' 'sky' with 'water,' and so forth." [10] Yes, we need to come back to the myth, but also and foremost to the practices and beliefs of a given society, which are our only source of information on those qualitative relations. This is the reason why we should give up pursuing the structural analysis of the myths of a society for which we lack an ethnographic context or, at any rate, a context that is independent from the information carried by the myths themselves. Such analysis would run on empty, deprived as it would be of concrete means of verification.

This is precisely the case for general mythology. It cuts off myths from those supports that, because of the generality of the approach itself, have become inaccessible. Emptied of their content, reduced to hollow forms, myths then receive as a substitute the content that the philosopher thinks himself permitted or forced to introduce in them. In so doing, he only replaces a content that lies beyond his reach with his fantasies or his desires.*

And yet, when the comparison of myths belonging to an ensemble of individual cultures—even one limited to a geographical area and to a period of history—risks becoming too general, not all is lost as long as we are conscious that this generalizing movement gradually reduces mythic thought to its form. The problem is not anymore to know what the myths are saying but to understand how they say it, even if, apprehended at that level, they say less and less. One would then expect that structural analysis shed light on the functioning—at, so to speak, a pure state—of a mind that, in emitting an empty discourse because it has nothing else to offer, unveils and lays bare the mechanism of its own operation.

---

*"The lives of saints are the most equivocal literature there is: to apply the scientific method to them *when one has no other documents available,* this seems to me to be doomed from the outset—it is just a simple entertainment for an idle scientist . . ." (Nietzsche, *'Antéchrist,* par. 28; emphasis in original).

17

The Last Return of the Bird-Nester

The preceding comments have a direct bearing on a problem I had formulated though not pursued in *The Naked
Man* (p. 368). Even if we take for granted that the Indians have
adopted a good number of French-Canadian tales and that they
have even integrated several of them into their own mythology,
how are we to understand that narratives so differently inspired
and coming from very distant areas of the world did spontaneously adjust to one another? If we had taken the Thompson myth
on the capture of the Wind at its face value—that is, without
putting in doubt its native origin—we would not hesitate to see
it as a straightforward inversion of the Pan-American myth of the
bird-nester: the very story that all along the course of *Mythologiques* I had chosen as a reference myth because it appeared the
most apt to articulate the mythological corpus of the two
Americas.

This interpretation would have seemed all the more convincing
in that, as I have shown in *The Naked Man* (pp. 152–59), the
Northwest of North America, the object of the present investigation, is also where the bird-nester myth coincides most neatly with
the South American versions. This resurgence of the same myth
in very distant points of the New World constitutes a supplementary argument, providing geographical and historical evidence to
back up the previously identified key position of this myth within
its logical and semantic settings.

Within Thompson mythology itself, the myth on the capture
of the Wind inverts that of the bird-nester. First, it commutes the
above and the below as the hero undergoes a disjunction through
a fall into the subterranean world instead of one through the

growth of a tree that lifts him up to the sky. This disjunction is the work of very close kin—in one case brothers, in another a father—who make the hero disappear so as to appropriate his wife or wives.

In all of their versions of the myth of the bird-nester, the Thompson attribute a hostile role to Coyote, the hero's father (*The Naked Man,* pp. 368–77). In contrast, in their version of the capture of the Wind, they turn Coyote into not only an invaluable helper (who carries the hero on his back all the way to the country where he will get married) but as well a rescuer: he pulls the hero out of the abyss where he had been thrown and thus enables him to recover the wife his brothers wanted to take.

Finally, while in the Thompson versions of the bird-nester the hero's father wants and appropriates his wife or wives, in the Thompson myth of the capture of the Wind, this same father protects the hero's wives against his other sons. Thanks to him, they are returned untouched to their husband. This attitude (which is found in none of the ninety-six versions of the tale of the princesses freed from the subterranean world listed by Delarue; see p. 181 above) is specific to the American narrative. Furthermore, this episode would seem to be unmotivated if we did not see it as an inversion of the corresponding episode of the bird-nester myth.

We can even extend the paradigm to the myths with which we began the present investigation. In the version of the story of Lynx featuring Coyote, this latter intervenes as his son's ally: there, too, he helps him conquer a faraway spouse. Moreover, Coyote fights at his son's side against the master of a destructive fire, while this son—congruent in this regard to the bird-nester—has, among other merits, that of producing a beneficial fire for human beings (see p. 19 above).

Thus the audience of a foreign narrative, far from accepting it passively, modifies or even transforms it so as to adapt it to its own traditions. To speak of borrowing would be too simple. Each time the problem is raised we must look behind appearances so as to untangle that which was truly borrowed, and we must particularly not let ourselves be fooled by the illusion that borrowing occurs without a motive or solely on account of a romantic attraction. This is because borrowing can fill a function; it can make up for the lack of something, the need for which was obscurely felt. Perhaps we should even reject the notion of borrowing in favor of the notion that often, when faced with allogeneic material, local minds recognize elements that, under different aspects, were already present or could be present in their own traditions. In this way, borrowing could help explicate latent elements and add to incomplete schemas.

Let us look at one case among others. We have seen in *The Naked Man* (pp. 425–28) that a Coeur d'Alene myth systematically transforms the neighboring versions of the bird-nester myth (Eagle → Crane; high → far; son → daughters; lust for daughters-in-law → hunger for the son-in-law's cooking; and so on). Once we have recognized this, can we, following Reichard,[1] treat as a borrowing from European folklore the episode in which women, exhausted from a long journey, devour edible bulbs tied to a door curtain without succeeding in satisfying their hunger? Or should we rather not take up the thread of the other transformations, which leads us to see that this bizarre motif actually shifts onto a vertical plane the flat celestial world in which the starving bird-nester pulls out edible bulbs with which he cannot quell his hunger because they are, in reality, stars? Depending on the perspective chosen, the same motif might thus appear as a borrowing or as a state of a transformation, a stage we might almost have been able to deduce a priori, so much it respects the internal logic of this transformation.

One of the most visible differences between the American myth of the bird-nester and the French tale of the princesses freed from the subterranean world is that, still on a vertical axis, the disjunction of the hero occurs downward in one and upward in the other. In both cases the hero, a denizen of the middle world, changes universes: he rises up to the celestial world or he goes down into the subterranean world. In both cases, more or less willing animals, who ultimately prove to be helpful, assist him in going back down to the terrestrial world or else in going back up to it.

Should we think of borrowing each time a version of the myth of the bird-nester sends the hero down from above, in contrast to the case in which the opposite occurs? Nothing is less certain. Already we hesitate when facing the versions coming from the inland Salish-speaking groups of the Sanpoil, the Okanagan (close neighbors to the Thompson), and the Shuswap (versions indexed M_{665} and M_{666} in *The Naked Man*, p. 368). Disjunction does occur downward, but the hero remains stuck in the middle on a ledge next to the nest of the Eagles, whose feathers he had intended to take. Against their will (as he captures them and ties them to his arms and legs), the birds transport him by flying to the bottom of the cliff, from which he goes back to his village through another itinerary, which we must assume to be easier.

Not only do these versions not mention one or more princesses brought back from the subterranean world, but the topology is not the same anymore. So, are these versions the weakened and almost unrecognizable echo of the French narrative, or was this particular construction already present in America before the imported tale and the native myth more or less succeeded in adapting to each other?

The versions of the bird-nester myth found south of the area we have dealt with so far seem even more puzzling. The Paiute and the Ute, speakers of a Shoshone language itself a branch of the great Uto-Aztecan language family, were immediate neighbors of the Sahaptian, notably the Nez Percé, whose myths we have already discussed. They were about two to three hundred kilometers inland and thus not too far either from the southernmost Coast Salish peoples.

I have discussed the Ute versions of the bird-nester (indexed M_{774} and M_{775} in *The Naked Man*, pp. 523–29) and will bring up here again only their essential points. The Paiute and the Ute, split into small nomadic bands, lived mostly from gathering in a semidesert environment whose resources they knew how to fully exploit. This environment did not prevent the penetration of the Spanish and then the Mexicans from the eighteenth century on—influences of which the myths and tales bear the traces. Within the very rich local versions of the myth of the bird-nester, do these influences provide a sufficient explanation for Coyote's throwing his nephew or son-in-law into an abyss and thus disjoining him downward? We would then also need to explain why a typical episode of the European folktale has, among the Indians, taken an inverted form: instead of the hero having to repair the helping bird's strength by feeding it meat (sometimes the hero's own flesh) during the ascent, he demands, before entrusting himself to it, that the bird demonstrate its strength.

Two remarks need to be made regarding this. The episode from the European tale has its concordant model in an already-summarized version of the myth (see p. 170 above), transposed only from the vertical axis to the horizontal one. The episode exists in this latter form in other Amerindian myths. It is typical of the cycle of the susceptible ferryman, in which the hero, so as to get a Serpent or other aquatic monster to carry him, commits himself to feed the animal each time its strength fails it (*The Origin of Table Manners*, pp. 435–56). Far from being the result of simple borrowing from European narratives, this episode constitutes a stage of a vast transformation that extends to the two hemispheres. The motif of the susceptible ferryman is found again in Japan in the story of the Hare of Inaba, as written in ancient texts. The Japanese stage of the transformation is also present in America (to fool the monster instead of feeding him). The motif is found as well in Indonesia, Malaysia, and India.[2] It thus might be conceivable that some elements of this story—such as the variant in which the monster demands food in exchange for his services—have been diffused from southern Asia to America on the one hand and, on the other, to Europe, through the intermediary of the Arabs, among whom this motif is well represented. In fact, the story of the hero thrown into an abyss from which a helpful animal helps him get out belongs to universal folklore. And thus the Indians, rather than borrowing from French folktales, instead recognized in them a story that had become common since distant time to both the old and the new continents.*

Second remark: The inversion that has just been discussed is not the only one. The Ute (Uintah) systematically invert the form taken by the myth of the bird-nester among their northern neighbors, the Sahaptian and the Salish: the hero is called Duck instead of Eagle; he is a stranger instead of close kin, an abductor of a married woman rather than a husband whose wife risks being taken away from him. And instead of the tree or the rock on which the Eagles were nesting rising up to the sky, it is the ground that gives in underneath: the rock does grow, but downward.

Finally, while these versions, which I will call straight for convenience' sake, make of the hero a human person bearing an animal name and receiving the help of animals, the Uintah version, which also gives him an animal name, replaces the helpful animals with human beings whom, before jumping down from the rock, the hero asks (as he does of an animal in the neighboring versions) to prove that they are strong enough to catch him.

Things get even more complicated when one takes into account the influence of the mythology of the Navajo (the Ute's southern neighbors) on that of the Ute. Navajo mythology is often presented in the form of theology. However, we find in it the same incidents as in the Ute narratives, notably the demonstration of strength asked of the helpful animal. The Navajo are Athapaskan speakers who came from the North during an unknown epoch but certainly predating the discovery of the New World by several centuries. In the course of a migration that led them from the northernmost regions of America all the way down to New Mexico,

---

*This hypothesis can be backed up by the argument that, shifted onto the vertical plane, the motif also exists in South America, though in a weak form: before coming to the aid of the bird-nester, Jaguar demands that he throw down the fledglings so that he could eat them (*The Raw and the Cooked*, pp. 68–77). According to a recently published version, the Carrion Vulture who helps the hero asks him for a dead rat (Schultz and Chiara, pp. 111–19). There are a number of various reasons precluding European influences here.

their mythology was enriched and transformed through contact with the cultures occupying the territories they were passing through. All of the myths we have dealt with come from recent or present-day representatives of these cultures. Consequently, borrowings from European folklore do not constitute a new kind of phenomenon. They take place in a long history of exchange among tribes, in the course of which the transformations spontaneously generated by mythological thought had already produced many of their effects. Indians adopted these tales of European origin because they completed or reinforced these effects.

One thing is certain in any case: there is nothing fortuitous about those borrowings. They are concentrated in certain domains, which they even seem to completely invade, while others remain better protected. Let us look, for instance, at the different ways the Thompson as well as the Shuswap treat two great mythical themes: the origin of the fog and the capture of the wind.

The episode of the capture of the wind by the hero Snánaz owes nothing to European influence: it is possibly a transformation of the myth of the capture of the sun (or of the moon) with a snare, a myth in which much is also made of a blanket or a coat (*The Origin of Table Manners*, pp. 390–96). This motif would rather lead us to wonder about the relation between American and Polynesian mythologies. We are at any rate struck by the reduced place that the Thompson and the Shuswap give to the major event that was the pacification of the wind. They place it, so to speak, as an hors d'oeuvre in a long story whose plot and details have been pulled out of the French folktales about John the Bear and the princesses freed from the subterranean world. But nothing similar can be observed when dealing with the fog. Let us take a closer look.

A version of a Shuswap myth collected between 1971 and 1975 confirms that this myth pertains to the origin of the fog.[3] The corresponding episode from Thompson mythology enabled us only to infer it (see p. 92 above). I had looked at this myth in

The Naked Man (pp. 471–86, indexed M_{738}) from another angle, as it also deals with the origin of the chickadee, a bird that, in the myths of this region, plays a decisive role in the conquest of fire in the sky. Myth M_{738} tells us that a Grizzly Woman used various materials to make herself four daughters, of whom only the last one survived. Seduced by the beauty of a Salmon (or a Trout), the young maiden wished to have him for her husband. He appeared in a human form, married her, and took her to live in the water. They had two children, who eventually wanted to visit their grandmother. These children were half-bear, half-fish. The old Grizzly transformed the boy, called Chickadee, into a human being, but she failed with the girl, who became a Dog. Her brother was ignorant of her original identity and beat her. She ran away and disappeared forever—whence the plaintive cry of the chickadee, which seems to call its lost sister.

Later the boy disobeyed his grandmother by climbing on a tree that grew and took him to the sky. There, he met either his grandfather or his great-grandfather. This old man, crippled and blind, promised to help him win a beautiful young woman, but on the condition that the young man incorporates [*sic*] his body into that of the old man and only leave this carnal envelope at night. The hero thus acquired the wisdom and the magical powers of the old man, and it was under his appearance that he succeeded in hitting an owl in a bow-and-arrow competition, for which the woman was the prize. He let his true nature be known to her only. All the others took him for the old man into whom he was incorporated during the day. Finally his secret was discovered, the old man was killed, the hero was pulled out of his envelope, and the skin was cut up into small pieces, which, once they were scattered, turned into the fog as it is known today.[4]

This myth is remarkable in that the successive episodes crisscross other myths, each time at a place where the same episode or an analogous one is featured. The narrative first cuts across a myth found from southern Oregon to northern British Columbia at the point at which a woman, either married or not married to a

Grizzly, changed herself into a Grizzly to punish either her children or her grandchildren, who were guilty of incest. I have discussed at length in *The Naked Man* (pp. 165–71, 261–74) the relation of this myth to that of the bird-nester, for which it constitutes what I called its "Overture IV." The next episode sends back to the great mythic cycle of the wives of the Stars (*The Origin of Table Manners,* pp. 199–225) with the only difference that the woman wishes to have as her husband a Fish instead of a Star. The failed humanization of the girl who becomes a Dog belongs to the cycle of the Dog husband, in which, of all the children, the girl alone keeps her animal nature even if only partially so in some versions (see pp. 155–56, 158 above). In the episode of the tree that grows and brings the hero up to the sky, we recognize, of course, the myth of the bird-nester. Finally, the hero who becomes part of the body of an old and crippled man or who hides under his skin (which gives birth to the fog) sends back to the story of Lynx and to that of the child stolen by Owl.

The Shuswap myth thus performs what one could call a sweeping of the native corpus.* And it does more: each episode imitates and inverts at the same time the corresponding episode in the other myths. Grizzly Woman, generally given a sexual connotation (at times menstruating, or lewd, or else incestuous), makes— as does Coyote in the local versions of the bird-nester (*The Naked Man,* p. 368ff)—an artificial child that owes nothing to nature: it is a manufactured product. The daughter becoming love struck for a Fish instead of a Star causes the axis *earth/sky* to shift onto the one of *earth/water;* from the point of view of the woman, the conjunction takes place from above downward instead of from below upward. Grizzly Woman's blunder, which led to the transformation of her grandson into a human being but of her grand-

---

*For other examples of this type of construction that are illustrated with diagrams, see *From Honey to Ashes,* pp. 353, 376–77. (In the first printings of the original French edition, on p. 324, line 7 (counting up from the bottom of the page) one should read *paradigmatique* instead of *syntagmatique*). See also *The Naked Man,* pp. 82–83, 171–72).

daughter into a Dog, excludes the possibility for the two siblings to commit incest, the more so in that the boy does not know that the animal is his sister and beats her outrageously. The next episode inverts that of the bird-nester, as the hero does not climb the tree because he was asked or coerced to but in spite of the fact that he had been forbidden to do so. Finally, shooting down an owl so as to receive a young woman as a prize gives this owl a conjunctive role instead of a disjunctive one as in the myth of the stolen child. The arrow shot from below toward a target—the metaphorical image of the young woman—is an inversion of Lynx's maneuver (and Lynx, too, had taken on the appearance of a sickly old man), impregnating—this time literally—a real young woman with a jet of saliva or of urine, which he sends down to her from above.

Consequently, though we would have assumed a parallelism between the mythical series pertaining to the fog and the one pertaining to the wind, as they both deal with meteorological phenomena, analysis reveals opposite constructions. One construction offers something that is much like a tracing of the syntagmatic chain in the French folktales, while the other brings together the main themes of Amerindian mythology onto a paradigmatic axis. It all happens as if one had to retake on the one side that which had been ejected on the other: the myth on the origin of the fog retells native motifs so much the more diligently as the myth on the capture of the Wind ignores them and seeks its inspiration elsewhere. In these constructions—which diverge to the point of becoming perpendicular to each other instead of parallel, as we wold have expected—we can easily perceive on the formal plane the reflection of the disparity inherent in the concrete entities of which the myths speak: the wind and the fog, twins as impossible as all the other candidates to union that Amerindian thought refuses to pair up.

ॐ

And yet these differences in the structures of the myths do not prevent heterogeneous materials, some native and some borrowed, from being organized within a system whose coherence has been progressively unveiled to us. I will first illustrate this system with a diagram enabling us to view it globally, and I will then analyze it in detail:

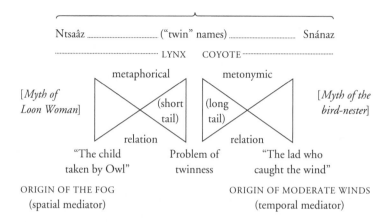

On the right of the diagram the myth of Snánaz, as we have seen (see p. 192 above), inverts that of the bird-nester. The same Snánaz, master of the wind, maintains a relation of contiguity—thus a metonymical one—with Coyote, who, when we look at the middle of the diagram, forms with Lynx, master of the fog, a pair of terms in correlation and opposition. This pair embodies the central theme of the whole system: the one I have just brought up again above, that of impossible twinness.

As for Lynx, he maintains a metaphorical relation with Ntsaâz (the name of the hero among Upriver Thompson, while he is called Tsa'au'z by the Downriver Thompson), the child stolen and raised by Owl. Instead of presenting himself openly in the village of the chief whose daughter he wishes to marry, Ntsaâz stops at the home of an old man whose sickly or dirty skin he dons, thereby taking on the appearance of a miserable character (which is what Lynx effectively is in the narratives about him). This sickly skin—a natural covering—is symmetrical to the black soot covering—a cultural product—that, at the other extreme of the diagram, is worn by an old man in whose home the hero does not stay but who gives him his magical powers and directs him to the house of a chief whose daughter he will marry.

According to the myths located on the left of the diagram, the sickly skin, once burned, gives birth to the fog, a spatial mediator between the sky and the earth. According to the myths on the right of the diagram, the robe or blanket of the hero, as a manufactured object belonging to the realm of culture, serves him as the means to capture the Wind, which will thenceforth be subject to seasonal rhythms. The blanket thus plays the role of temporal mediator.

Lynx's son—or his double, Ntsaâz—is a child whom the myth describes positively or negatively *sub specie culturae:* positively when given a legitimate identity in the course of a public ceremony (the test of his recognition by his father); or negatively as afflicted with an antisocial temperament when he shows himself to be a nuisance. On the other side of the diagram, the hero Snánaz too is given either positive or negative qualities but through attributes that are either supernatural, or, so to speak, subnatural: capable of accomplishing miraculous feats according to the Thompson version, physically ugly according to the Shuswap, or even an idiot according to the Shuswap tale of the Seven-headed Beast, in which he commits one blunder after another before his gifts manifest themselves.

We have seen (see p. 169 above) that the Inland Salish sometimes think of "owl" (more specifically of the "great horned owl") as the signified of the given name Snánaz. This is the name of the hero who puts an end to the damages the Wind used to cause in the past, particularly those resulting in the loss of many human lives. In establishing the regime of the winds, the hero thus added to human life expectancy. There is a version of the myth of the child stolen by Owl (which in the diagram is the counterpart of the capture of the Wind) that specifies that from being a child abductor, Owl becomes the annunciator of an impending death, thereby connoting as a signifier a motif that I had named "the shortness of life"* in *Mythologiques*. The link comes out even more clearly for the Okanagan, the eastern neighbors of the Thompson. According to their version of the myth, a brother and a sister stolen by Owl Woman escaped as soon as they could because she was an ogress. A helpful old man carried them across the river in his canoe. When it was the turn of the ogress to cross, he drowned her; when she fell into the water, she lost all her teeth, which turned into Ducks.[5] When I cited this myth (indexed M_{744}) in *The Naked Man* (pp. 477–79), I was reminding my readers that Ducks are the masters of spring and that myths frequently turn the loss of teeth (which transforms the victim of such an accident into an elderly person) into the symbol of the shortness of life. Finally, the Nez Percé myths put the loss of teeth in relation to the origin of the periodicity of the winds. "In this way the meteorological code," I concluded, "effects a kind of compromise between the astronomical and biological codes." The fact that, in another context, a symmetry should appear between myths on the periodicity of the winds and other myths sending back to the shortness of life confirms all the better the correspondence between the three codes, a correspondence that has been unveiled as the needs of the analysis of the present myths led us to have recourse to the astronomical code (see chap. 12–14 above).

For the mention in the diagram of twinness and for the designation of the two given names as "twins," one should look to pages 88 and 169 above. On either side of the diagram, the myth on the capture of the Wind hooks up to that of the bird-nester, and the myth of the stolen child (as well as that of the dentalia thieves, of which it is the continuation) hooks up to the myth of Loon Woman (see pp. 87–88, 108, 206–7), which—see *The Naked Man* (pp. 107–17)—inverts the forms taken by the myth of the bird-nester in the north of California and in Oregon. Not all of these inversions are located on the same axis; if they were, the myth of Ntsaâz would reconstitute that of the bird-nester (as

*TN: In the original French, *la vie brève*. Sometimes translated as "man's mortality" in the English version of the four volumes of *Mythologiques*.

the inversion of an inversion). But the schema of the reconstruction of the system is nonetheless justified by the appearance of the myth of the bird-nester in filigree in the myth of Ntsaâz. This filigree appearance is due to the effects of inversions that themselves are distinct from those I had noted at the other end of the diagram and that were at play between the bird-nester myth and that of Snánaz. Let us focus briefly on this point.

In the Northwest of North America, myths account for the birth of the bird-nester in drastically opposite manners. According to the versions from the borders of California and of Oregon discussed at the beginning of *The Naked Man*, the demiurge saved a baby from the pyre, where his mother was about to drag him. Not knowing what to do with the child, the demiurge incorporated him into himself; having thus become a pregnant man, he had to give birth to this baby and raise him. In the interior of British Columbia, the Thompson tell an entirely different story. Wishing to have a son, Coyote, the trickster, set out to make one. He tried several materials before finding one that was suitable (cf. in *The Naked Man* M$_{529}$, pp. 29–30; M$_{667}$, p. 368; and M$_{670a}$, p. 394). The Shuswap myth on the origin of the fog makes use of both devices, each at a different moment of the narrative—a supplementary proof that it transversely crisscrosses other myths (see pp. 199–200 above). Grizzly Woman first makes herself a daughter through technological methods; later her grandson incorporates himself into the old man, who thus becomes a pregnant man—repetitively, I might add, as he carries the hero during the day and gives birth to him each night. Thus the Shuswap myth pairs up within a single plot two methods of producing a child—one technological and the other organic—of which the versions of the bird-nester myth choose either one or the other to explain how the hero was born.

Both in the myth of the bird-nester and in that of Loon Woman, which inverts it, we note the presence of what I have called a cell (see p. 87 above). The hero, reduced to a lamentable condition, near death from cold or hunger or because only fragments of his body remain, is saved by two sisters—either animal or human ones—who take him in and give him back his physical integrity and whom he marries (cf. in *The Naked Man* M_{530}, M_{531}, M_{538}, M_{546}, and M_{550}). We find this cell in a prominent place again in the Chilcotin version of the myth of the stolen child (see pp. 95–98 above), in which a skin of mud replaces the skin of fog of the Thompson and Shuswap versions (without excluding the possibility that this skin too might be the origin of the fog, because, except for this detail, the Chilcotin version follows exactly that of the Shuswap). If we take into account that at the moment when the sisters intervene, the bird-nester finds himself stuck at the top of a tree or a rock against his will while the other hero has chosen to live underneath the water, a microstructure emerges. This structure brings to light the relation of symmetry, occurring on both sides of the myth of the bird-nester, between the myth of the origin of the fog and the one of the origin of the capture of the wind:

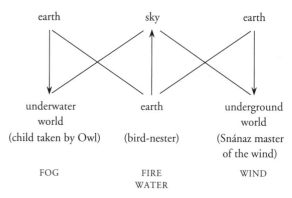

At least one version of the bird-nester illustrates this microstructure, of which it is, in some ways, the empirical actualization. This version comes from the Yurok of northern California whom, following Kroeber, I have already used to shed light on the beliefs and the myths of the Salish (see pp. 35, 114–15). In one of their myths (indexed M_{557a}, *The Naked Man*, p. 153), the Yurok tell that, in order to prevent the bird-nester from coming down from his tree, his father caused a destructive wind to rise, which broke the big branches; once he was freed, the hero hid his escape with a saving fog. We can add that in the course of this escape he succeeded in taking all of the dentalia shells, whose sole possessor he became. We might still add that the versions of the myth of the bird-nester that include the motif of the pregnant man end on the origin of adornments (in this case made with porcupine quills). The myth of the dentalia thieves and that of the stolen child, which is its continuation, are also concerned with the origin of body adornments, specifically those of dentalia shells (cf. *The Naked Man,* pp. 153–59 and 203–5, and *The Origin of Table Manners,* pp. 31–32, on the transformation at play in both types of adornments).

We thus can observe a sort of to-and-fro exchange of positions of the motifs within a semantic field in which two mythical systems—one pertaining to water and fire and the other to wind and fog—insert themselves into each other and, depending on the chosen perspective, alternatively play the roles of container and content. The system pertaining to the wind and the fog is *in* the macrosystem formed by the myths of the bird-nester and that of Loon Woman. I have shown this at length in the preceding pages in regard to the first of these myths. In regard to the myth of Loon Woman, I will only remind the reader that in most of the versions (indexed M_{540}, M_{546}, M_{550}, M_{551}, and M_{553} in *The Naked Man;* cf. pp. 112–13) the hero, who is the object of the incestuous desire of his sister, is named Lynx. Furthermore, because several versions of the myth claim to explain why it will not be possible anymore to resuscitate the dead (M_{554}, M_{555} in *The Naked Man,* pp. 132, 136–39), a place had to be made in the present book for a Thompson myth in which the outcome of a brother-and-sister incest is the impossibility of resuscitating the dead (see p. 162 above). Indeed, the party responsible for this state of affairs is called Loon, which makes the linkage manifest.

But inversely, the macrosystem formed by the great myths on the origin of fire and water (those studied in *The Raw and the Cooked*) is reflected within the myths on the wind and the fog in the form of, so to speak, a reduced model. It might be remembered that Coyote's son or son-in-law has the ability to cause a fire to spring forth with a kick. This fire is not a cooking fire, but rather it is aimed at warming up his chilled companions (see pp. 19, 21 above; cf. *The Naked Man,* p. 360). For his part, the son of the Root (whose place, as we have seen, lies closer to the side of Lynx) possesses a symmetrical gift of making, also with a kick, a thirst-quenching water spring forth from the ground (see p. 111 above). Thus two relatively modest functions are assigned here to elements called upon to fill bigger roles elsewhere. The reason for this play of mirrors, which makes things alternatively bigger and smaller and sends back and forth the same images, is that, when all is said and done, on the reduced scale of meteorology, the wind and the fog have homologous relations to those at play between fire and water on the cosmic scale. Like fire—in one case celestial and in the other domestic—fog unites the sky and the earth, or else it separates them by interposing itself in between. And just as celestial water puts out fire (thereby making cooking impossible) while terrestrial water is propitious to cooking (because of the fish it provides), unleashed wind destroys all life on earth (like the general conflagration lit by Loon Woman) while regularized wind helps domestic fire burn by fanning it. Since the time, the Thompson say, Coyote stole the fire from its first owners, "there have been smoke and fire in the world, and the two are inseparable. Smoke is always a sign of fire, and wind makes fire blaze up."[6]

18

Rereading Montaigne

The discovery of the New World does not seem to have had much of an impact on European consciousness in the following decades. Like other historians of ideas, Lucien Febvre points out the indifference of these

> cosmographers who, forty years after the publication of Vespucci's voyages in French, continued simply to pass over the two Americas in silence in books devoted to the description of the globe. . . . We tend to think [mistakenly] that the discovery of the new continent brought about in all of Europe a sort of intellectual and philosophical revolution that was without precedent.

And further on he writes:

> There was not even, at the time of Rabelais, the argument we would have expected to see exploited by the contemporaries of Columbus, Cortez, Cabral and Magellan: that Christianity did not extend over the ecumene but kept outside its authority and its benefits, and, above all, outside salvation, eternal salvation, a mass of men and peoples whom the navigators had suddenly revealed to the Old World. . . . So the discovery of a New World, a fourth "part of the world," for several decades caused only moderate amazement. That is a fact, and one that says a great deal about a state of mind.[1]

But what about Montaigne? Besides being born in 1533, he began the *Essays* as the century entered its last quarter; thus he could write with a certain degree of temporal distance. His attitude toward the things and the peoples of the New World turns out to be more complex than some famous pages have led us to think. True, the New World is everywhere present in his work, and he broaches the topic directly in at least three chapters: "On the Cannibals" (book 1, chap. 30); "On Coaches" (book 3, chap. 6); plus a crucial passage in "An Apology for Raymond Sebond" (book 2, chap. 12). To which we can add, even though the references are less direct, "On Habit: and On Never Easily Changing a Traditional Law" (book 1, chap. 23). And yet Montaigne does not say the same thing in each of these chapters, or, rather, his reflections are not all located on the same plane.

The chapter "On Coaches," written last (book 3 appeared only in the 1588 edition), limits his vision of the Americas to what we might call today the high cultures: Mexico and Peru. And it is as historian that Montaigne focuses on the most tragic episodes of the conquest; he condemns them by pointing out all that brought these high American cultures close to ours and that would have justified the establishment of a fruitful collaboration between the natives and the invaders instead of the massacres, pillages, and destructions that these latter perpetrated:

> What a renewal that would have been, what a restoration of the fabric of this world, if the first examples of our behaviour which were set before that new world had summoned those peoples to be amazed by our virtue and to imitate it, and had created between them and us a brotherly fellowship and understanding.[2]

Regarding the low cultures, which make up the subject matter of "On the Cannibals," Western conscience does not make the same reproaches to itself. This is first because—and how one wishes that the course of history had confirmed this prediction!—very primitive peoples were thought to be better protected from the enterprises of the conquerors, who would find among them "none of the merchandise they were after, no matter what other delights* could be found there. Witness my cannibals."[3] And yet, these peoples too are probably doomed, but not because

*TN: Lévi-Strauss has provided a number of clarifications to the published translation of Montaigne's works used here. These are indicated here and in the rest of the text as follows: LÉVI-STRAUSS: "no matter what other goods could be found there."

of destructions and massacres such as those that reduced to nothing "the awe-inspiring magnificence of the cities of Cuzco and Mexico."[4] They are to live out their decline in a gradual and passive manner,

> unaware of what price in peace and happiness they would have to pay to buy a knowledge of our corruptions, and unaware that such commerce would lead to their downfall.[5]

This is because while Mexico and Peru possess at least the seed of civilization, the Indians of Brazil "are still governed by the laws of Nature and are only very slightly bastardized by ours";[6] they remained even in such a "purity" that Montaigne regrets that the contact was not established earlier, in the times of the Greeks,* who were perhaps closer than ourselves to these natural laws, even though the Ancients were already incapable of imagining

> a state of nature so simple and so pure as the one we have learned about from experience; they could not even believe that societies of men could be maintained with so little artifice, so little in the way of human solder.[7]

And it is indeed because a culture that has remained close to natural law and one like ours, depending entirely on artifice, are not comparable that Montaigne offers the reader a very well documented précis of Tupinamba ethnography. He doesn't allow himself to be judgmental of their customs and beliefs, even though they are apt to shock Christian souls, except to remark that customs that at first appear revolting are no more so and perhaps even less so than some of ours, which he takes care to list.

In Montaigne's argument, the call to reason comes up over and over like a refrain. We must "bring matters back to truth and rea-

---

*Likewise, in the chapter "On Coaches," Montaigne regrets that the conquest of the New World had not occurred during the times of the Greeks and Romans: their respective armaments would have been similar so that instead of the "Tradesmen's victories" [Lévi-Strauss: "victories due to superiority in the mechanical arts"] from which resulted the crushing and extermination of the weakest, these would have fallen "into hands which would have gently polished those peoples, clearing away any wild weeds" (Montaigne, p. 1031).

son"; "we should judge . . . by the ways of reason."[8] One can of course characterize a given people as "barbarians by the rules of reason"[9] as long as we do not forget that in the end "every man calls barbarous anything he is not accustomed to"[10] and vice versa: as, writes Montaigne,

> I reckon that there is no notion, however mad, which can occur to the imagination of men of which we do not meet an example in some public practice or other and which, as a consequence, is not propped up on its foundations by our discursive reason.*[11]

Social philosophy was to later learn at its own expense that the recourse to reason can have two different implications. Today, an ambiguity already present in the *Essays* still embarrasses and sometimes even paralyzes our thinking. All societies appear savage or barbarian when their customs are judged by the criterion of reason; but judged by this same criterion, no society should ever appear savage or barbarian, since a well-conducted discourse can find a foundation for any custom replaced in this custom's context. Thus one perspective leads to the philosophy of the Enlightenment—that is, to the utopia of a society that would finally have a rational basis. The other perspective leads to cultural relativism and the rejection of any absolute criterion that one culture could use to judge another. Montaigne navigates between these two extremes by following the dictates of practical, if not speculative, reason: since all customs are equal to one another, whether in good or in bad, wisdom advises conforming to those of the society in which we are born and continue to live.

This ethics permeates as well "An Apology for Raymond Sebond," but it doesn't keep Montaigne from using ethnographic data in a much more radical manner than in all the other chapters.

---

*I did not have this sentence in mind when writing the beginning of chapter 20 of *Tristes Tropiques,* and I will not call on it to turn Montaigne into a precursor of structuralism . . .

Montaigne had first written *raison* ["reason"] and later on crossed the word out and replaced it with *discours* ["discourse"]—that is, a chain of reasons. [TN: Lévi-Strauss is referring to the term translated as "discursive reason" by M. A. Screech in the English edition of Montaigne's *Essays* used here.]

He does not drag to the tribunal of reason various customs and beliefs in order to legitimize all of them or to recognize in them only a relative value; he uses them to take reason itself to court.

ૐ

By far the longest chapter of the *Essays,* the "Apology" takes up almost one-third of Book 3, which includes thirty-seven chapters. The discussion of ethnographic data takes up a few pages, but it occurs at a moment of strategic import: soon after the solemn warning opening up the last third of the chapter. In order to show wrong those who claim to prove religion with speculative reasons, Montaigne is resigned, he explains to the unknown lady for whom he is writing this essay, that "it is a desperate act of dexterity, in which you must surrender your own arms to force your opponent to lose his" [12]—that is, to refuse any power to reason. Montaigne was not doing this in the manner of his contemporaries, who, rather than doing their own thinking, relied on ancient authorities. Since "the freedom and vigor of minds in Antiquity created many Schools holding different opinions in philosophy and the humanities," what credit could one give to a thinking that, even then, admitted its inability to grasp first causes and principles and limited its ambition to speak of the probable? Even the philosophy of the Ancients, so much superior to ours, does not offer something to fall back on. The world of the Likely envelops that of the True; the one does not go without the other: "We judge entirely, or entirely not." [13] How can we even rely on our natural senses when perception varies in each subject according to his states and, as well, varies from one subject to another? There is no perception, no doctrine, no truth that will not be contradicted one day by another. This can be seen in physics, in medicine, in astronomy, and even in geometry, "which claims to have reached the highest degree of certainty among the sciences." [14] Ptolemy believed that he had identified the limits of our world: "A thousand years ago, if you had questioned the data of cosmography, you would have been accused of Pyrrhonizing—of doubting opinions accepted by everybody." [15] And yet, "in our century new discoveries have revealed, not the odd* island or the odd in- dividual country, but an infinite landmass, almost equal in size to the part we already knew." [16]

To dismiss the power of reason, Montaigne appeals for help successively to philosophy, psychology, and the sciences. But when he comes to the latest scientific revolution—the discovery of the New World, which too puts in question prior certitudes— he changes scale at the same time as he turns this object of thought inside out. What matters for him is not so much anymore the fact of the discovery seen from the outside but the particular teachings he draws from an inside and magnified perspective. What he does reveal to us are "those strange examples of past and present simi- larities and resemblances to be found between our world and that New World of the West Indies." [17] "I have often been struck with wonder," continues Montaigne,

> at the resemblances there are—separated by immense spaces of place and time—between many savage beliefs or fantastic popular opinions which, whatever way you look at them, do not seem to arise from our natural reasoning. The human mind is a great forger of miracles. [18]

Then follows on the next several pages a list that Montaigne himself characterizes as eclectic, a mess of customs and beliefs that are either common to or opposite in the Old and New Worlds. It is a list on which one would be tempted to see a first inventory of that which anthropologists call "culture universals" if it were not for the fact that Montaigne is concerned with bringing out differ- ences as much as resemblances, setting up on the same plane the identical and the contradictory, as if it were equally significant that the customs and beliefs of exotic peoples were identical to or op- posite ours. Indeed, either possibility shows that always and every- where these customs and these beliefs are arbitrary. When they resemble one another, the ignorance that the two worlds had of each other excludes the hypothesis of borrowing, which would be

---

*Lévi-Strauss: "not [a mere] island or [some sizeable] country."

a rational explanation; and when they are different or even contradictory, this proves their lack of natural basis.

We are thus far from "Cannibals" and from the conceptualization of a society whose "solder" would owe very little to men and almost everything to natural law.* In the "Apology," Montaigne pushes cultural relativism to its extreme by denying the existence of laws

> perpetual and immutable, whose essential characteristic consists in their being imprinted upon the human race. There are said to be three such laws; or four; some say less, some say more: a sign that the mark they bear is as dubious as all the rest,†

because

> there is not one of these three—or four—selected laws, which has not been denied and disowned by several nations, not just one.[19]

And since meanings too are misleading, we have to acknowledge that, as much in the order of nature as in that of culture, "we have no communication with Being."[20] This formula, the strongest perhaps one can read in the whole of philosophy, comes at the start of a long passage recopied from Amyot's translation of Plutarch, and it is remarkable that this is the only place where Montaigne does not follow his model. Amyot had written: "We have no participation from‡ the real being" (because being belongs to its sole divinity)§ to translate *Hèmin mèn gar ontos tou einai métestin oudén.* In modifying this statement, Montaigne appears to displace the problem, which in this new formulation belongs less to ontology than to the theory of knowledge. More exactly, this claimed disability of human nature in relation to being intervenes as a supplementary argument, one that is probably not indispens-

---

*"[T]hose peoples who are said still to live under the sweet liberty of Nature's primal laws." But already in book 2, chap. 8, p. 434: "If there is truly a Law of Nature . . . (which is not beyond dispute)."

†Lévi-Strauss: "some say more: [uncertainty that shows the notion itself to be equally dubious]."

‡Lévi-Strauss: "We have no participation [into] the real being."

§TN: In the French original, *Nous n'avons aucune participation du vrai estre.*

able, to back the thesis that we do not have the power to know anything—except, concedes Montaigne, through the divine: "Only such things as come to us from Heaven have the right and the authority to carry conviction; they alone bear the mark of Truth." [21] But is this still an act of knowledge, properly speaking?

The only mooring in which we can take shelter from the skepticism that the "Apology" pushes to the point of philosophical nihilism is that provided by Christian faith and divine grace. Still, Montaigne brings in this conclusion in a paradoxical way: yielding the floor to Plutarch for two pages, sweeping Seneca along on the way, and limiting himself to recapitulate in six lines the broad concerns of the beginning of the "Apology." Thus it is doubtful that this adherence, repeated as if halfheartedly, does not lose much of its fervor at the close of a ravaging critique that, anticipatorily sending away back to back the universalism of the Enlightenment and the transcendental claims of phenomenology, reduces any rational mode of knowing to nothing.

There has been much questioning of Montaigne's beliefs. Was he a sincere Catholic, or did he show religious sentiments out of prudence and perhaps as well for the good of society? To pose the question in these overly simple terms would be to cheapen a thought whose radical intent is so often ignored by Western philosophy (it would have been better understood in the Far East). At any rate, some of Montaigne's successors, such as Descartes and Pascal, were alarmed by the audacity of his philosophy to the point of taking on, perhaps as their main tasks, the search for ways to go around it.

After following all the meanderings of the formidable project of refutation of knowledge that Montaigne was engaged in with a rigor and meticulousness made apparent by the corrections in successive editions; after following him through the *Essays* and, mostly, through the roughly two hundred pages of the "Apology," in which the whole work is reflected as a microcosm, it becomes unquestionably apparent that Montaigne was thoroughly a skeptic. "We have no communication with Being": everything is summarized in these decisive words, which one does not tire from citing. And once we are convinced of this lack, we do not even know if this knowledge that denies itself is knowledge.*

And yet, on the other hand, life would be impossible if we had to base all our thoughts and our actions on this radical skepticism. A consistent skepticism would only lead to suicide or to the most extreme asceticism, if it were not for its butting against an empirical fact: without having to justify them in another way, human beings find sensory satisfactions in living life as if it had a meaning, this even though intellectual honesty assures us that this is not so.†

*In my view, the alleged giving up of Pyrrhonism at the end of the chapter "On the Lame" (book 3, chap. 11) merely amounts to this disabused observation.

†In his deep meditations on Montaigne and in the ensemble of his work, M. Marcel Conche leads an unrelenting fight against all metaphysical idols. We admire the greatness and salubrity of his project but not without noting that he does not push it to the point at which he would have to deny a philosophical foundation for ethics—as if this at least should be salvaged. For M. Conche, the rights of moral conscience would remain intact in Montaigne; they would be practiced in and through the use of reason.

I myself have cited some texts that might go in this direction (see p. 210), but it was in order to point out how much, in the "Apology," Montaigne shows himself to be more radical and refuses any power to reason, including that one. Thus M. Conche feels the need to limit the implications of the "Apology," in which, he writes, "Montaigne, aiming to bring down an adversary and showering him with arrows, comes up with a number of arguments which he doesn't necessarily adopt" (*Montaigne et la philosophie*, p. 112).

It seems to me rather that Montaigne makes use of a rhetorical device. Taking as his excuse the verbal excesses one is compelled to in a polemical debate, he uses this cover to deliver the very essence of his thought. This ruse would mesh well with the one he uses in giving the title of "Apology" to something that is in fact a demolition.

And yet there is certainly in Montaigne an ethic for more intimate uses beyond conventional morality: just as it is wise to live in accord with the society in which one is born, it is also wise to live in accord with oneself—but without seeking in this behavior any other basis than the sensory satisfaction I discussed above. Are even corporal pleasures not "double . . . sensed through the understanding, understood through the senses" [LÉVI-STRAUSS: "sensed through the [intellect, intellectualized] through the senses"] ("On Experience," book 3, chap. 13, p. 1257)? "Natural enjoyment" is thus felt without the intervention of reason, from the sole fact, Montaigne further states, of behaving "by the consent of

All philosophies recognize the existence of contradictions, but they believe they can overcome them to reach certainties, though these certainties are not all cut from the same pattern. Montaigne's philosophy states that any certainty has the a priori form of a contradiction and that there is nothing to seek underneath it. Knowledge and action are forever placed in an awkward position: they are stuck between two mutually exclusive systems of reference that are imposed on them though even temporary faith in one destroys the validity of the other. And yet we need to tame them so that they can live together in each of us without too much drama. Life is short; it is just a matter of a little patience. The wise person finds intellectual and moral hygiene in the lucid management of this schizophrenia.

Skepticism reduces the religious profession of faith to an act of convenience. In return, the respect of this convenience (among others) in regard to all the acts of practical life allows the world to look upon the profession of skepticism as a matter of temperament.* The two neutralize each other: knowing that they are unavoidable even though mutually incompatible keeps us from being a slave to either one—which is not too difficult—and as well forces us to do the more difficult task of setting our course day after day on both.

Though profoundly subversive, this relativism manifesting itself by falling back takes a conservative coloration. This ambiguity continues to poison our debates, and it is true that Montaigne offers the reader no refuge other than religion—more specifically, Catholicism—against the dangers of a critique whose reflection on the customs of the Indians of America marks a decisive mo-

---

almost all my parts, without schism or inner strife" ("On Repenting," book 3, chap. 2, pp. 910, 915).

*I would not be so rash of speech if it were my privilege to be believed on this matter. And I replied thus to a great nobleman who complained of the sharpness and tension of my exhortations [LÉVI-STRAUSS: "of the sharpness and [heat] of my exhortations"]. It is certain that I have not only a great many humours but also quite a few opinions which I would willingly train a son of mine to find distasteful, if I had one that is. ("On the Lame," book 3, chap. 11, p. 1170).

ment: "And thus, by God's grace, without worry or a troubled conscience, I have kept myself whole, within the ancient beliefs of our religion." And also: "That is why the Christian, wiser and more humble and more aware of what he is, refers himself to his Creator to choose and command what he needs." And finally (and these are the last words of the "Apology"): "Man . . . will rise if God proffers him his hand; he will rise by abandoning and disavowing his own means, letting himself be raised and pulled up by purely heavenly ones."[22]

Thus, taken literally, Montaigne's answer does not stray from the sixteenth- and seventeenth-century answers the explorers' and missionaries' contemporaries, such as Father Joseph de Acosta or Father Gabriel Sagard, provided to the questions raised by the discovery of America: before anything else, they felt it led them to "gratefulness to this God of all the world who has allowed us to be born in a Christian country and from Catholic parents."[23] On the practical and speculative planes, only "our old beliefs," as Montaigne puts it, can counterbalance the effects of the revulsion felt upon contact with strange customs and of the seed of philosophical doubt that they might sow and lead one to believe.

However, let us not forget that to the people of the sixteenth century the discovery of America confirmed the diversity of customs more than it revealed it. In their eyes, this discovery came mixed with others that were of greater importance: those of the Egyptian, Greek, and Roman customs that the study of the great authors of antiquity had led them to know. Too many new things at once made the heads of scholars and thinkers spin. What they expected from exotic cultures was mostly the contemporary evidence that would confirm those things ancient writings had begun to teach them: not only the reality of the devil and his works,* but also that of strange races called Plinean, as Pliny had compiled

---

*This turned out to be a tenacious conviction. In the middle of the nineteenth century, when learning of the human sacrifices of the Pawnee and the refined vengeance of the Sioux, Father de Smet exclaimed, "Who could not recognize upon seeing so many horrors the invisible influence of the enemy of the human species" (Smet, p. 124). An ethnologist specialist in the Coast Salish in

their list, and bizarre encounters that were recognized without any hesitation (if only by analogy) as the Eden of the Bible, the Golden Age of the Ancients, the Garden of Hesperides, Atlantis, the Fountain of Youth of the Fortunate Isles . . .

The recently discovered peoples only corroborated these traditions, which had been handed down from antiquity. The existence of the Indians was not surprising since, thanks to them, things were ordered again: encountering them did not bring anything that was not already well known. It was only after the publication of the first works by travelers who had lived in the New World that questions began to be asked. But for a long time and, at any rate, in conformity with etymology, only a slight difference in degree was perceived between the savages (*silvaticus,* "of the forest") and the pagans (*paganus,* "peasant").

In fact, Las Casas liked to compile lists of all the similarities between the customs of the Indians and those of the societies of antiquity. Acosta advised people surprised by the customs and rites of the Indians to refer to authors such as Eusebius of Caesarea, Clement of Alexandria, Theodorus of Cyrene, Pliny, Dionysius of Halicarnassus, and Plutarch to find similar and even worse ones.[24] There was nothing in the customs of the inhabitants of the

---

British Columbia reported that, in 1902, the local bishop was persuaded that the shamans received their powers from the devil:

> The bishop's long experience with the native shamans, and his observations of their undoubted supernatural powers, led him to the conviction that they were assisted, after the manner of the witch of Endor, by "familiar spirits." (Hill-Tout, "Ethnological Studies of the Mainland Halkōm'ēlem," p. 412)

To be fair, we must add, however, that the Indians gave back what they got to the Catholic priests, though with more moderation. The Shuswap said that

> although they were possessed of much magic, and did some good, still they did more evil. They were descendants of the Coyote, and like him, although very powerful, they were also very foolish, and told many lies. They were simply the Coyote returning to the earth in another form. (Teit, *The Shuswap,* 612–22)

Thus the two cultures confronting each other did not question the powers each attributed to itself: without doubting their supernatural character, each pictured the other in ways that enabled it to integrate it into its own system.

New World that warranted any excitement. All of this was, if not already seen, at least already known.* This voluntary retreat onto oneself, this reluctance, this blindness were the first response of a humankind that had believed itself full and complete when, from one day to the next, it was faced with the evidence that it made up only half of the human species.

❧

At the end of the preceding chapter I formulated a problem: a large part of the mythology of the Indians of Oregon and of British Columbia is made up of borrowings from French-Canadian folklore. However, this mythology shows itself to be solidly organized, as if in its initial state it had had omissions, empty spaces, while it was awaiting, so to speak, external contributions that would fill them and only thanks to which its structure could be completed.

Could we not see in this the effect of the reaction, in a confused form and a rudimentary state, that the Indians of the two Americas had in the presence of the envoys from another world, a reaction so very different from that of the Europeans I just described? In chapter 5 I already pointed out the ease with which distant tribes that had no relationships with one another integrated the Whites into their mythology, and this almost in the same ways. I noted that this phenomenon would be incomprehensible unless we accept that the place of the Whites was already marked in the form of a hollow space within systems of thought based on a dichotomous principle that at each stage forces the terms to become double, so that the creation of the Indians by the demiurge necessitated as well the creation of non-Indians.

On the main, the minor phenomenon that we are perusing—that is, of how the mythology of one area of America acquired its character of structured totality only through borrowings from a foreign folklore—appears as an echo or a reflection of

*TN: Lévi-Strauss makes a pun on the French *déjà vu,* which in French does not have the specific mystical meaning it has in English, with *déjà-su* ("already known").

a mindset common to all the peoples of the New World, one that was observed in all its consequences at the time of the conquest in Mexico and in Peru.

It is well known that the fall of the Aztec and the Inca, who had been unable to put up an effective resistance against their conquerors, can be explained in great part by the fact that the natives thought they recognized in the latter disappeared gods whose sacred traditions presaged and even encouraged the hope of their return. When Quetzalcoatl, the civilizing god of the Toltec (from whom the Aztec, who arrived in the region of Mexico in the thirteenth century, acquired their culture) was persecuted by a rival god and had to leave his people (see p. 183 above), he announced that the day would come when, across the sea, from the place where the sun rises, would appear beings similar to himself. The Indians imagined them in the form of a tall man, with white skin, wearing a long and rounded beard. Thus said the chronicles, and when the Indians saw the Christians, they took them for gods—brothers and sons to Quetzalcoatl. The Maya were aware of the same prophecy: "Welcome your guests," we can read in one of their sacred books, "who are bearded and come from the country of the East." [25]

Likewise, in Peru, the eighth Inca, who lived at the end of the fifteenth and beginning of the sixteenth centuries, received from the god Viracocha (whose name he took) the revelation that bearded and unknown men would put an end to his empire and religion. This prediction was repeated by the eleventh (according to the conventional chronology) and last Inca, Huayna Capac, and we can see in it one of the causes for the paralysis that took hold of 20,000 armed men in the face of 160 Spaniards. On the morrow of his vision, the Inca Viracocha had wanted to have a statue of the god raised, showing him as he had appeared to him: "A large man with a foot-long beard and a robe in the shape of a cassock which reached the ground. He was leading with a chain a very strange animal of unknown shape which had the nails of a lion." Garcilasso writes that the native sculptors "could not capture the look of this figure," which represented a type of being that had never been seen. As for the Spanish, they felt no such difficulty: they recognized Saint Bartholomew and concluded that this saint must have preached the Gospel in Peru,* which did not prevent them, as they imagined that treasures were hidden underneath, from demolishing the temple in which the statue was kept.[26]

These prophecies are known only through texts written after the discovery. It might thus be possible that the chroniclers or their informants arranged things so as to give more coherence to the incredible events that they had directly or indirectly witnessed. And yet it does seem difficult to doubt the welcome the Aztec gave Cortez and his companions as it was described to Sahagún some thirty years later. Convinced that the god Quetzalcoatl had returned, Montezuma sent emissaries laden with all the regalia of the gods: masks inlaid with turquoise, earrings, ceremonial armor ornamented with precious feathers, necklaces of gold and jade, sumptuous headdresses, and so on. They covered Cortez with these sacred clothes and gave him the worship due a god.[27]

It might be thought surprising that we would seek in concepts better illustrated in the high civilizations of Mexico and Peru the ultimate reason for a syncretism that some myths from the North American Northwest first brought to our attention. However, it must be remembered that they, along with all the other mythical representations we have dealt with, belong to the bedrock of American mythology. Even when casting our gaze in the distance, our feet remain solidly planted on this base. Already in chapter 4, we had to recognize that the structure of Salish myths only became transparent in the light of myths collected in Brazil from the ancient Tupinamba. We can add as well Aztec mythology in regard to the problem of twinness—the key, as we have seen, to the whole system. This is because while the peoples of the Northwest of North America identified twins with certain animals such as bears or salmon, in Aztec language the word *coatl* has the double meaning of "serpent" and "twin." The name of the god Quetzal-

*Just as they recognized Saint Thomas in the Aztec's Quetzalcoatl and in the Tupinamba's Sumé (see p. 45).

coatl can thus be understood at the same time as "feathered serpent" and "magnificent twin"—this latter term perhaps stemming from the fact that, in the astronomical register, Quetzalcoatl stood for the planet Venus, a twin through its two aspects of evening and morning star.

We could also conceive of a dialectical relationship between these two meanings. Each unites two terms: one serpent and bird, the other twins. These terms evoke in one case a maximal opposition (between heaven and the chthonic world) and in the other case a minimal one (between twins). This way, the name Quetzalcoatl connotes through its two meanings the upper and lower limits of the category of opposition. Like the pair of names Ntsaâz–Snánaz (see p. 202 above), but by itself alone, Quetzalcoatl is a "twin name." this is moreover the case for many gods of Central America and Mexico: Mayan gods often bear twin names. The names of Aztec gods exemplify this internal doubling: Two-Reed, Two-Lord, Two-Woman, and so on. If, as it appears, a relation of identity, or at least of filiation—or perhaps of twinness—exists between Quetzalcoatl and another god, Xolotl, one could not fail to be struck by the fact that this latter appears in all his avatars as a double ear of corn or a double maguey plant and that he was in charge of twin births. Finally, the mythology of the Mixtec, a people neighbor to the Aztec, corroborates these interpretations by giving an important role to two divine brothers capable of transforming themselves, one into an eagle, the other into a serpent—in other words, into the two types of beings the name Quetzalcoatl unites in one.[28] Quetzalcoatl would feature all by himself a twin who would, so to speak, be fissioning, as do twins in all Amerindian myths in which their respective origins and their different natures are seated progressively farther apart.

The North American Northwest and Mexico also have in common the myth of the creation of the Sun and the Moon, according to which the gods or the ancestors decided to put two of their numbers to a test; these are the twin sons of Lynx in the Kutenai version, Coyote's two sons in that of the Okanagan, Coyote and Lynx elsewhere, and so on. The character who failed in the role of the Sun was given that of the Moon, or vice versa. We can recognize here a famous Mexican myth, of which Sahagún gives two versions (there are more). In very olden days, when the two celestial bodies did not yet exist, the gods got together to choose one amongst them to light up the earth after self-immolating on a pyre. A god offered himself, but no one came forward to be the needed second volunteer. The task was assigned to the smallest and lowliest being, whose body was covered with sores. At the moment of throwing himself into the flames, the first god took a step back, but the other one did not hesitate and induced his companion to follow. The gods did not know where the celestial bodies would rise, and they were looking for them in all directions. The Sun finally appeared in the east, then the Moon. In order to make their light unequal, a Rabbit was thrown into the face of the god, who had sacrificed himself last. He would have been the Sun if he had been more courageous.[29] According to other traditions there was at the origin only a half-sun, which did not shed much light. Quetzalcoatl threw his son into a fire, and he became the Sun; Tlaloc, another god, also threw in his son, who became the Moon.

19

The Bipartite Ideology of the Amerindians

The mythology of the two Americas is certainly not the only one in which twinness occupies a large place. We could say as much for the myths of the entire world. Vedic India sets into play successive generations of twins, while Zoroastrian religion rests on the antithetical pair formed by Ohrmazd and Ahriman. And of course the rich mythology of twinness among the Dogon of Mali brought to light by Griaule and Dieterlen readily springs to mind, a mythology that meshes well with the beliefs pertaining to twins observed in the whole of Africa.

Still, we need to differentiate between two formulas. The twins are at times of opposite sexes and are doomed to an incest already prefigured by their promiscuousness in the maternal womb. In general, this couple procreates children, boys and girls: from their union, likewise incestuous, the first humans are born. Even though it is also encountered in America, I have set this mythological scheme aside because it answers a specific question: how can duality be produced (that of the sexes and subsequently that which is implied in marriage) from unity, or, more exactly, from an image of unity, ambiguous enough so as to be able to conceive of the diversity emerging from it? The Rig-Veda offers a first example with the hymn (X.10) featuring a dialogue between Yama and Yamī—that is, "male twin" and "female twin"—the boy saying the even stanzas and the girl the uneven ones. They are born of another twin, the wife of the Sun, from whom she tries in vain to escape because she cannot withstand his heat (cf. p. 148n above).

And yet the Sun will beget twins, the Asvin, themselves progenitors of other twins. The text does not clearly state that Yamī succeeded in convincing Yama to unite with her. However, in the old Japanese mythology, the primordial female twin, who too is overly enterprising (whence a first birth of a defective child), has several pairs of twins among her descendants.*

The other formula, in which twins are of the same sex, either male or female, answers a question that is the inverse of the preceding one. Can duality resorb itself into the image of the unity through which it is represented, or is it irreversible to the point that the minimal gap between its terms must fatally become greater? In between these extreme solutions the myths conceive a whole series of intermediaries. Irreducible, the duality will take the form of antitheses: a good twin, a bad twin; one associated with life, the other with death; one in the sky, the other on the earth or in the chthonic world. Then come the systems in which the opposition between the twins loses its absolute character in favor of relative inequality: clever or stupid, agile or clumsy, strong or weak, and so on. American myths give us a good sampling of these graduated solutions. These range from the antithetical pair formed by the good and the bad demiurge in the myths of southern California[1] to the respectively beneficent and maleficent twins of the Iroquois and include the twins featured in a Coeur d'Alene myth. This myth tells that a woman surprised her twin sons while they were arguing in secret. One was saying, "It is better to be alive," while the other was arguing, "It is better to be dead." When they noticed their mother, they became silent, and since then, from time to time, some people die. There are always some who are born and some who die at the same time. If the woman had

---

*Izanagi and Izanami have sex after having turned, he leftward and she rightward, around the celestial pillar and met on the other side. But the woman errs by speaking first instead of leaving the initiative to her male partner.

There is a good parallel in a Chilcotin myth: "As they journeyed they came to the foot of a high mountain; and the brother said to his sister that they should separate and go around the mountain, one on one side and one on the other: and if they should meet face to face on the opposite side they would marry each other, otherwise not" (Farrand, *Traditions of the Chilcotin Indians*, p. 22).

not shown herself and had let her children finish their discussion, one of the twins would have won over the other and there would have been either no life or no death. Another Salish myth, this time from the coast, deals with the theme of twins in a picturesque vein: two Siamese brothers were linked through their backs so that one had to walk backward while the other walked forward, and, when armed with bows and arrows, they were shooting in opposite directions.[2]

In South America, companions who are either twins or not and who have unequal physical or moral qualities cooperate and share the same adventures. The more intelligent or the stronger fixes the blunders of the other; he even resuscitates him if he dies, the victim of his own lack of abilities. Thus we have the Kraho Pud and Pudlere, the Bakairi Keri and Kame, the Bororo Meri and Ari, the Tukana Dyoi and Epi, the Carib Makunaima and Pia, and so on.[3] But in general, American myths stop at that point, as if they were giving up making the twins homogeneous in the manner of Castor and Pollux, famous for their fraternal friendship and even, writes Plutarch, "the indivisible union binding them"; "a highly egalitarian pair" notes Marcel Detienne,[4] even though they had different fathers, one divine and the other human. The Dioscuri erased this initial disparity by sharing the mortality of one and the immortality of the other. Thus, initially their situation did resemble that of Amerindian "twins" born of different parents or at least different fathers (see p. 49 above). In America, however, inequality is maintained and gradually takes over in all domains; it is to this that native cosmology and sociology owe their internal dynamics.

The Old World favors extreme solutions in response to the problem of twinness: its twins are either antithetical or identical. The New World prefers intermediate forms that were known as well by the ancient Greeks and Romans: the way Plato tells it (*Protagoras,* p. 321), the myth of Prometheus and Epimetheus could have been Brazilian! However, it does appear that in the mythology of the Old World this formula yielded, so to speak, a small return, while in the mythology of the New World it constitutes a sort of seminal cell.*

Dumézil insisted at length on the equality or even the indistinctness of twins in Indo-European tradition: Vedic hymns treat the Asvin or Nasatya as one entity, while the Mahabharata turns their twin sons, Nakula and Sahadeva, into humble characters playing inconsequential roles. The authors of the hymns, notes Dumézil, showed little interest in differential theology; everything occurs as if a constant tendency drove Indo-European thought to erase the difference between twins, a difference that, as various clues indicate, had been more pronounced originally. The case of Romulus and Remus shows the persistence of ancient conceptions, whose existence might also be evidenced, albeit in very weak form, by the different skills attributed to Castor and Pollux (one a specialist in horsemanship and the other in wrestling) and, in another register, the attributes—wisdom and beauty, respectively—of the two sons of the Asvin.[5]

Out of myths dealing with an identical conjuncture—the mortal twin receives a burial while the mortal one goes to reside in the sky in the form of a luminous body[6]—the Greek myth rejects this disparity and renders the two conditions equal, while the American myth accepts them and has no need to change the disparity. In the whole of Europe, popular ideas pertaining to twins embroider on the theme of their complete identification: they are physically indistinguishable from each other except

*According to Claudie Voisenat (p. 1), Greek mythology likens twinness to pollution and lack of restraint and thus, in this view, gives it a negative sense. But it is clear from her article that these connotations come out mostly from a reading of "hot" history: actions stemming from the impact of politics on mythology and not the other way around. The case of Sparta appears to be significant, as it is clear that the practice of dual kingship gave birth retroactively to the origin myth: "Lathria and Anaxandra . . . were female twins, and consequently the sons of Aristodemus [Procles and Eurysthenes, the stems of the two Spartan dynasties], who were also twins, married them" (Pausanias, vol. 3, pt. 1, p. 7, and pt. 16, p. 6). This is certainly not a myth that would have produced in Sparta alone a form of political organization of which there are numerous examples in Greece itself (Michell, pp. 101–4) as well as in other areas of the world.

through recourse to clothing or to cosmetic means; they have the same tastes, same thoughts, same characters; they are either in love with the same woman or are so identical that the woman confuses one with the other; they are sick at the same time, incapable of surviving each other, and so on. A sort of epitome of these beliefs can be found in George Sand's novel *La Petite Fadette*.

Amerindian thought, on the other hand, rejects this notion of twins between whom there would be a perfect likeness. Lynx and Coyote fathered the same twins (like the Dioscuri's fathers, Zeus and Tyndareus),* and they were themselves—either at the origin or temporarily—identical according to an already-cited myth (see p. 49 above). We need to add that peoples as different through their language and culture as the Kutenai, the Wichita, and the Sia tell this myth in the same terms, in spite of the distances separating Montana, New Mexico, Oklahoma, and Texas.[7] But in between these groups, we also come across a good number of kindred versions. Lynx, who had cause to complain of Coyote, stretched out the mouth, the ears, and the legs of his enemy. In return, Coyote pushed in Lynx's mouth, ears, and tail—this is the reason why this canine and this feline bear so little resemblance to each other today.† They might have been identical in the past, or

---

*In addition, some traditions make of them both the sons of Zeus alone or of a father who had a double nature, at once divine and human.

†In a slightly different vein, the Kaska, a small Athapaskan people of northern British Columbia, tell that Lynx smashed his nose against a wall of ice (Teit, "Kaska Tales," p. 455). Living in a vast territory around Lake Superior, halfway between the Atlantic and the Pacific (thus very much eastward from the area on which the present book is focused), the Ojibwa explain that Lynx suffered a burn that caused his face to become ugly, flat, and wrinkled. This is the reason why his testicles, which he retracted into his body, are today barely visible, like those of the cat (W. Jones, vol. 2, pp. 125, 705; Radin, p. 37; Speck, pp. 67, 68). Lynx is thus opposed to Coyote through this introverted [*introverti*] physical appearance, in contrast to Coyote, whose physical appearance is "extroverted" [*extraverti*].

To conclude with Lynx's morphology, it must be noted that while the Old World attributes a piercing gaze to him, in North America the Ojibwa have him afflicted by a squint ever since he tried to take in too big a panorama in one glance (W. Jones, vol. 2, p. 131).

they might have been so during the short moment when their respective physiognomies coincided while they were both in the process of undergoing opposite transformations. In both hypotheses, their likeness is a revocable or temporary state; it cannot last.

Amerindian thought thus gives to symmetry a negative, even evil value. I have discussed in *The Naked Man* the sinister connotations of the parhelions the myths put in relation with stories about twins, who are often issued from a character who has been vertically cut into two individuals who then become incestuous.* According to the Haida, when a supernatural being is beheaded, the head and the body come back together; but if it is split vertically and a grinding stone is placed in between the two halves, the supernatural being grinds itself and reduces itself to powder. This procedure is the only one capable of destroying a supernatural being.[8]

It is also deserving of note that in America one of the twins almost always holds the job of trickster: the principle of disequilibrium is located within the pair itself. In ancient Greece, the principle of disequilibrium can only come from outside, which makes harmony rule between the Dioscuri. The role of trickster falls to a third character, Eurymas or Eurymnos, whom Pherecydes described as *diábolos* (which is pretty well translated as "trickster") and about whom we unfortunately hardly know anything, except that Pollux killed him with a blow of his fist because he was trying to cause discord between him and his brother.[9]

Consequently, even though the Indo-Europeans held an archaic notion of twinness that was close to that of the Amerindians, they gradually discarded it. In contrast to the Indians and as Dumézil would have said, "they did not draw an explanation of the world from it."[10] For the Indo-Europeans, the ideal of perfect twinness could be achieved in spite of contrary initial conditions.†

---

*A Chinese myth takes the opposite path. It speaks of incestuous siblings who died and came back to life in the form of a single character with two heads, four arms, and four feet (Mathieu, pp. 158–59).

†The Greek Dioscuri had both as doubles and as adversaries a pair of brothers, their patrilineal cousins, called Idas and Lynceas. That in America a character

In Amerindian thought, a sort of philosophical bias seems to make it necessary for things in any sector of the cosmos or of society to not remain in their initial state and for an unstable dualism to always yield another unstable dualism, regardless of the level on which it might be apprehended. This philosophy has accompanied us all along the two parallel paths we have followed in this book, paths that have led to the theme of impossible twinness: that of the Indians and the Whites on the one hand and that of the fog and the wind on the other. The proof for this convergence of these two itineraries has been provided by the formally heterogeneous constructions of a myth on the origin of the fog, which reflects, as in a microcosm, the universe of Amerindian mythology and of myths on the origin of the winds, condensing everything the Indians knew of European folklore (see p. 200 above).

Undoubtedly, there are objective reasons for the importance the peoples of this area of America give to the fog and the wind. In the carved-out maritime zone where sounds, gulfs, and fjords penetrate to the heart of the mountains and that is blessed with a mild climate and abundant rain, the fog imposes itself as one of the givens of experience. This remains true, though to a lesser degree, on the inland plateau, where the barrier formed by the coastal chain prevents maritime air from penetrating. The climate there is semidesertic (the annual precipitation average is 25 centimeters in the valley of the Thompson River, in contrast to 275 centimeters on the western coast of Vancouver Island) with drastic changes in temperature between summer and winter. Going from the interior toward the coast, the yearly average of days of thick fog goes up from about twenty to more than forty-five, with two maximal periods in March and October.[11]

---

called Lynx has led us to twins and that in Greece twins lead back to a character whose name is derived from the word *lynx* is one of the accidents of which comparative mythology offers other examples; in most cases, nothing can made of these except for poetic satisfaction.

This fog is not always of the same type. Meteorologists differentiate several types: diffusional or advectional, cold or warming, and so on. While Lynx caused a winter fog that made hunting impossible and caused famine (see p. 4 above), according to other myths, only the Dog brothers, out of all the animals, had the magical power to end the harshness of winter and the lack of food.

> "If we are successful," they said, "mist will settle along the mountain ridge when dawn comes. . . . There will be snow, the snow will turn to water, rain will come. . . . We shall lead the deer down. . . . We shall have enough to eat; never again shall we hunger." The land became warm, and spring came.[12]

The change in seasons, from fair weather to cold or vice versa, is thus linked to two characters: Lynx on the one hand, Dogs on the other, protagonists in myths whose respective structures, as we have seen, are both correlative and opposite (see chap. 14 above).

As for the winds, their import in native thought can be measured by the fact that, for instance, the Twana of Puget Sound define the directions of space in terms of wind direction:

> Probably no terms had primary reference to cardinal directions. However, a set of wind-direction terms apparently denoted specific directions.[13]

The peoples of this area tell many myths on the war of the winds, principally the one between the northeastern and the southwestern ones, one cold and the other warm (cf. *The Naked Man,* M_{754}, M_{756}, M_{780}, M_{783}, and M_{785}). The Indians of Cape Flattery, who are "excellent judges of the weather, and can predict a storm or calm with almost the accuracy of a barometer," distinguish six winds: from the north, the south, the east, the southeast, the west, and the northwest.[14] In mythological narratives, winds formed a family. West Wind Woman and East Wind Man have two sons, Northern Wind and Southern Wind (see p. 131 above); or again, Rain Wind (from the southwest) has as his wife the daughter of Cold Wind (north), who ends up killing his son-in-law. The victim's son, Stormy Wind, avenges him.[15]

The wind from the southwest, called Chinook (after a people from the mouth of the Columbia River), comes, as its name suggests, from the ocean. Tempestuous and laden with rain when it arrives on the coast in January or February, it loses its humidity when crossing the mountainous barriers formed by the coastal chains, the Cascades and then the Rockies. Having become a warm and dry foehn, it then rages over the plains, where it provokes drastic rises in temperature. These rises are already marked in between the Cascades and the Rockies. An observer from the turn of our century described them in lyrical terms for what was then called the Oregon Territory (comprising the present-day states of Oregon, Washington, Idaho, and a part of Montana), from which many of the myths used here have come:

> Scarcely anything can be imagined in nature more picturesque and dramatic than this Chinook wind. The thermometer may be down nearly to zero, a foot of snow may rest like a pall on the earth, or a deadly fog may wrap the earth in its cold embrace, when suddenly, as if by the breath of inspiration, the fog parts, the peaks of the mountains may be seen half-stripped of snow, and then, roaring and whistling, the warm south wind comes like an army. The snow begins to drip like a pressed sponge, the thermometer goes with a jump to sixty, and within two hours we find ourselves in the climate of southern California. No wonder the Indians personified this wind. We personify it ourselves.[16]

For the coastal fishing people, the wind from the south nonetheless posed a threat. They tell that the animals waged war against it and beat it. But they did not kill it; thus it blows only for several days in a row and then it calms down.[17] According to another myth, the demiurge had to intervene to stop the war between the brothers Northeast Wind and the brothers Chinook. The demiurge who moderated them all but left the advantage to the Chinook.

> And thus at the present time in the perpetual flux and reflux of the oceans of the air, when the north wind sweeps down from the chilly zones of Canada upon the Columbia basin, his triumph is

but transient. For within a few hours or days at most, while the cattle are threatened with destruction and while ranchers are gazing anxiously about, they will soon discern a blue-black line in the southern horizon, in a short time the mountain ridges can be seen bare of snow, and deliverance is at hand. For the next morning, rushing and roaring from the south, comes the blessed Chinook, and the icy grip of the north melts as before a blast from a furnace. The struggle is short and Chinook's victory is sure.[18]

The war of the warm wind against the cold wind corresponds closely, in another register, to that waged by the earth people against the celestial people for the conquest of fire (cf. *The Naked Man,* pt. 7, chap. 2). Indeed, while the warm wind from the southwest comes from the sea—that is, from below—the cold northeastern wind lives in the sky.[19] This parallelism comes out clearly in a Shuswap version. In olden days, the animals suffered from the cold [instead of from lack of fire]. Hare and Fox left toward the south, where the masters of the Chinook wind and of the warm weather lived. After they arrived, they punctured the bag that contained the wind. The people from the South tried to stop their flight by causing a burning heat that set the whole country ablaze, but the two heroes ran faster:

> Henceforth warm winds shall blow over the north, melting the snow and drying the earth. The people of the cold shall not always rule the weather nor plague the Indians too much with their cold winds.[20]

However, in contrast to the other cycle resulting in an irreversible outcome—that is, the breakdown of communication between the two worlds—here the struggle ends with a compromise. Neither side wins a decisive victory, and thus the cold wind and the warm wind shall alternate. The Coeur d'Alene can describe the arrival of fair weather in categorical terms: "We see the killing of Cold by his brother." But they immediately qualify the formula by specifying "each spring."[21]

๛

This fundamental notion of a dualism in a perpetual state of disequilibrium does not only come through in ideology but is also reflected in the social organization of large groups of people, whether it be in North America (where I have brought it out for the Winnebago)[22] or in South America. In central and eastern Brazil, the tribes of the linguistic family Gê, as well as others surrounding, illustrate this.

A recent collective work, whose authors had the generous thought of dedicating it to me (at the same time as to the memory of W. H. R. Rivers, which makes it an even more overwhelming honor), contributes many new facts and insightful analyses to dualism. Professor David Maybury-Lewis, who is one of the editors of the volume, along with Professor Uri Almagor, expounds in it views on Gê social organization that I have many reasons to find judicious:

> The dual organizations of central Brazil . . . are comprehensive social theories, linking cosmos and society. . . . They are dependent on no particular institution. They are capable of generating new institutional arrangements when and where it may be necessary.[23]

It is surprising that the author of these lines believes that he is distancing himself from me, while for more than forty years I have ceaselessly said and written exactly the same things on dualist organizations in general and those of Brazil in particular.

Already in *The Elementary Structures of Kinship* I refuted the thesis (the very one Maybury-Lewis attributes to me) according to which dualist societies would be reducible to moiety systems, and these latter to a means of ensuring the equilibrium of matrimonial exchanges:

> Dual organization is not in the first place an institution. . . . It is, above all, a principle of organization, capable of widely varying and, in particular, of more or less elaborated, applications. In

some cases, the principle applies only to sporting competition. In others, it extends to political life . . . in others again, to religious and ceremonial life. Finally, it may extend to the marriage system.[24]

All the facts assembled in the course of this chapter, I concluded,

tally . . . in revealing dual organization less as an institution with certain precise and identifiable features than as a method for solving multiple problems.[25]

Likewise, when Professor Maybury-Lewis writes that "hierarchy . . . is neither logically nor sociologically incompatible with thoroughgoing and persistent dual organization,"[26] I agree all the more with him in that I have previously dealt with the problem of the relationship of reciprocity and hierarchy (in a text absent from his bibliography, along with one by J. Christopher Crocker, who has specified that he wrote it as a continuation of mine).[27] In it I showed that though, among the Bororo, moieties are linked through a network of reciprocal rights and obligations, they are nonetheless in a dynamic disequilibrium in relation to each other.* I also noted that South American moieties are

in no way comparable to the Australian systems since in the first case there are never more than a pair of moieties playing the role of matrimonial classes.[28]

And finally, I went ahead of Maybury-Lewis's reflections when I wrote, still in the same text:

A probably unilateral analysis of dual organization has all too often propounded the principle of reciprocity as its main cause and

---

*I am criticized (Maybury-Lewis and Almagor, pp. 110–13) for having stated that diametrical dualism is static in essence. But it was precisely because I had demonstrated this by using formal arguments (*Structural Anthropology*, p. 148; *Structural Anthropology*, vol. 2, p. 73) that I could conclude, contrary to the views of my predecessors, that diametrical dualism does not constitute in itself a model that is adequate for understanding the functioning of dual organizations, whose dynamism requires us to call upon other principles. The whole of my 1944 text already showed that, in my view, a society such as that of the Bororo gets its dynamism from the play of reciprocity and hierarchy.

result. . . . However, we should not forget that a moiety system can express not only mechanisms of reciprocity but also relations of subordination.* However, the principle of reciprocity is at play even in these relations of subordination; this because subordination itself is reciprocal: the moiety who wins the top spot in one plane concedes it to the opposing moiety in another.

I concluded:

> It is possible that systems typical of dual organization in South American in which multiple pairs of moieties crisscross each other . . . can be understood as an attempt to overcome these contradictions.[29]

Consequently, among a vast ensemble of South American peoples, a social organization "in close correspondence with meta-

---

*It would, however, be naive to limit the relevance of these considerations to Brazil. Finding myself in 1983 in some small islands of the Ryukyu archipelago, I observed the same alternating disequilibrium between moieties. One of these was linked with the east, with men, and with the profane world, while the other was linked with the west, with women, and with the sacred. In the political and social order, superiority belonged to the masculine principle, while in the religious orders, it belonged to the feminine principle. In the villages I visited, the rite of the rope-pull, in the course of which the moieties opposed each other, gave rise to ambiguous feelings. The superiority of the eastern camp was recognized, but the victory of the western camp was considered beneficial to human fertility and the prosperity of the fields (Lévi-Strauss, "Herodole en mer de Chine," pp. 25–26; cf. Yoshida, pp. 65–66).

In the southernmost island of the Ryukyu, C. Ouwehand (pp. 26, 34, 197) has noted analogous contradictions inherent to the system. It would appear that the people may have even renounced the rope-pull because they could not agree on the prominence of one or the other camp. This is perhaps the result of the eastern camp having the sun as symbol while the western camp has the moon, which was considered inferior to the sun.

An article by T. Yoshida and A. Duff-Cooper clearly brings out, in Okinawa as well as in Bali, the dialectical relations between systems of oppositions: north/south, west/east, feminine/masculine, sea/mountain, external/internal, and so on. In them, the relative values attributed to the terms of each pair become inverted when passing from the sphere of the sacred to that of the profane, from the world of the living to that of the dead, and so on. There, as elsewhere, dualism is translated into a seesaw play between reciprocity and hierarchy.

physical ideas"[30] seems also conceived on the model of a dynamic disequilibrium between terms: beings, elements, social groupings which it would have been tempting to associate in pairs because, at first sight and considered two by two, they appeared equivalent, equal, and even sometimes identical. At this point, we are rejoining the theme developed all along in the present book.

It is true that, among the so-called "low" cultures of South America, this type of social organization appears peculiar only to the Gê. Seeger notes this with humor:

> The first reaction of many ethnographers who work in lowland South America is that the dualism described for the Gê cannot be applied to the ethnographer's own group of study. "It is not Tupi," they object. As soon as anyone suggests a general form for the analysis of a group of societies, another anthropologist rushes in to say that it is different somewhere else (in Brazil this group includes the Tupi, Arawak, and Karib language families).

No doubt, continues Seeger,

> the "It is not Tupi" criticism is absolutely correct. . . . Instead of stressing distinctions, the Tupi groups tend to negate them and to unite poles. . . . Among the forest Tupi, especially, there are no complex, cross-cutting social groups such as those found among the Gê, but instead spirits (hundreds of them), which are not necessarily ordered in a binary way.[31]

All this is quite true, and yet, even though the Tupi have not made a place for dualism in their social organization or in their pantheon, dualism nevertheless organizes their mythology. I showed this in chapter 4 and the end of chapter 5 (pp. 61–64) of the present book. In this regard, the Arawak and the Carib, who also have the cycle of the twins, are not very different from the Tupi, and we have seen (chap. 5) that it is possible to pass through transformations from Tupi mythology to that of the Gê. Finally, the social organization of Andean civilizations at the time of discovery offered striking analogies with the still-existing one of the Bororo and the Gê.[32]

Contrary to what Seeger imagines,[33] I do not see in dual organization a universal phenomenon resulting from the binary nature of human thought. I only note that certain peoples, occupying an immense though bounded geographical area, have chosen to explain the world on the model of a dualism in perpetual disequilibrium, whose successive states are embedded into one another—a dualism that is expressed coherently at times in mythology, at times in social organization, and at times in both at once.

A schematic illustration of this particular form of dualism was provided to me by the contrast between the Dioscuri of the Greco-Roman tradition and the Amerindian twins. In both cases they are unequal on account of their birth, but the first set of twins succeeds in becoming and remaining similar while the second, during the whole of the length of their terrestrial life and beyond, works to widen the difference existing between them. Could we thus infer from this that in terms of twinness, hot societies can make do with a cold philosophy while cold societies, perhaps because they are so, feel the need for a hot philosophy? I would not go this far, particularly since there is much evidence that in other respects, the myths contradict this hypothesis. Occasionally, within this all-encompassing domain general mythology holds as an ideal (although it would form a network too connex to disengage meanings out of it), it sometimes happens that a crossroads lights up with a brief phosphorescence. It surprises us, it stops us, we give it a curious glance, and then it all fades away and we continue on our way. The mythology of twins offers a propitious terrain for this type of illusion.

Among the sacred attributes of the Greek Dioscuri was a plant, Silphium,[34] to which the ancient Greeks and Romans attributed extraordinary properties. Cargoes of it were imported from Libya, where it grew wild, for food and many medicinal uses. It was thought to be so precious that when Caesar seized the public treasure of Rome, large quantities of preserved Silphium were found in it. Since at least the sixth century before our era, the harvest of Silphium in the territory where it grew spontaneously (it has never been possible to cultivate it) was controlled by rigid rules. When, toward the end of the first century B.C., local administrators loosened their control either through neglect or because of self-interest, the overexploited species disappeared in about fifty years.[35] At the beginning of the Christian era, the Romans knew it only by name and by reputation.[36]

Silphium was not the *Peucedanum officinale,* known and utilized in Europe since the classical era (see p. 111n above), but according to L. Hahan it was nonetheless probably a member of the same family (now reclassified among the Lomatium),[37] or at any rate an Umbellifer of a genus close to it, producing a resinous juice.

The belief associating Silphium with the Dioscuri stemmed possibly from nothing more than an allusion to the passage of the two heroes thorough Cyrene, a city from which Silphium was exported (unless this visit was invented to give more credibility to the belief itself). And we should attach only an anecdotal interest to the reuse of the available term *Silphium* (since the plant it used to designate is unknown to us) for the scientific name of an American Compositae producing sticky secretions (popular names: rosinweed, compass plant).[38] Unknowingly, Linneaus reproduced with this choice, limited to nomenclature,* one the Indians had made by using a close member of the Compositae family to replace in their rituals a Lomatium that did not grow in their territory (see p. 112 above). This is, indeed, an intriguing

---

*"True *Silphium* whose name Linnaeus was perhaps wrong to assign to a genera of the corymbifer family originary from Louisiana as it likewise had its leaves close together and even linked from the bottom" (*Dictionnaire des sciences naturelles,* vol. 49, entry, "Silphium"). But was not there, in Indian thought, a certain terminological ambiguity between diverse Umbellifers of the genus *Peucedanum = Lomatium* and a Compositae close to the genus *Silphium* (cf. see p. 113n)? A species (*Silphium lacinatum* L.) was held as sacred by the Omaha and the Ponca, both Siouan-speaking Indians in the region of the Missouri River. They avoided setting up camp where the plant was growing because, according to them, lightning would strike there frequently. On the other hand, they believed they could protect a spot from thunder with the smoke of a fire made with the dried roots of the plant. The Winnebago of the area of the Great Lakes used *Silphium perfoliatum* as an emetic for ritual purification (Gilmore, p. 80).

encounter, which might be taken as a sign that the specter of the Silphium plant could be haunting the neighborhood . . .

Finally, how can we avoid being troubled when keeping in mind the nutritive as well as the magical and religious value given in the Northwest of North America to various Lomatium species (they, too, being different from *Peucedanum officinale* L.); the required use of a given Umbellifer or of the Compositae mentioned above for the ritual preparation of the first salmon; and, most of all, the likening in native thought of twins with salmon? All the more so that according to the Kwakiutl, the chewing and spitting out of grains of Lomatium made marine monsters go far away, and, according to the Thompson, made wind and storm abate— thus, the very same qualities the ancient Greeks and Romans attributed to the Dioscuri. In North America, the use of resinous plants in ritual cooking can probably be explained as an implicit reference to primordial fire (see p. 116 above). The ancient world, too, set the Dioscuri in a relation with fire[39] and, as is well known, with luminous meteors.

The apparent coherence of all these facts would lead us to believe that, for reasons that escape us, in the Old and New Worlds there was a similar association between certain Umbellifers and twins. This is probably only an optical illusion. But illusions have their charms, and we can be forgiven for being sensitive to them as long as we know to cut it short.

Could it be that, on rare occasions, this powerful instrument that structural analysis is succeeds in breaking through the nearest limits of our world and in perceiving, in the furthest reaches of the mythological sky, that which, borrowing from the vocabulary of astrophysicists, we could call singularities? These would have no more connections with the superficial similarities that satisfied the old comparative mythology than the mysterious objects revealed by radio telescopes have with the celestial bodies the first astronomers observed with the naked eye.

In the face of the facts of the type I have invoked, the habitual categories of thought totter. One does not know what one seeks: A community of origin, unprovable because of the tenuousness of the traces that might bear witness to its existence? Or a structure reduced through successive generalizations to such evanescent contours that one feels hopeless to ever grasp it? And yet, the change in scale might enable us to catch a glimpse of an aspect of the moral world in which—as the physicists say of the infinitely big and of the infinitely small—space, time, and structure become one: a world whose existence we would be able to conceive only from very far while abandoning the ambition of entering it.

1989–90

Notes

Preface

1. Rohrlich: 1253, 1255.
2. Lévi-Strauss 3: chap. 8; 9: chap. 6.

3. Lévi-Strauss 12: 211–16.
4. Ibid.: 59–63.

1. An Untimely Pregnancy

1. Boas 4: 195–96.
2. Phinney: 456–88.
3. Spinden 3: 207; Haines: 14.
4. Boas 4: 196–97.
5. Jacobs 1: 161.
6. Haines: 14.
7. Phinney: 483.
8. Haines: 14.
9. Boas 28: 16–17; Krause: 178.
10. Boas 20: 206, 230.
11. Lévi-Strauss 8: 393.
12. Lévi-Strauss 5: 293.
13. Hill-Tout 10: 556. (Cf. Lévi-Strauss 8: 378.)
14. Teit 10: 337.
15. Boas 21: 569.
16. Teit 6: 176.
17. Chamberlain: 575.
18. Teit 8: 466–67; McKennan: 203–4.
19. Cline: 236; Jacobs 6: 140; Teit 5: 309; Farrand 1: 114; Andrade: 177–81; Marx: 275.
20. Jacobs 1: 27–30; Adamson: 193–95.

21. Reichard 3: 109–19.
22. Adamson: 188.
23. Hill-Tout 7: 534–35.
24. Teit 6: 177.
25. Ray 2: 138–42.
26. Hoffman 2: 28–29.
27. Ray 1: 177; Teit 6: 291; Cline: 167.
28. Boas 4: 10; Teit 10: 344.
29. Teit 1: 643.
30. Teit 11: 282.
31. Barnett 3: 38; Swan 1: 180.
32. Elmendorf 1: 252.
33. Smith 2: 127.
34. Teit 6: 267.
35. Sproat: 24.
36. Haeberlin 1: 414–16.
37. Boas 9: 119.
38. Turney-High 1: 41; Barnett 3: 63; Teit 6: 225, 227; Hill-Tout 6: 79; Sapir 3: 36 n. 55. On the American species of the genus Lynx, see Bailey; Hall–Kelson: vol. 2, 966–72.

2. Coyote, Father and Son

1. Teit *4:* 36–40; *5:* 209–10; Hill-Tout *10:* 534–40.
2. Lévi-Strauss *9:* chap. 14.
3. Boas *4:* 11.
4. Cf. Lévi-Strauss *8:* 360–61, 378–79, 425; Hill-Tout *10:* 684.
5. Teit *4:* 53–55; *2:* 296–97, 352–56.

6. Boas *13:* 9–10; Hill-Tout *6:* 228–42; Teit *1:* 684.
7. Hill-Tout *10:* 534–40.
8. Lévi-Strauss *8:* 368ff.
9. Ibid.: 426, 440–43, 459–61.
10. Boas *4:* 12; Teit *10:* 255.
11. Lévi-Strauss *14:* 126–29.
12. Boas *9:* 49, 69, 121, 286.

3. The Dentalia Thieves

1. Teit *5:* 213–17.
2. Ibid.: 373.
3. Teit *4:* 77–78.
4. Ibid.: 78–79.
5. Hill-Tout *8:* 154–58.
6. Boas *9:* 119, 287.
7. Reichard *3:* 165–70. On the identification of the grebe, cf.

Pearson: 5, 8; Bent: 44; Brasher. On the robin, cf. Lévi-Strauss *8:* 488–90.
8. Lévi-Strauss *11:* 105–10.
9. Kroeber *1:* 41.
10. Kroeber *14:* 391 n. 7, 392, passim.

4. A Myth to Go Back in Time

1. Thevet; Métraux *1.*
2. Métraux *1:* 15.
3. Lévi-Strauss *13:* 86.
4. Métraux *1:* 235–39.
5. Nimuendaju *1;* Cadogan *4;* Wagley–Galvão: 137–40; Huxley: 217–22.
6. Teit *5:* 217, 243.

7. Métraux *3:* 55–56.
8. Cardim: 44–45.
9. Boas *9:* 165, 296, n. 4. Cf. Lévi-Strauss *11:* 193–95.
10. Métraux *2; 6.*
11. Avila: 23, 29.
12. Métraux *1:* 11, 44.
13. Ibid.: 9, 11.

5. The Fateful Sentence

1. Wilbert–Simoneau: 126–54.
2. Da Matta: 93–141; Carneiro da Cunha *1; 2.*
3. Lévi-Strauss *4; 5; 6; 7; 8; 9:* 175–90; *11:* chap. 12–15; *12:* 59–63, 111–17, 214–16.
4. Teit *5:* 215.
5. Nimuendaju *8:* 246.
6. Teit *5:* 215, 301.

7. Hill-Tout *8:* 156.
8. Golder: 290–91; Swanton *2:* 80–81; Boas *2:* 306–7; *7:* 158; *9:* 158, 161, 187; Jacobs *1:* 123; Lowie *4:* 190–91; etc.
9. Lévi-Strauss *11:* chap. 12.
10. Boas *9:* 89–127.
11. Adamson: 83; Gayton–Newman: 48–50; Lévi-Strauss *11:* 283.

12. Cadogan *4:* 70–71.
13. Wagley-Galvão: 70; Lévi-Strauss *10:* 277–84.
14. Cadogan *4:* 74.
15. Nimuendaju *8:* 317–22.
16. Métraux *5:* 95.

6. *A Visit to the Mountain Goats*

1. Turney-High *1:* 40.
2. Teit *10:* 230; Barnett *3:* 106.
3. Bouchard–Kennedy *1:* 44–53.
4. Hall–Kelson: vol. 2, 1027.
5. Teit *1:* 513.
6. Ibid.: 748; Boas *13:* 12–13.
7. Hall–Kelson: vol. 2, 1027.
8. Teit *5:* 258–60.
9. Ibid.: 262.
10. Ibid.: 263.
11. Cline: 240–41.
12. Teit *2:* 358–59.
13. Boas *4:* 40–43.
14. Hill-Tout *3:* 191–97.
15. Hill-Tout *7:* 539–41. Cf. Lévi-Strauss *10:* 108–9.
16. Haeberlin *1:* 384–85, 418–20.
17. Boas *13:* 12–13.
18. Teit *1:* 748.
19. Lévi-Strauss *9:* chap. 9.
20. Boas–Hunt *1:* 1, 7–25.
21. Swanton *2:* 58–60.
22. Boas *4:* 42; Hill-Tout *3:* 196.
23. Lévi-Strauss *5:* 85.
24. Wagley-Galvão: 70, 102.
25. Hill-Tout *9:* 368–69; Duff: 21, 43–44.
26. Teit *1:* 656–57.
27. Boas *4:* 40.
28. Teit *5:* 262.
29. Hill-Tout *3:* 194.
30. Boas *4:* 41.
31. Teit *1:* 579 n. 1.
32. Hill-Tout *3:* 195–96.

7. *The Child Taken by the Owl*

1. Merriam: 433; Farrand *1:* 122; Boas *3:* 324.
2. Boas *4:* 26–30; Teit *4:* 63–64.
3. Boas *4:* 26–30.
4. Teit *5:* 241.
5. Ibid.: 265–68.
6. Hill-Tout *2:* 347–50.
7. Ibid.: 350.

8. *Jewels and Wounds*

1. Lévi-Strauss *7:* 263–73; *8:* 537–60; *9:* 184–85, 260; *10:* passim; *11:* 110–15; *13:* passim; etc.
2. Farrand *2:* 36–37.
3. Cline: 228 (indexed M$_{744a}$, Lévi-Strauss *8:* 479).
4. Hill-Tout *2:* 350.

9. *The Son of the Root*

1. Hill-Tout *10:* 566–74; Teit *2:* 340; Boas *13:* 37, 124.
2. Teit *4:* 83; *1:* 725; Boas *13:* 247.
3. Teit *2:* 335 (indexed M$_{579a}$, Lévi-Strauss *8*).
4. Boas–Hunt *2:* 544–49.
5. Spinden *3:* 203–4; Turney-High *1:* 31, 34.
6. Merriam, A. P.: 115.
7. Spinden *3:* 203–4;

Turner–Bouchard–Kennedy: 115, 116.

8. Boas *4:* 15; Teit *4:* 95; *5:* 224, 319; *2:* 350–52; Hill-Tout *10:* 564; Reichard *3:* 57ff; Dawson: 31; Teit *1:* 644–52.

9. Teit *2:* 351–52; *5:* 220, 225–26; Reichard *3:* 57–63; Boas *9:* 119.

10. Hill-Tout *10:* 540.

11. Teit *9:* 508.

12. Boas *16:* 569, 577, 580.

13. Boas *27:* 242–43; Boas–Hunt *2:* 175, 608.

14. Turner–Bouchard–Kennedy: 65, 80.

15. Teit *10:* 349.

16. Eells *4:* 51.

17. Dawson: 20.

18. Elmendorf *1:* passim.

19. Kroeber *1:* 66; *14:* 292.

20. Kroeber *14:* 454–56.

21. Ibid.: 388, 402, 221–22, 231.

22. Kroeber–Gifford: 60.

23. Spott–Kroeber: 177.

24. *Relations des Jésuites:* 40.

25. Jacobs *1:* 159–62; Hill-Tout *2:* 343; *3:* 188; Adamson: 211–13. (Cf. M₇₄₀₋₇₄₂, Lévi-Strauss 8).

26. Boas *2:* 87–88; Frachtenberg *3:* 14–19, 28–29; *1:* 91ff; *2:* 214–16; *4:* 65ff; Teit *2:* 306.

27. Delaby: 397; Krejnovic *1:* 68; *2:* 197–205.

28. Packard: 327–29.

29. Gunther *5:* 166.

10. Twins: Salmon, Bears, and Wolves

1. Boas *20:* 206.

2. Hill-Tout *7:* 841; Barnett *3:* 136.

3. Boas *20:* 206; Boas–Hunt *2:* 631–35.

4. Jones, C. F.: 33, 121, 162–63.

5. Ibid.: 162–63.

6. McCormick Collins: 277–78.

7. Barnett *1:* 179; *2:* passim.

8. Barnett *1:* 179; Curtis: pt. 4, 82.

9. Ballard *2:* 131. (Cf. Lévi-Strauss *8:* 541.)

10. Stern: 14–15.

11. Cline: 121; Teit *6:* 166, 279, 381.

12. Eells *4:* 194–95.

13. Barnett *2; 3:* 136.

14. Boas *20:* 203.

15. Boas–Hunt *2:* 673–94.

16. Ibid.: 685–86.

17. Boas–Hunt *2:* 689–91.

18. Boas–Hunt *1:* 322–49, 375.

19. Gunther *5:* 154–55.

20. Teit *10:* 310–11.

21. Teit *11:* 263.

22. Boas *16:* 644.

23. Teit *1:* 586–87.

24. Elmendorf *1:* 420–22.

25. Olson *2:* 101.

26. Boas *20:* 237; *16:* 613.

27. Sproat: 156–57; Boas *16:* 591–92; Drucker: passim.

28. Stern: 36.

29. Boas *13:* 111.

30. Cline: 226; Ray *2:* 145; Hill-Tout *6:* 228.

31. Adamson: 112.

32. Delaby: 400.

33. Krejnovic *1:* 71–73.

34. Carlson: 1, 5.

35. Borden *1; 2.*

11. Meteorology at Home

1. Andrade: 177–81; Farrand–Mayer: 269–71.
2. Gunther 2: 120–21.
3. Teit 2: 310–11; 4: 55–56; Hill-Tout 3: 204–5.
4. Teit 2: 310.
5. Ibid.: 311; 4: 56.
6. Teit 1: 652.
7. Teit 2: 309.
8. Ballard 1: 103.

12. Jewels and Food

1. Teit 5: 267.
2. Boas 4: 173–75, 186–87.
3. Teit 1: 701–2 n. 1.
4. Boas 9: 127–41, 298–99.
5. Reichard 3: 75.
6. Sapir 5: 131.
7. Jacobs 1: 139–42; Adamson: 158–77; Hill-Tout 7: 541–42.

Sixteen versions of this myth are indexed M$_{375a–p}$ in Lévi-Strauss 7; 8.
8. Jacobs 1: 159–63.
9. Boas 9: 132–33.
10. Adamson: 248–49. Cf. Reichard 3: 17.
11. Boas 5: 172ff; Adamson: 378.

13. From the Moon to the Sun

1. Teit 5: 91–92, 229.
2. Teit 4: 53–55; Boas 4: 43.
3. Boas 13: 15; Teit 4: 110 n. 169.
4. Elmendorf 1: 367–69.
5. Jacobs 1: 125.
6. Ibid.: 33–39.
7. Boas 7: 9–19.
8. Teit 4: 54–55.
9. Haeberlin 1: 430–32.
10. Boas 9: pt. 5.
11. Uhlenbeck: 68; Grinnell 3: 258.
12. Grinnell 3: 167–68.
13. Uhlenbeck: 91.
14. Wissler–Duvall: 31–32; Josselin de Jong 2: 7–9.

14. The Dog Husband

1. Teit 5: 277; 10: 296–97; 11: 259.
2. Waterman 1: 27–30.
3. Teit 2: 316.
4. Boas 4: 30, 130; Teit 4: 62–63; Haeberlin 1: 418–20; Teit 5: 354; Adamson: 96–109; Hill-Tout 7: 536–39; Farrand 1: 127–28.
5. Teit 10: 303.
6. Adamson: 103–9.
7. Boas 4: 130.
8. Teit 8: 464; Petitot: 311–16.
9. Kroeber 11: 168–69; Boas 8: 165–67.
10. Teit 4: 62–63.
11. Teit 2: 316–17; Haeberlin 1: 418–20.
12. Teit 2: 316–17.
13. Teit 5: 313–14.
14. Boas 9: 287.
15. Barnett 3: 22; Hill-Tout 5: 336–38; Teit 2: 340–41; 5: 287–88.

16. Hill-Tout *10:* 566–74.
17. Ibid.: 570 n. 1.
18. Myth indexed M₅₈₇ₐ₋ᵦ, summarized in Lévi-Strauss *8:* 210–11. Cf. Cline: 212–14.
19. Cline: 214; Ray *2:* 133, 135.
20. Hill-Tout *2:* 364; *10:* 574; Boas *4:* 48.
21. Boas *13:* 92–94.

22. Hill-Tout *7:* 534.
23. Teit *4:* 113 n. 204.
24. Sapir *1:* 141, 261.
25. Teit *2:* 298, 353–54.
26. Teit *2:* 354–56.
27. Teit *4:* 51–52; *5:* 230.
28. Boas *13:* 241–42.
29. Adamson: 71, 233, 346, 370; Teit *1:* 642; *4:* 33.

15. The Capture of the Wind

1. Teit *1:* 702 n. 3; Boas *4:* 26 n. 3; Teit *5:* 393.
2. Teit *4:* 87–88.
3. Ibid.: 118 n. 283.
4. Ibid.: 118 n. 20; Boas *4:* 20.
5. Boas *4:* 124; Reichard *3:* 146; Ray *2:* 163; Jacobs *1:* 147–48.

6. Teit *1:* 702–7.
7. Farrand *2:* 42–43.
8. Suttles *3.*
9. Teit *5:* 393–94.
10. Teit *1:* 753–55; *12:* 307.

16. Indian Myths, French Folktales

1. Dumézil *1:* 42–44, 128–30; *3:* 136–38; *5:* 219–21.
2. Barbeau *3* (1917): 4.
3. Teit *1:* 753; *12:* 315–16.
4. Teit *4:* 88; *5:* 358–60; *14:* 189–90. Cf. Boas *29;* Hallowell.
5. Barbeau *3* (1917): 21, 61, 82, 86.

6. Delarue: pt. 1, 39–40, 242–63; Fabre; Barbeau *3* (1917): 93–98; *5:* 96–97.
7. Sahagún: pt. 3, 5, 6.
8. Hamayon: 615–16. Cf. Reichard *2.*
9. Lorrain: 26.
10. Ibid.: 58.

17. The Last Return of the Bird-Nester

1. Reichard *3:* 4 n. 2.
2. Kojiki: 93–95, 406–7; Antoni.
3. Bouchard–Kennedy: 47–57.
4. Ibid.: 47–56; Teit *1:* 691–96. Cf. Teit *4:* 72; Farrand *2:* 19.

5. Cline: 228–29.
6. Boas :*4:* 2; *9:* 299.

18. Rereading Montaigne

1. Febvre: 416, 457, 459. Cf. Ryan: 519–38.
2. Montaigne: book 3, 1031.

3. Ibid.: book 3, 1032.
4. Ibid.: book 3, 1029.
5. Ibid.: book 1, 240.

6. Ibid.: book 1, 232.
7. Ibid.: book 1, 232–33.
8. Ibid.: book 1, 132, 228.
9. Ibid.: book 1, 236.
10. Ibid.: book 1, 231.
11. Ibid.: book 1, 125.
12. Ibid.: book 2, 628.
13. Ibid.: book 2, 633.
14. Ibid.: book 2, 643–44.
15. Ibid.: book 2, 644.
16. Ibid.
17. Ibid.: book 2, 646.
18. Ibid.
19. Ibid.: book 2, 654.

20. Ibid.: book 2, 680.
21. Ibid.: book 2, 635.
22. Ibid.: book 2, 642, 649n, 683.
23. Sagard: vol. 1, xli.
24. Las Casas: pt. 1, 17; Acosta: 346.
25. *Chilam Balam:* 186.
26. Vega: pt. 5, xxii, xxviii; pt. 9, xv.
27. Sahagún: pt. 12, iii–vii.
28. Garcia: 327–28; Dahlgren de Jordan: 294–98; *Codice Chimalpopoca.*
29. Sahagún: pt. 7, ii. Cf. *Popol Vuh:* pt. 2, chap. 141.

19. The Bipartate Ideology of the Amerindians

1. Cf. Lévi-Strauss *13:* 139–40.
2. Boas *4:* 125 (indexed M$_{755}$, Lévi-Strauss *8:* 494n); Adamson: 83–87 (indexed M$_{716b}$, Lévi-Strauss *8*).
3. Métraux *6.*
4. Detienne: 87.
5. Dumézil *2:* vol. 1, 78ff, 87–89.
6. Lévi-Strauss *13:* 137–38.
7. Boas *9:* 296; Stevenson: 148–49; Dorsey *3:* 282–83.
8. Swanton *9:* 376–78.
9. Pherecyde: pt. 10, §92; Plutarch *1:* vol. 1, 267; *2:* 160; Roshcer: article "Eurymos."
10. Dumézil *6:* 188.
11. Sproat: 13; Elmendorf *1:* 21; Myers; Farley.
12. Jacobs *1:* 30–33. Cf. Lévi-Strauss *8:* 522.
13. Elmendorf *1:* 21–22.
14. Swan *2:* 92.
15. Ballard *1:* 55–63 (indexed M$_{754a-g}$, Lévi-Strauss *8:* 493).
16. Lyman: 237–38.

17. Ballard *1:* 69.
18. Lyman: 240. Cf. Kerr.
19. Adamson: 75.
20. Teit *1:* 624–25.
21. Boas *4:* 124.
22. Lévi-Strauss *3:* chap. 8.
23. Maybury-Lewis–Almagor: 114–15.
24. Lévi-Strauss *2:* 75.
25. Ibid.: 82.
26. Maybury-Lewis–Almagor: 113. Cf. 10.
27. Lévi-Strauss: *1; 3:* 135–50, 158; Crocker.
28. Lévi-Strauss: *2:* 268.
29. Ibid.
30. Ibid.
31. Maybury-Lewis–Almagor: 199–200.
32. Ibid.: 255–73.
33. Ibid.: 200.
34. Pausanias: vol. 3, xvi; Daremberg–Saglio: entry "Silphium"; Pauly-Wissowa: entry "Silphion"; Roscher: 1171.

35. Andrews.
36. Pliny the Elder *2:* pt. 19, chap. 3 and 111–14; pt. 22, chap. 23 and 108.
37. *Grande Encyclopédie:* entry "Silphium."

38. Rydberg: 924; Abrams: vol. 4, 105; Gleason: vol. 3, 367–69.
39. Dumézil *4:* 265–66.

Bibliography

In order to facilitate research, whenever possible, the same numbers have been used for titles already cited in the bibliographies of *Mythologiques*.

Abbreviations

AA   *American Anthropologist*
ARBAE   *Annual Reports of the Bureau of American Ethnology,* Washington,
          D.C.
BAMNH   *Bulletins of the American Museum of Natural History,* New York
BBAE   *Bulletins of the Bureau of American Ethnology,* Washington, D.C.
CUCA   *Columbia University Contributions to Anthropology,* New York
JAFL   *Journal of American Folklore*
JRAI   *Journal of the Royal Anthropological Institute of Great Britain and
          Ireland*
MAAA   *Memoirs of the American Anthropological Association*
MAFLS   *Memoirs of the American Folk-Lore Society*
MAMNH   *Memoirs of the American Museum of Natural History,* New York
RBAAS   *Reports of the British Association for the Advancement of Science*
UCPAAE   *University of California Publications in American Archaeology and
          Ethnology,* Berkeley
UWPA   *University of Washington Publications in Anthropology,* Seattle

Abrams, L.
   Illustrated Flora of the Pacific States, 2nd ed., 4 vol., Stanford University Press,
   1950.
Acosta, J. P.
   Historia Natural y Moral de las Indias [1590], Mexico, Fundo de Cultura
   Economica, 1940.
Adamson, Th.
   Folk-Tales of the Coast Salish, MAFLS, 28, 1934.
Andrade, M. J.
   Quileute Texts, CUCA, 12, New York, 1931.

Andrews, A. C.
"The Silphium of the Ancients: A Lesson in Crop Control," *Isis*, t. 33, 1941: 232–36.

Antoni, K. J.
Der weisse Hase von Inaba. Vom Mythos zum Märchen, Münchener Ostasiatische Studien, Band 28, Wiesbaden, Franz Steiner Verlag, 1982.

Avila, F. de.
Dioses y Hombres de Huarochiri, Edicion bilingüe, Lima, Museo Nacional de Historia y Instituto de Estudios Peruanos, 1966.

Bailey, Th.-N.
"The Elusive Bobcat," *Natural History*, October 1972.

Ballard, A. C.
(1) *Mythology of Southern Puget Sound, UWPA*, 3–2, 1929.
(2) *Some Tales of the Southern Puget Sound Salish, UWPA*, 2–3, 1927.

Barbeau, C. M.
(3) "Contes populaires canadiens," *JAFL*, 30, 1917; 32, 1919.
(5) "Contes populaires canadiens," *JAFL*, 53, 1940.

Barnett, H. G.
(1) *Culture Elements Distribution: VII, Oregon Coast*, Anthropological Records, 1, Berkeley, 1937–39.
(2) *Culture Elements Distribution: IX, Gulf of Georgia Salish*, Anthropological Records, 1, Berkeley, 1937–39.
(3) *The Coast Salish of British Columbia*, University of Oregon Monographs, Studies in Anthropology, 4, 1955.

Bent, A. C.
Life Histories of North American Diving Birds, New York, Dover Publications [1919], 1963.

Boas, F.
(2) *Tsimshian Mythology*, 31st *ARBAE*, 1909–10, Washington, D.C., 1916.
(3) *The Social Organization and the Secret Societies of the Kwakiutl Indians*, Reports of the United States National Museum, Washington, D.C., 1895.
(4) ed.: *Folk-Tales of Salishan and Sahaptin Tribes, MAFLS*, 11, 1917.
(5) "Zur Mythologie der Indianer von Washington und Oregon," *Globus*, 65, 1893.
(7) *Kathlamet Texts, BBAE*, 26, Washington, D.C., 1901.
(8) *The Eskimo of Baffin Land and Hudson Bay, BAMNH*, 15, New York, 1901–7.
(9) *Kutenai Tales, BBAE*, 59. Washington, D.C., 1918.
(13) *Indianische Sagen von der Nord-Pacifischen Küste Amerikas*, Sonder-Abdruck aus den Verhandlungen der Berliner Gesellschaft für

Anthropologie, Ethnologie und Urgeschichte, 23–27, Berlin, 1891–95.

(16) "Second General Report on the Indians of British Columbia," *RBAAS,* 60, 1890.

(20) "Current Beliefs of the Kwakiutl Indians," *JAFL,* 45, 1932.

(21) "Fifth Report on the Indians of British Columbia," *RBAAS,* 65, 1895.

(27) *The Religion of the Kwakiutl Indians, CUCA,* 10, 1930.

(28) Tsimshian Texts, BBAE, 27, Washington, D.C., 1902.

(29) "Notes on Mexican Folklore," *JAFL,* 25, 1912.

Boas, F. (and G. Hunt)

(1) *Kwakiutl Texts, MAMNH,* 5, 1902–5; 14, 1906.

(2) *Ethnology of the Kwakiutl,* 35th *ARBAE,* 2 vol., Washington, D.C., 1921.

Borden, Ch. E

(1) *Origins and Development of Early Northwest Coast Culture to about 3000 B.C.,* Archaeological Survey of Canada, Paper 45, Ottawa, National Museum of Man, 1975.

(2) "Peopling and Early Cultures of the Pacific Northwest," *Science,* vol. 203, 4384, 1979.

Bouchard, R. and D. I. D. Kennedy

(1) *Knowledge and Usage of Land Mammals, Birds, Insects, Reptiles and Amphibians by the Squamish Indian People of British Columbia* (mimeo.), Victoria, *British Columbia Indian Language Project,* 1976.

(2) eds.: *Shuswap Stories,* Vancouver, CommCept Publishing Ltd, 1979.

(3) "Shuswap Indian Use of the Squilax Area," Appendix 1 in *Archaeological Excavation Sites . . . near Squilax, B.C.* (mimeo.), Areas Consulting Archaeologists Ltd., Coquitlam, B.C., March 1990.

Brasher, R.

Birds and Trees of North America, 4 vol., New York, Rowman and Littlefield, 1961.

Cadogan, L.

(4) *Ayvu Rapita. Textos míticos de los Mbya-Guarani del Guairá,* Antropologia, 5, Boletim 227, Universidade de São Pualo, 1959.

Cardim, F.

Tratados da terra e gente do Brasil, n. ed., São Paulo, Bibliotheca pedagogica brasileira, 1939.

Carlson, R. L. ed.

Indian Art Traditions of the Northwest Coast, Burnaby, B.C., Archaeology Press, Simon Fraser University, 1983.

Carneiro da Cunha, M.

(1) "Logique du mythe et de l'action. Le mouvement messianique Canela de 1963," *l'Homme,* 13, 1973/74: 5–37.

(2) *Antropologia do Brasil. Mito, História, Etnicidade,* São Paulo, Editora da Universidade, 1986.

Chamberlain, A. F.
"Report on the Kootenay Indians of South-Eastern British Columbia," *RBAAS,* 62, 1892.

Chilam Balam
Libro de Chilam Balam de Chumayel . . . por Antonio Mediz Bolio, Mexico, Ediciones de la Universidad Nacional Autonoma, 1941.

Cline, W. et al.
The Sinkaietk or Southern Okanagon of Washington, General Series in Anthropology, 6, Menasha, 1938.

Codice Chimalpopoca
Anales de Cuauhtitlan y Leyendas de los Soles, trad. por P. F. Velasquez, Mexico, 1945.

Conche, M.
Montaigne et la philosophie, Villers-sur-Mer, Éditions de Mégare, 1987.

Crocker, J. C.
"Reciprocity and Hierarchy among the Eastern Bororo," *Man,* 4(1), 1969.

Curtis, E. S.
The North American Indian, vol. 9, Norwood, MA, 1903.

Dahlgren de Jordan, B.
La Mixteca. Su cultura e historia prehispanica, Mexico, Imprenta Universtaria, 1954.

Da Matta, R.
"Mito e autoridade doméstica: una tentativa de análise de un mito timbira em suas relações com a estructura social," *Revista do Instituto de Ciências sociais,* 4, 1, Rio de Janeiro, 1967: 93–141.

Daremberg, Ch. and E. Saglio
Dictionnaire des antiquités grecques et romaines, 9 vol., Paris, Hachette, 1877–1912.

Dawson, G. M.
"Notes on the Shuswap People of British Columbia," *Proceedings and Transactions of the Royal Society of Canada,* 9(1891), Montréal, 1892.

Dealby, F.
"A Propos d'un plat sibérien du Musée de l'Homme," *Objets et Mondes,* 15, 4, 1975.

Delarue, P.
Le Conte populare français, Paris, Éditions Erasme, 1957.

Detienne, M.
L'Écriture d'Orphée, Paris, Gallimard, 1989.

Dictionnaire des sciences naturelles . . . *par plusieurs professeurs du jardin du roi,* 72 vol., Strasbourg-Paris, Levrault, 1816–30.

Dorsey, G. A.
(3) *The Mythology of the Wichita,* Carnegie Institution of Washington, Publ. 21, 1904.

Drucker, Ph.
The Northern and Central Nootkan Tribes, BBAE, 144, Washington, D.C., 1951.

Duff, W.
The Upper Stalo Indians of the Fraser Valley, British Columbia, Anthropology in British Columbia, Provincial Museum, Victoria, reprinted by Indian Education Resources Centre, Vancouver, University of British Columbia, 1972.

Dumézil, G.
(1) *Horace et les Curiaces,* Paris, Gallimard, 1942.
(2) *Mythe et épopée,* 3 vol., Paris, Gallimard, 1968–73.
(3) *Heur et malheur du guerrier,* Paris, P.U.F., 1969.
(4) *La Religion romaine archaïque,* Paris, Payot, 1974.
(5) *Heur et malheur du guerrier,* Paris, Flammarion, 1985.
(6) *Entretiens avec Didier Eribon,* Collection Folio/Essais, Paris, Gallimard, 1987.

Eells, M.
(4) *The Indians of Puget Sound. The Notebooks of Myron Eells,* edited by G. P. Castile, Seattle–London, Univ. of Washington Press, 1985.
(5) "The Chinook Jargon," *AA,* 7, 3, 1894: 300–312.

Ehrenreich, P.
Die Mythen und Legenden der südamerikanischen Urvölker und ihre Beziehungen zu denen Nordamerikas und der alten Welt, Zeitschrift für Ethnologie 37, Suppl., 1905.

Elliot, W. C.
"Lake Lilloet Tales," *JAFL,* 44, 1931: 166–81.

Elmendorf, W. W.
(1) *The Structure of Twana Culture [with] Comparative Notes on the Structure of Yurok Culture [by] A. L. Kroeber,* Research Studies, Monographic Supplement 2, Pullman, 1960.

Fabre, D.
"Recherches sur Jean de l'Ours," *Folklore. Revue d'ethnographie méridionale,* 21, 131/132, 1968, and 22, 134, 1969.

Farley, A. L.
Atlas of British Columbia, Vancouver, The University of British Columbia Press, 1979.

Farrand, L.
(1) (assisted by W. S. Kahnweler) *Traditions of the Quinault Indians, MAMNH,* 4, New York, 1902.
(2) *Traditions of the Chilcotin Indians, MAMNH,* 4, New York, 1900.

Farrand, L. and Th. Mayer
"Quileute Tales," *JAFL*, 32, 1919.

Febvre, L.
The Problem of Unbelief in the Sixteenth Century. The Religion of Rabelais, translated by B. Gottlieb, Cambridge, MA, Harvard University Press, 1982.

Frachtenberg, L.
(1) *Coos Texts, CUCA,* 1, New York–Leiden, 1913.
(2) "Shasta and Athapascan Myths from Oregon. Collected by Livingston Farrand," *JAFL*, 28, 1915.
(3) *Lower Umpqua Texts, CUCA,* 4, New York, 1914.
(4) *Alsea Texts and Myths, BBAE,* 67, Washington, D.C., 1920.

Garcia, G.
Origen de los Indios del Nuevo Mundo y Indias Occidentales, etc., [Valencia, 1607] Madrid, 1729.

Gayton, A. H. and S. S. Newman
Yokuts and Western Mono Myths, Anthropological Record, 5, 1, Berkeley, 1940.

Gibbs, G.
Alphabetical Dictionary of the Chinook Language, New York, Cramoisy Press, 1863.

Gilmore, M. R.
Uses of Plants by the Indians of the Missouri River Region [1919], Lincoln–London, University of Nebraska Press, 1977.

Gleason, M. A.
Illustrated Flora of the Northeastern United States and Adjacent Canada, 3 vol., The New York Botanical Garden, 2nd ed., 1958.

Goddard, P. E.
Life and Culture of the Hupa, UCPAAE, 1, Berkeley, 1903.

Godfrey, W. E.
Les Oiseaux du Canada, Musée national du Canada, Bull. 203, Série biologique, 73, Ottawa, 1967.

Golder, F. A.
"Tlingit Myths," *JAFL*, 20, 1907.

Grande Encyclopédie (La)
Inventaire raisonné des sciences, des lettres et des arts . . . sous la direction de MM. Berthelot, etc., Paris, Société anonyme de la Grande Encyclopédie, s.d. (1885–1903).

Grinnell, G. B.
(3) *Blackfoot Lodge Tales,* New York, Ch. Scribner's Sons, 1892.

Gunther, E.
(2) *Klallam Folktales, UWPA,* 10, 1, 1945.
(5) *A Further Analysis of the First Salmon Ceremony, UWPA,* 2, 1928.

Haeberlin, H. K.
(1) "Mythology of Puget Sound," *JAFL,* 37, 1924.
Haines, F.
The Nez Percés. Tribesmen of the Columbia Plateau, Norman, University of Oklahoma Press, 1955.
Hall, E. R. and K. R. Kelson
The Mammals of North America, 2 vol., New York, Ronald Press Company, 1959.
Hallowell, A. I.
"'John the Bear' in the New World," *JAFL,* 65, 1952: 418.
Hamayon, R.
La Chasse à l'âme. Esquisse d'une théorie du chamanisme sibérien, Nanterre, Société d'ethnologie, 1990.
Hill-Tout, Ch.
(2) "Ethnological Report on the Stseélis and Sk.aúlits tribes of the Halōkmēlem Division of the Salish of British Columbia," *JRAI,* 34, 1904.
(3) "Report on the Ethnology of the Stlatlumh of British Columbia," *JRAI,* 35, 1905.
(5) "Report on the Ethnology of the Southeastern Tribes of Vancouver Island," *JRAI,* 37, 1907.
(6) *The Natives of British North America,* London, 1907.
(7) "Notes on the Sk.qómic of British Columbia," *RBAAS,* 70, 1900.
(8) "Report on the Ethnology of the Okanak.ēn of British Columbia," *JRAI,* 41, 1911.
(9) "Ethnological Studies of the Mainland Halkōm'ēlem, a Division of the Salish of British Columbia," *RBAAS,* 72, 1902.
(10) "Notes on the N'tlakápamuQ of British Columbia, a Branch of the Great Salish Stock of North America," *RBAAS,* 69, 1899.
Hoffman, W. J.
(2) "Selish Myths," *Bulletin of the Essex Institute,* 15 (1883), Salem, MA, 1884.
Hugh Jones, St.
The Palm and the Pleiades. Initiation and Cosmology in Northwest Amazonia, Cambridge University Press, 1979.
Hunn, E. S. (with James Selam and Family)
Nch'i-Wána, "The Big River". Mid-Columbia Indians and Their Land, Seattle and London, University of Washington Press, 1990.
Huxley, F.
Affable Savages, London, Rupert-Hart-Davis, 1956.
Ihering, R. von
Diccionario dos Animaes do Brasil, São Paulo, 1940.

Jacobs, M.
(1) *Northwest Sahaptin Texts, CUCA,* 19, 1–2, New York, 1934.
(4) *Kalapuya Texts, UWPA,* 11, 1945.
(6) *Coos Myths Texts, UWPA,* 8, 2, 1940.
(7) "Notes on the Structure of Chinook Jargon," *Language,* 8, 1932.
Jenness, D.
(2) "Myths of the Carrier Indians," *JAFL,* 47, 1934.
Jones, C. F.
A Study of the Thlingets of Alaska, New York, 1914.
Jones, W.
Ojihwa Texts, Publications of the American Ethnological Society, 7, vol. 2, New York, Steichert, 1919.
Josselin de Jong, J. P. B. de
(2) *Blackfoot Texts,* Verhandelingen der Koninklijke Akademie van Wetenschappen te Amsterdam, Afdeeling Letterkunde Niewe Reeks, Deel 14, 4, 1914.
Kerr, A.
"Chinook Winds Resemble Water Flowing over a Rock," *Science,* 231, 1986: 1244–45.
Kojiki
translated with an introduction and notes by Donald L. Philippi, University of Tokyo Press, 1968.
Krause, A.
The Tlingit Indians, translated by E. Gunther, Seattle, University of Washington Press, 1956.
Krejnovic, E. A.
(1) "La Fête de l'ours chez les Ket," *l'Homme,* 11, 4, 1971.
(2) "La Fête de l'ours chez les Nivx," *l'Ethnographie,* n.s., 74–75, 2, 1977.
Kroeber, A. L.
(1) *Handbook of the Indians of California, BBAE,* 78, Washington, D.C., 1925.
(11) "Tales of the Smith Sound Eskimo," *JAFL,* 12, 1899.
(14) *Yurok Myths,* Berkeley–Los Angeles, University of California Press, 1976.
Kroeber, A. L. and E. W. Gifford
World Renewal. A Cult System of Native Northwest California, Anthropological Records, 13, Berkeley–Los Angeles, University of California Press, 1949.
Las Casas, B. de
Historia general de las Indias [1552], Mexico City, 1951.
Lévi-Strauss, C.
(1) Reciprocity and Hierarchy," *AA,* 46, 1944: 266–68.

(2) *The Elementary Structures of Kinship,* translated by J. H. Bell, J. R. von Sturmer, translation ed. R. Needham, Boston, Beacon Press, 1969.

(3) *Structural Anthropology,* translated by C. Jacobson and B. G. Grundfest Schoepf, Garden City, N.Y., Doubleday (Anchor Books), 1967.

(4) *The Savage Mind,* Chicago, University of Chicago Press, 19966.

(5) *The Raw and the Cooked,* translated by J. and D. Weightman, New York, Harper & Row (Harper Torchbooks), 1969.

(6) *From Honey to Ashes,* translated by J. and D. Weightman, New York, Harper & Row (Harper Torchbooks), 1973.

(7) *The Origin of Table Manners,* translated by J. and D. Weightman, New York, Harper & Row (Colophon Books), 1978.

(8) *The Naked Man,* translated by J. and D. Weightman, New York, Harper & Row, 1981.

(9) *Structural Anthropology,* vol. 2, translated by M. Layton, New York, Basic Books, 1976.

(10) *The Way of the Masks,* translated by S. Modelski, Seattle, University of Washington Press, 1982.

(11) *The View from Afar,* translated by J. Neugroshel and P. Hoss, New York, Basic Books, 1985.

(12) *Anthropology and Myth: Lectures, 1951–1982,* translated by R. Willis, Oxford, Blackwell, 1987.

(13) *The Jealous Potter,* translated by B. Chorier, Chicago, University of Chicago Press, 1988.

(14) "De la Fidélité au texte," *l'Homme,* 27(1) 1987: 117–40.

(15) "Hérodote en mer de Chine," in *Poikilia,* Études offertes à. J.-P. Vernant, Paris, ed. de l'École des hautes études en sciences sociales, 1987: 25–32.

Lorraine, F.
Réseaux sociaux et classifications sociales. Essai sur l'algèbre et la géométrie des structures sociales, Paris, Hermann, 1975.

Lowie, R. H.
(4) "Shoshonean Tales," *JAFL,* 37, 1924.

Lyman, W. D.
"Myths and Superstitions of the Oregon Indians," *Proceedings of the American Antiquarian Society,* 16, 1904: 221–51.

McCormick Collins, J.
Valley of the Spirits. The Upper Skagit Indians of Western Washington, Seattle–London, University of Washington Press, 1974.

McKennan, R. A.
The Upper Tanana Indians, Yale University Publications in Anthropology, 55, New Haven, 1959.

Marx, J
  La Légende arthurienne et le Graal, Paris, P.U.F., 1952.
Mathieu, R.
  Anthologie des mythes et légendes de la Chine ancienne, Paris, Gallimard, 1989.
Maybury-Lewis, D. and U. Almagor, eds.
  The Attraction of Opposites. Thoughts and Society in the Dualistic Mode, Ann Arbor, University of Michigan Press, 1989.
Merriam, A. P.
  "Ethnomusicology of the Flathead Indians," *Viking Fund Publications in Anthropology,* 44, New York, 1967.
Merriam, C. Hart
  "Transmigration in California," *JAFL,* 22, 1909.
Métraux, A.
  (1) *La Religion des Tupinamba,* Paris, Ernest Leroux, 1928.
  (2) "Mitos y cuentos de los Indios Chiriguano," *Revista del Museo de La Plata,* 23, Buenos Aires, 1932.
  (3) *Myths and Tales of the Matako Indians,* Ethnological Studies, 9, Göteborg, 1939.
  (5) *Myths of the Toba and Pilagá Indians of the Gran Chaco, MAFLS,* 40, Philadelphia, 19946.
  (6) "Twin Heroes in South American Mythology," *JAFL,* 59, 1946: 114–23.
Michell, H.
  Sparta, Cambridge University Press, 1952.
Montaigne, M. de.
  The Essays of Michel de Montaigne, translated and edited by M. A. Screech, London, Allen Lane (The Penguin Press), 1991.
Morice, A. G.
  "The Great Déné Race," *Anthropos,* 1–5, 1906–10.
Myers, J. N.
  "Fog," *Scientific American,* 219, 6, 1968: 74–82.
Nietzsche, F.
  L'Antéchrist. Suivi de *Ecce Homo,* translated by Jean-Claude Hémery, Paris, Gallimard (Folio/Essais), 1990.
Nimuendaju, C.
  (1) "Die Sagen von der Erschaffung und Vernichtung der Welt als Grundlagen der Religion der Apapocúva-Guaran," *Zeitschrift für Ethnologie,* 46, 1914.
  (8) *The Eastern Timbira, UCPAAE,* 41, Berkeley–Los Angeles, 1946.
Olson, R. L.
  (2) *The Quinault Indians,* Seattle–London, University of Washington Press, 1967.

Ouwehand, C.
Hateruma. Socio-Religious Aspects of a South-Ryukyuan Island Culture, Leiden,
E. J. Brill, 1985.

Packard, R. L.
"Notes on the Mythology and Religion of the Nez Percé," *JAFL,* 4, 1891.

Pauly-Wissowa
Real-Encyclopädie der classischen Altertumswissenschaft, Stuttgart, 1927.
Zweite Reihe [R–Z]: 103–14.

Pausanias
Description of Greece, 6 vol., translated with a commentary by J. G. Frazer,
London, Macmillan [1897], 1913.

Pearson, T. G.
Birds of America, Garden City, N.Y., G. C. Publishing Co., 1936.

Petitot, E.
Traditions indiennes du Canada nord-ouest, Paris, Maison-neuve Frères et Ch.
Leclerc, 1886.

Pherecyde
"Pherecydis Fragmenta," in *Fragmenta Historicum Graecorum,* ed. Theod.
Muller, vol. 1, Paris, Didot, 1841.

Phinney, A.
Nez Percé Texts, CUCA, 25, New York, 1934.

Pliny the Elder
(1) *L'Histoire du monde* . . . mis en françois par Antoine du Pinet, etc.
3rd ed., 2 vol., Lyon, Antoine Tardif, 1584.
(2) *Histoire naturelle,* 19 and 22, translated and with commentary by J.
André, Paris, Les Belles Lettres, 1964, 1970.

Plutarch
(1) Les Œuvres Meslées, translated by . . . J. Amyot 2 vol., Pars, G. de la
Nouë, 1584.
(2) *Plutarchi Scripta Moralia,* ed. F. Dübner, vol. 2, Paris, Firmin Didot,
1890.
(3) *Plutarch's Moralia in Fifteen Volumes,* with an English translation by
Frank Cole Babbitt, Cambridge, MA–London, Harvard University
Press–W. Heinemann Ltd., vol. 5, 1962.

Popol Vuh
The Sacred Book of the Ancient Quiché Maya, English version by Delia Goetz
and Sylvanus G. Morley from the translation of Adrián Recinos, Norman,
University of Oklahoma Press, 1950.

Radin, P.
Some Myths and Tales of the Ojibwa of Southeastern Ontario, Canada Depart-
ment of Mines, Geological Survey, Memoir 48, 2, Anthropological Series,
Ottawa, Government Printing Bureau, 1914.

Ray, V. F.
(1) *The Sanpoil and Nespelem,* reprinted by Human Relations Area Files, New Haven, 1954.
(2) "Sanpoil Folk Tales," *JAFL,* 46, 1933.
Reichard, G. A.
(2) "Literary Types and the Dissemination of Myths," *JAFL,* 34, 1921.
(3) *An Analysis of Cœur d'Alene Indian Myths, MAFLS,* 41, 1947.
Relations des Jésuites
6 vols., Montréal, Éditions du Jour, 1972.
Rohrlich, F.
"Facing Quantum Mechanical Reality," *Science,* vol. 221, 4617, 1983: 1251–55.
Roscher, W. H.
Ausführliches Lexicon der griechischen und römischen Mythologie, 7 vol., Leipzig, Teubner, 1884–1924.
Ryan, M. T.
"Assimilating New Worlds in the Sixteenth and Seventeenth Centuries," *Comparative Studies in Society and History,* 23, 4, 1981: 519–38.
Rydberg, P. A.
Flora of the Rocky Mountains and Adjacent Plains, New York, Hafner [1922], 1954.
Sagard, G.
Histoire du Canada [1636], 4 vol., Paris, Tross, 1865–66.
Sahagún, B. de
Florentine Codex. General History of the Things of New Spain, in 13 parts, translated by A. J. O. Anderson and Ch. E. Dibble, Santa Fe, N. M., The School of American Research and the University of Utah, 1950–63.
Sapir, E.
(1) *Wishram Texts,* Publications of the American Ethnological Society, 2, Leyden, 1909.
(3) *Yana Texts, UCPAAE,* 9, 1, Berkeley, 1910.
(5) *Takelma Texts,* University of Pennsylvania, The Museum Anthropological Publication, 2, 1, Philadelphia, 1909.
Schultz, H. e V. Chiara
"Mais lendas Waura," *Journal de la Société des Américanistes,* LX, 1971: 105–36.
Smet, R. P. de
Voyages dans les montagnes Rocheuses et séjour chez les tribus indiennes de l'Oregon, n. ed., Bruxelles, Devaux-Paris, Repos, 1873.
Smith, M. W.
(2) *The Puyallup Nisqually, CUCA,* 32, New York, 1940.

Speck, F. G.
Myths and Folk-lore of the Timiskaming Algonkin and Timagami Ojihwa,
Canada Department of Mines. Geological Survey, Memoir 71, 9, Anthro-
pological Series, Ottawa, Government Printing Bureau, 1915.

Spinden, H. J.
(3) *The Nez Percé Indians, MAAA,* 2, 1908.

Spott, R. and A. L. Kroeber
Yurok Narratives, UCPAAE, 35, 9, Berkeley, 1942.

Sproat, G. M.
Scenes and Studies of Savage Life, London, 1868.

Stern, B. J.
The Lummi Indians of Western Washington, CUCA, 17, New York, 1934.

Stevenson, M. C.
The Sia, ARBAE, 11, Washington, D.C., 1894.

Suttles, W.
(3) "The Early Diffusion of the Potato among the Coast Salish," *Southwestern Journal of Anthropology,* 7, 3, 1951: 272–88.

Swan, J. G.
(1) *The Northwest Coast. On Three Years Residence in Washington Territory,*
New York, 1857.
(2) *The Indians of Cape Flattery* [1868], facsimile reproduction, 1964.

Swanton, J. R.
(1) *Myths and Tales of the Southeastern Indians, BBAE,* 88, Washington,
D.C., 1929.
(2) *Tlingit Myths and Texts, BBAE,* 39, Washington, D.C., 1909.
(9) *Haida Texts and Myths, BBAE,* 29, Washington, D.C., 1905.

Teit, J. A.
(1) *The Shuswap, MAMNH,* 4, Leiden–New York, 1909.
(2) "Traditions of the Lilloet Indians of British Columbia," *JAFL,* 25,
1912.
(4) *Traditions of the Thompson Indians, MAFLS,* 6, 1898.
(5) *Mythology of the Thompson Indians, MAMNH,* 12, Leiden–New York,
1912.
(6) *The Salishan Tribes of the Western Plateaus, ARBAE,* 1927–28, 45,
Washington, D.C., 1930.
(8) "Kaska Tales," *JAFL,* 30, 1917.
(9) *Ethnobotany of the Thompson Indians of British Columbia,* 45th
ARBAE, 1927–28, edited by E. V. Steedman, Washington, D.C.,
1930.
(10) *The Thompson Indians of British Columbia, MAMNH,* 2, 1900.
(11) *The Lilloet Indians, MAMNH,* 4, 1906.

(12) "European Tales from the Upper Thompson Indians," *JAFL*, 29, 1916.

(14) "More Thompson Indian Tales," *JAFL*, 50, 1937.

Thevet, A.

Cosmographie universelle, etc., 2 vol., Paris, L'Huilier, 1575.

Thompson, S.

(2) European Tales Among the North American Indians," *Colorado College Collection*, Colorado Springs, 1919.

(3) *Tales of the North American Indians*, Cambridge, MA, Harvard University Press, 1929.

Tozzer, A. M.

A Comparative Study of the Mayas and the Lacandones, Archaeological Institute of America, Report of the Fellow in American Archaeology, 1902–5, New York, 1907.

Turner, N. J.

Food Plants of British Columbia Indians. Part II—Interior Peoples, British Columbia Provincial Museum, Handbook 36, Victoria, 1978.

Turner, N. J., R. Bouchard, J. van Eijk and I. D. Kennedy

Ethnobotany of the Lilloet Indians of British Columbia, Unpublished manuscript, 1987.

Turner, N. J., R. Bouchard, D. I. D. Kennedy

Ethnobotany of the Okanagan-Colville Indians of British Columbia and Washington, British Columbia Provincial Museum, 21, Occasional Paper Series, Victoria, 1980.

Turner, N. J., L. C. Thompson, M. T. Thompson, A. Z. York

Thompson Ethnobotany. Knowledge and Usage of Plants by the Thompson Indians of British Columbia, Royal British Columbia Museum, Memoir 3, Victoria, 1990.

Turney-High, H. H.

(1) "Ethnography of the Kutenai," *RBAAS*, 62, 1892.

Uhlenbeck, C. C.

Original Blackfoot Texts. A New Series of Blackfoot Texts, Verhandelingen der Koninklijke Akademie van Wetenschappen te Amsterdam, Afdeeling Letterkunde, Nieuwe Reeks, Deel 12, 1–13, 1, 1911–12.

Vega, G. de la

Histoire des Yncas, rois du Pérou, etc., 2 vol., Amsterdam, J. F. Bernard, 1737.

Voisenat, C.

"La Rivalité, la séparation et la mort. Destinées gémellaires dans la mythologie grecque," *L'Homme*, 28, 1, 1988: 88–104.

Wagley, Ch. and E. Galvão

The Tenetehara Indians of Brazil, CUCA, 35, New York, 1949.

Wateman, T. T.

(1) "The Explanatory Elements in the Folk-Tales of the North American Indians," *JAFL,* 27, 1914.

Wilbert, J. ed. with K. Simoneau

Folk Literature of the Gê Indians, 2 vol., Los Angeles, UCLA, Latin American Center Publications, 1978 and 1984.

Wissler, C. and D. C. Duvall

Mythology of the Blackfoot Indians, Anthropological Papers of the American Museum of Natural History, 2, New York, 1908.

Yoshida, T.

"The feminine in Japanese folk-religion: polluted or divine?," in F. Ben Ari, B. Moeran, and J. Valentine, eds., *Unwrapping Japan,* Manchester University Press, 1990.

Yoshida, T. and A. Duff-Cooper

"A Comparison of Aspects of Two Polytheistic Forms of Life: Okinawa and Balinese Lombok," *Cosmos,* 5, Edinburgh, 1989: 213–42.

Index

Locators in boldface indicate complete myths. Italicized locators refer to illustrations in the text.